Microsoft® Publisher 2007 For Dummies®

Navigation Keys

Home	Go to the beginning of current text line
End	Go to the end of current text line
Up arrow	Move up one text line
Down arrow	Move down one text line
Right arrow	Move right one character
Left arrow	Move left one character
Ctrl+Home	Go to the beginning of current text box
Ctrl+End	Go to the end of current text box
Ctrl+Up	Go to the beginning of current paragraph
Ctrl+Down arrow	Go to the beginning of next paragraph
Ctrl+Right arrow	Move right one word
Ctrl+Left arrow	Move left one word
Ctrl+Tab	Move to next connected text box
Ctrl+Shift+Tab	Move to previous connected text box
Ctrl+G	Go to a specific page

If text is highlighted, pressing the left- or right-arrow key positions the insertion point at the beginning or end of that highlighting and then removes the highlighting.

Ten Design Tips

1. Design your publication for the right audience.
2. Talk to your printer early in the project
3. Check with your print shop to be sure that you're using the right printer driver.
4. Use white space.
5. Use a simple design that highlights the important parts of your publication.
6. Add contrast to spice up your pages and keep readers interested.
7. Plan carefully for the number of copies that you need — don't print extra!
8. Try to substitute less expensive elements or processes to avoid going over your budget.
9. Be aware of copyright laws and follow them.
10. Scan graphics at the resolution you will use to print them.

For Dummies: Bestselling Book Series for Beginners

Microsoft® Publisher 2007 For Dummies®

Cheat Sheet

Formatting Keystrokes

Ctrl+B	Bold selected text
Ctrl+I	Italicize selected text
Ctrl+U	Underline selected text
Ctrl+=	Superscript selected text
Ctrl+Shift+K	Change text to small caps
Ctrl+Spacebar	Change text to plain text and remove all styles
Ctrl+Shift+>	Increase the font size one half point
Ctrl+Shift+<	Decrease the font size one half point
Ctrl+Shift+P	Activate the Font Size list box in the Format toolbar
Ctrl+Shift+F	Activate the Font list box in the Format toolbar
Ctrl+Shift+S	Activate the Style list box in the Format toolbar
Ctrl+Shift+[	Decrease kerning in selected text
Ctrl+Shift+]	Increase kerning in selected text
Ctrl+Shift+"	Insert an inch mark and defeat smart quotes
Ctrl+Shift+'	Insert foot mark and defeat smart quotes
Ctrl+1	Single space lines of text
Ctrl+2	Double space lines of text
Ctrl+5	1½ space lines of text
Ctrl+L	Left align text
Ctrl+R	Right align text
Ctrl+E	Center align text
Ctrl+J	Fully justify text
Ctrl+Q	Return paragraph to standard format
Ctrl+Enter	Insert a column or page break

Ten Questions for Your Printing Service

1. Are you comfortable working with Windows files?
2. How do you want to receive my files?
3. What is your usual turnaround time?
4. What kind of imagesetter do you use?
5. What kind of equipment do you have in your shop?
6. Do you have the fonts in my publication?
7. Do you have the creator applications for the EPS graphics that I create?
8. How much do you charge?
9. Can you outsource the work that you can't do?
10. Can you give me some references?

For Dummies: Bestselling Book Series for Beginners

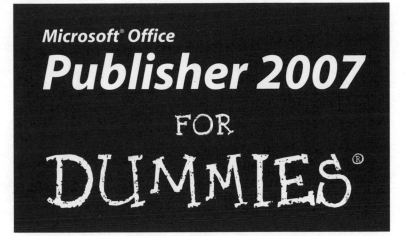

Microsoft® Office

Publisher 2007

FOR

DUMMIES®

Microsoft® Office

Publisher 2007

FOR

DUMMIES®

by Jim McCarter
and Jacqui Salerno Mabin

Wiley Publishing, Inc.

Microsoft® Office Publisher 2007 For Dummies®

Published by
Wiley Publishing, Inc.
111 River Street
Hoboken, NJ 07030-5774

www.wiley.com

Copyright © 2008 by Wiley Publishing, Inc., Indianapolis, Indiana

Published by Wiley Publishing, Inc., Indianapolis, Indiana

Published simultaneously in Canada

For general information on our other products and services, please contact our Customer Care Department within the U.S. at 800-762-2974, outside the U.S. at 317-572-3993, or fax 317-572-4002.

For technical support, please visit www.wiley.com/techsupport.

Wiley also publishes its books in a variety of electronic formats. Some content that appears in print may not be available in electronic books.

Library of Congress Control Number: 2007941223

ISBN: 978-0-470-18496-7

Manufactured in the United States of America

10 9 8 7 6 5 4 3 2

WILEY

About the Authors

Jim McCarter attended Webster University in Vienna, Austria, where he minored in foreign languages and graduated with a bachelor's degree in computer studies. There he also launched his career as a computer consultant, which spanned more than 18 years. Jim has authored several books and served as technical reviewer for more than 80 books. He now works as a project manager in the field of wireless communications. Jim lives in Greenfield, Indiana, with his wife, Kathy, and two children, Rebecca and James. He spends his free spare time (there is no such thing as free time) learning and teaching taekwondo at Indianapolis ATA Black Belt Academy with his family, geocaching with his children, and being humbled by his son at just about any video game you care to mention.

Jacqui Salerno Mabin lives in the Seattle area with her husband, Jay and their dog, Marley. After graduating from the University of Illinois, Chicago, with a Bachelor's degree in English, Jacqui worked as a copy editor for a local newspaper. Later, she filled several roles with a startup software company, working as a software tester and technical writer, creating the user manuals for their document storage solution software. Currently, she is a software development test engineer with a deep interest in Microsoft Publisher 2007 software.

Authors' Acknowledgments

Jim: I want to acknowledge the efforts of the many people who made this book possible. In particular, thanks to Kyle Looper, for giving me the opportunity to write this book, and to Paul Levesque, for taking my random jumble of thoughts, words, and phrases and turning them into a real book.

A special thanks to Ric Caldwell for allowing me the flexibility in my schedule to take on this project.

Jacqui: Working on this book has been very exciting and I especially thank Kyle Looper and Paul Levesque for taking a chance on a relatively untested writer. I also want to thank my managers and colleagues at my 'day job' for their support and for giving me time to contribute to this book.

Thanks also to Tony (my dad) and Toni (my sister), to my husband Jay and to my step-daughters, Nicole and Tia, just for being who they are.

Publisher's Acknowledgments

We're proud of this book; please send us your comments through our online registration form located at www.dummies.com/register/.

Some of the people who helped bring this book to market include the following:

Acquisitions and Editorial

Senior Project Editor: Paul Levesque

Acquisitions Editor: Kyle Looper

Copy Editor: Rebecca Whitney

Technical Editors: JoAnn Paules and Jacqui Salerno

Editorial Manager: Leah Cameron

Editorial Assistant: Amanda Foxworth

Sr. Editorial Assistant: Cherie Case

Cartoons: Rich Tennant (www.the5thwave.com)

Composition Services

Project Coordinator: Erin Smith

Layout and Graphics: Jonelle Burns, Reuben W. Davis, Barbara Moore, Ronald Terry, Alissa D. Walker, Christine Williams

Proofreader: Toni Settle

Indexer: Broccoli Information Management

Anniversary Logo Design: Richard Pacifico

Publishing and Editorial for Technology Dummies

 Richard Swadley, Vice President and Executive Group Publisher

 Andy Cummings, Vice President and Publisher

Mary Bednarek, Executive Acquisitions Director

 Mary C. Corder, Editorial Director

Publishing for Consumer Dummies

 Diane Graves Steele, Vice President and Publisher

 Joyce Pepple, Acquisitions Director

Composition Services

 Gerry Fahey, Vice President of Production Services

 Debbie Stailey, Director of Composition Services

Contents at a Glance

Table of Contents

Introduction

● ●

*W*elcome to *Microsoft Publisher 2007 For Dummies.* If you've never used desktop publishing software and really aren't much interested in becoming an expert at it, congratulations! The book you hold in your hands is an excellent choice: It can help you complete your current project quickly — and with the least effort possible. (I'm pretty good at that "least effort possible" stuff. Just ask our editors.)

Many computer users simply don't have the time or resources to become experts on all the complicated software programs they use. Oh, sure, some of you like to spend your spare time learning the most minute details about the software you use — We won't mention any names, Kevin — but most of us are content to learn just enough to get the job done in an efficient manner. We don't want to read page after page of esoteric information, presented by some computer books, that doesn't pertain to the job at hand. If you want to know a simple answer to a single question about desktop publishing with Microsoft Publisher 2007, this book is for you.

Microsoft Publisher 2007, designed for Windows XP, Windows Vista, Windows 2003 Server (Service Pack 1 required), and newer operating systems, is an inexpensive desktop publishing program. In fact, if you purchased any of the following versions of Microsoft Office 2007, you already own it: Microsoft Office Small Business 2007, Microsoft Office Professional 2007, Microsoft Office Ultimate 2007, Microsoft Office Professional Plus 2007, or Microsoft Office Enterprise 2007. You use this program to create professional-looking marketing materials — brochures and flyers, for example — as well as Web pages.

Even though Microsoft Publisher 2007 is low priced ($169 for a full-package version or $99 to upgrade from a previous version), it's definitely not under-powered. You can do things with Microsoft Publisher 2007 that a few years ago would have made the big boys (you know, those expensive desktop publishing programs) sit up and take notice. For example, you can create publications automatically by using the wizards in Microsoft Publisher (something that you can't do with your Quirks and PageMonsters). You can freely borrow any of the professionally designed templates from Microsoft Office online — and customize it to your heart's content. You can even personalize the contents of your publications so that each of the 10,000 recipients thinks you created a document expressly for him or her.

We want to carry on with the *For Dummies* tradition and help you have fun with Microsoft Publisher 2007 as you use this book. After all, if a 5-year-old can find happiness with a set of crayons, you should be able to find bliss with all the bells and whistles that you'll uncover in Publisher 2007! We do have to warn you that creating a wealth of publications might prove hazardous to the front of your refrigerator, because you'll want to share your artistic achievements with your significant others.

About This Book

You can read this book from cover to cover, but you don't necessarily have to; you can use it as a reference book. When you need to know something about a particular aspect of Microsoft Publisher 2007, just jump to the appropriate section and read about it. And don't worry that you'll feel lost if you start on page 231 rather than on page 1; most chapters are self contained, so you can dip your toes in at any point.

If you're curious about what you might find, here are some typical sections you might stumble across:

- ✔ You Want Fast? Well, Meet Mr. Wizard
- ✔ Things You Can Do with Files
- ✔ Keeping Good Margins
- ✔ Hide and Seek: Find and Replace
- ✔ Collecting and Using Type
- ✔ How Color Improves Your Page
- ✔ Printers and Output Quality

The information you need to know is in this book. Don't bother memorizing the contents, and don't even think about using this book to *learn* Microsoft Office Publisher 2007. What you find in this book is only the information that you need to get your work done. Because we tend to babble on, from time to time we post a Technical Stuff icon (which features the *For Dummies* guy — check out the margin) to warn you in case you want to ignore our rantings.

Conventions Used in This Book

Because this book is a reference, you can look up a topic of interest in the table of contents or in the index, in the back of this book. These tools refer you to the sections that talk about that topic. If you need to know something specific in order to understand a section's content, we tell you so. We know that computer technology is loaded with confusing words and phrases and tech-nobabble. (Sometimes we can't avoid slinging this stuff about like a short-order cook in a cheap diner.) But in some cases, we may send you off elsewhere to help you figure out the confusing terms.

We like to give you examples of how to do something. Because Microsoft Publisher 2007 is a Windows-based program, most instructions tell you to "click here" or "click there" or to "choose File⇨Print from the menu" or "press Alt+F,P on the keyboard." Notice two things about these instructions: First, the File⇨Print business is our shorthand way of saying "Open the File menu and then choose Print from the choices that appear"; second, we show you that you press and hold the Alt key while you press the F key, by placing the plus sign (+) sign between them. Then you release both keys and press the *P* key. This keyboard combination produces the same action as using your mouse to choose the menu command. It's all standard Windows fare.

If we want you to enter information from your keyboard, you may see a line that looks like the following (this comes up just a few times):

```
ENTER THIS STUFF
```

In this example, you type the words **ENTER THIS STUFF** after the prompt and then press the Enter key. Notice that we don't use quotation marks around the text ("ENTER THIS STUFF") because we don't want you to enter quotation marks. We then explain why you do what we've told you to do and point out what happens after you do, so don't worry.

Desktop publishing can be a complicated endeavor, with many things that you may (or may not) want to know about. We include in this book a few sections on more advanced topics, such as selecting paper, working with outside print services, and choosing color processes. Of course, if all you want to do is create a greeting card or gift certificate and print the results from your inkjet printer, you might not need to look at these topics. We try to warn you when a section tends toward technical talk or is limited to specific interests. But you can read these sections, and doing so will earn you a gold star in the Desktop Publishing Hall of Fame (although that's not what this book is meant to do).

Foolish Assumptions

We make only three assumptions about you in this book. The first, we've already stated: You don't want to waste time studying useless trivia. You're in a hurry, and you want to get your work done.

Our second assumption is that you have a PC that has at least Microsoft Windows XP installed — although Vista would be nice. Maybe you have set up your computer, or maybe someone else has. But it's working, and you can get the help you need to keep it working.

Our third assumption is that you know your way around your computer's operating system well enough to perform simple operations in that environment. You already know how to move your mouse and stroke your keyboard. You should know how to select a menu command, know how to work with dialog boxes and windows, and be familiar with common desktop items, such as the Recycle Bin. We cover some of these topics (when the discussion is directly applicable to Microsoft Publisher 2007), but we don't go into any great detail.

By the way, if finding your way around your new computer or your operating system is still one of the mysteries of life for you, check out the following books, published by Wiley Publishing:

- *PCs All-in-One Desk Reference For Dummies,* by Mark L. Chambers
- *Windows XP For Dummies,* by Andy Rathbone
- *Windows Vista For Dummies,* by Andy Rathbone

How This Book Is Organized

Topics in this book are generally arranged as though we were directing you through a desktop publishing project from start to finish. In the progression of topics, we try to address the issues you commonly tackle first, first, and the issues that you tackle last, last. Clever, eh? This book has seven major parts; each part has two or more chapters. (Our editors insist that each divided topic should have at least two subdivisions, and we slavishly follow their teachings.)

Aside from these considerations, you'll find that most chapters stand by themselves. You can start reading at any section. Great teachers tell us, "Tell them (the audience) what you are going to tell them." So, we outlined the entire book as follows.

Part 1: Getting Acquainted with Publisher 2007

When you create a project in Microsoft Publisher 2007 to print something, you're doing desktop publishing (DTP). When you create a project to place on the Internet, you're Web spinning. Desktop publishing replaces technology of past decades and centuries with something new and special. For many folks, desktop publishing is the reason they bought computers. Part I tells you what desktop publishing is, how it came about, and where it's going. Also in Part I, we give you the skinny on design issues and provide the nickel tour on the basics that you need to know to run and use the program.

Part II: Mark This Page

Microsoft Publisher 2007, like most desktop publishing programs, uses the metaphor of a pasteboard. In this part, you work on creating a page, defining the layout, and then adding things to your page. You add objects to Microsoft Publisher 2007 pages inside frames, which we tell you how to work with in this part. ("We're innocent, we tell ya. We've been framed!")

Part III: 10,000 Words, One Maniac

An important part of desktop publishing is marrying text and figures on a page. In this part, you discover how to work with text on your page; not just how to enter text into a text frame, mind you, but also how to select and work with type. This part also guides you through the process of importing text from Microsoft Word 2007 and including tables from Microsoft Excel 2007 and Microsoft Access 2007 in your Microsoft Publisher 2007 publications. We'll leave you to figure out who the maniac is.

Part IV: A Picture Is Worth $6.95

A picture is worth a thousand words. That works out to be about $6.95. Honest, we did the math ourselves! You always knew talk was cheap. Now you know *how* cheap. Microsoft Publisher 2007 lets you enhance your page with all kinds of pictures: drawings, images, and other forms of art, including Microsoft PowerPoint 2007 slides and a chapter on using Microsoft Picture Manager. In this part, we tell you what you need to know to create and work with different kinds of pictures — and where to get help if you need it. We also use a chapter to talk about the related topic of using color in your publications.

Part V: Proof Positive

This part contains a cornucopia of important fruits of knowledge for you to nibble on. You see how to fine-tune your page: Edit copy, hyphenate, add flourishes, and assemble your project. You also find a chapter in this part with a discussion on paper, printing, and working with commercial print services.

Part VI: Publishing on the Internet

Publishing on the Internet is almost a requirement. In this part, you learn how to create and edit a Web site, including adding graphics and hyperlinks and adding color and texture to the background. You also find tips on previewing your Web site. Finally, we tell you how to publish your Web site.

Part VII: The Part of Tens

Other people have their lists, and we have our lists. In this part, The Part of Tens, you see lists of ten things on topics that you will want to know about. We give you lists on design issues, printing, commercial print services, and other topics. Have fun reading this part, and when you're done, we will part.

Icons Used in This Book

You won't find a lot of icons in this book, but you will find some. Here is what they mean:

This information may appeal to the nerd in you. If it doesn't, you can safely skip it.

Tips are intended to save you time or help prevent heartburn. We think you will find them worth the read.

Our friendly Design icon points out principles that you may want to employ.

These paragraphs point out tidbits of information that you should, well, remember.

We point out some of the little "gotchas" that life (or Microsoft Publisher 2007) has to offer. (*Hint:* Don't do this!)

Where to Go from Here

You're ready to use this book. Start by reviewing the table of contents to find a topic of current interest to you. Then dive right in and read about it. Try some of our suggestions in your work and experiment. Microsoft Publisher 2007 is a very friendly and forgiving program. (If you save copies of your publication as you go, little can go wrong that you can't fix.)

When you find something that doesn't work quite the way you expect or something that you want to know more about, return to this book. Repeat the process. Finding out about Microsoft Publisher 2007 and Windows XP or Windows Vista can and should be an exploration. Microsoft meant for these programs to be a "discoverable environment" — that is, to be like a well-designed computer game that you can figure out as you play. We're here to get you past any bumps or tilts that you might encounter.

Desktop publishing is fun. That's why so many people do it. And Microsoft Publisher 2007 makes it easier to do than any other program we know of.

Part I

Getting Acquainted with Publisher 2007

The new desktop publishing software not only lets Rags produce a professional looking greeting card quickly and inexpensively, but it also allows him to say it his way.

In this part . . .

*E*veryone wants to create publications that people will read. The quality of your printed work can directly influence your income, your career advancement, the list of attendees at your parties, and more. Attractive résumés open the door to interviews, attractive books get bought, attractive birthday cards get picked up in the store more often, attractive ads pull orders, and attractive people date more often. (No, Microsoft Publisher 2007 doesn't make you more beautiful or handsome.) It's fair to say that the appearance of your designs affects what people think of you as a person.

Some people are born designers; most people are not. Microsoft Publisher 2007 lets you create professional-quality publications and marketing materials easily, even if you're not artistically inclined. You do need to know something about the elements that separate good design from poor design and enough about the technology to create publications or page layout documents in Publisher. That's what Part I is all about. The chapters in this part provide an overview of desktop publishing, tell you what constitutes good design principles, and give you some basic information that you need to know in order to get started working in Microsoft Publisher 2007.

Chapter 1

Own the Printing Press

- -

In This Chapter

▶ Deciding when to use Microsoft Publisher 2007

▶ Understanding desktop publishing

▶ Exploring the design process

▶ Using Publisher templates

- -

Desktop publishing uses page layout software and a personal computer to combine text, type, drawings, and images on a page to create books, newsletters, marketing brochures, flyers, greeting cards, and Web sites, for example. Anything you can print on a page can be put into a page layout program. Microsoft Publisher 2007 lets you place elements on a page, precisely position them, modify them, and specify a print job by using techniques that commercial printers require. Whether you print to your inkjet or laser printer, run down the street to Quick Copy Shop, or send your files to a commercial printer, Microsoft Publisher 2007 helps you prepare your work for that level of quality.

When Should You Use Microsoft Publisher 2007?

Many programs let you design and print pages to various levels of sophistication. These programs include word processors such as Microsoft Word 2007 and Corel WordPerfect Office X3; graphics programs such as CorelDRAW and Adobe Illustrator; and even low-end integrated packages such as Microsoft Works and Broderbund ThinkFree Office 3. The program I use for writing, Microsoft Word 2007, enables me to type text, format text, import pictures, create drawings, and even work with images.

If you can do all that in Microsoft Word 2007, why do you need a desktop publishing or page layout program like Microsoft Publisher 2007? The short answer is control. Microsoft Publisher 2007 lets you control these elements with finer precision and also offers you many special tools.

What's new in Microsoft Publisher 2007?

If you've used a previous version of Microsoft Publisher you may be wondering why you should bother with this latest version. Well, here is a partial list of new features to be found in Microsoft Publisher 2007:

✔ **Apply your brand in one step:** Microsoft Publisher 2007 lets you easily apply and view logos, colors, fonts, and other information in one step.

✔ **Search templates:** It's easier than ever to find templates within Microsoft Publisher 2007, and now you can even preview templates online. Just point your Web browser to the Microsoft Office Online Web site to access hundreds of Microsoft Publisher templates — without ever having to leave Microsoft Publisher 2007!

✔ **Publisher Tasks:** The new Publisher Tasks pane in Microsoft Publisher 2007 provides help with common publication creation and distribution procedures.

✔ **Reuse design elements:** The Content Library lets you store and reuse text, graphics, and other design elements in any of your Microsoft Publisher publications.

✔ **Publish in PDF or XPS format:** Download a free add-in and you can save your Microsoft Publisher 2007 files in PDF or XPS format.

✔ **Create a new marketing campaign:** If you have Microsoft Outlook 2007 with Business Contact Manager, you can create and track your own marketing campaigns!

So, if you just want to stick your company's logo at the top of your letters and insert a copy of your scanned-in signature at the bottom, you don't need Publisher to do that. If you want to create a company logo by combining a couple of graphics from different sources, write some text, add some color, and then separate the output to give to a commercial print service to print, Publisher is a better choice. If you want to create high-quality marketing materials that will help you attract new customers and keep existing customers, Publisher is definitely the way to go. It does these things well.

How Desktop Publishing Works

Page layout software combines various parts into a single document, or *publication*. The following list briefly covers the parts you can meld. In Figure 1-1, you can see that I labeled a few sample elements.

Nearly all objects on a page are in frames or blocks that are created when you import or create the object:

✔ **Text:** Okay, I know that you know what text is. Text is the stuff you type: all those individual characters that form words, sentences, and paragraphs, for example.

✔ **Type:** Man/woman does not live by text alone. Type and typography are the various letter forms you can use to make your text more attractive. Publisher lets you access WordArt, a text manipulation program that lets you add fancy effects to your text.

✔ **Picture:** Computers make two kinds of pictures: drawn (*vector,* or object-oriented) and painted (*raster,* or bitmapped) images. You can import both types into a picture frame.

While Publisher doesn't ship with a ton of clip art, you can go to the Microsoft Office Web site to access a huge amount of clip art, including thousands of clip art images, photographs, Web-related graphics, animated GIFs (those cute pictures that seem to wiggle around on Web pages), and more! In fact the Microsoft Office Web site has more than 150,000 free images and sounds. Check it out at `http://office.microsoft.com/clipart`.

✔ **Drawn object:** Publisher isn't a drawing program, although some tools on its Objects toolbar enable you to create drawn images, such as lines, ovals and circles, rectangles and squares, and a whole bunch of custom shapes.

✔ **Table:** Although you can import tables from other programs as objects, as either drawings or Object Linking and Embedding (OLE) objects managed by other applications, Publisher has its own Table tool.

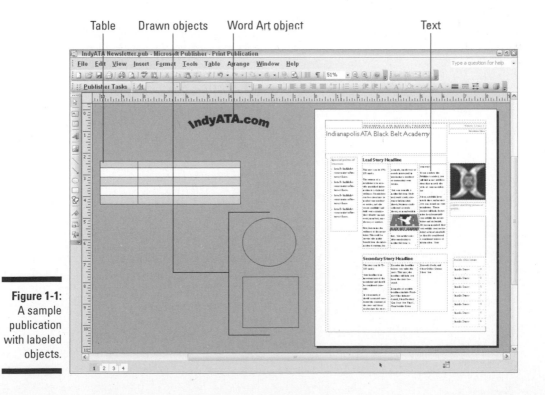

Figure 1-1:
A sample publication with labeled objects.

You can use Publisher to create these elements from scratch, or you can use other programs to create the objects and then use Publisher to place them in your publication.

If you have used a previous version of Publisher or Microsoft Office, most things you see on the screen will seem familiar. However, if your first exposure to Publisher and/or Office is with version 2007, you might need a brief tour. The first thing you'll probably notice is that the user interface in Microsoft Publisher 2007 is quite a bit different from the rest of the Microsoft Office 2007 products. Microsoft Publisher 2007 utilizes the more traditional menu system found in Microsoft Office 2003 and earlier. The "other" Microsoft Office products use Microsoft's new Ribbon interface that is intended to make it easier and faster to find the commands and features when you need them.

Let's take a moment to get familiar with the Microsoft Publisher 2007 screen. Figure 1-2 shows you Publisher with an open publication. If you look closely, you'll find the following:

✔ **Title bar:** At the very top of the Publisher window, you'll find the Title bar. The Title bar shows you the name of the current publication and whether the publication is a Print Publication or a Web Publication.

✔ **Menu bar:** Just below the Title bar you'll find the Menu bar. The Menu bar contains, (yes, you guessed it!) the menus. The Menu bar gives you access to all the features and functions of Publisher. Everything from creating publications to specifying program settings to getting help.

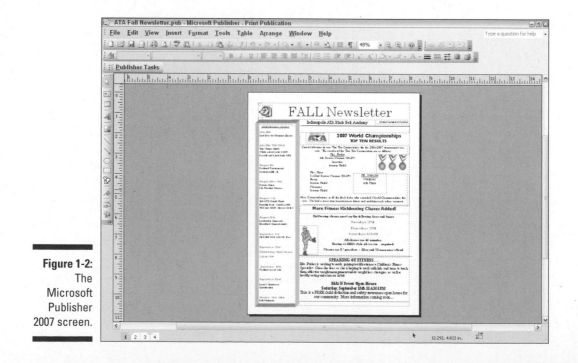

Figure 1-2:
The
Microsoft
Publisher
2007 screen.

- ✔ **Standard toolbar:** This toolbar is located right below the Menu bar. The Standard toolbar's main job is to let you control the appearance of the text in your publication.

- ✔ **Publisher Tasks pane:** This little guy likes to hang out on the left side of the screen just under the Standard toolbar. Although often hidden, it expands to provide links that guide you through the steps necessary to complete the design of your publication.

- ✔ **Objects toolbar:** This toolbar is located on the left side of the screen. It has the tools to help you create Text boxes, Tables, Pictures, and the like.

- ✔ **Publication workspace:** In the middle of the screen you'll see a large white box. The shape of this box varies with the type of publication you are creating. This white box represents the page upon which you create your publication.

- ✔ **Rulers:** The rulers located above and to the left of the publication work- space are provided to help you lay out and properly align objects on your page.

- ✔ **Scroll bars:** On the right and bottom of the screens you see scroll bars that let you scroll vertically and horizontally when your entire document doesn't fit on the screen.

- ✔ **Page Selection bar:** The Page Selection bar, located at the bottom left of the screen, lets you quickly go to any page in your publication. This may not seem like a big deal in a one-page flyer, but if you are working on a 300-page catalog, that feature comes in mighty handy.

The Design Process

Page design is an iterative process. You can always find a better way to make a point with design, to use type and color, or to refine a graphical image, for example. You can always return to a publication later and find something you could have done better. Like all creative endeavors, a well-designed publication can be improved by planning before the fact, experimenting, and offering thoughtful criticism at all stages. The sections that follow describe some methods that designers use to make their pages stand out from the crowd.

Storyboarding

To get a good start on the design process, you can block out the way you want your publication to look. One block-out method is storyboarding. *Storyboards* are like block diagrams. Cartoonists use storyboards to show a story's progression. Movie designers use storyboards to illustrate key frames in a movie, which enables them to present the movie in a preproduction form that others can view and understand. You can use this same technique.

Many people like to mock up their design projects with pencil and paper. They create a dummy of their publication and, when the publication spans several pages, create storyboards. But this is all a matter of preference: The important thing is to plan your publication before you create it.

I find Publisher so easy to work with that I prefer to create my dummies inside the program. The tools for creating frames, lines, and boxes make these page elements easy to create and modify inside Publisher. I also find that working inside the program forces me to think, right from the start, about how I'll break apart a sample design and implement it.

Publisher has a collection of templates that help you create professional-looking publications. When you first launch Publisher, you see the templates in the Catalog window as a collection of thumbnails showing sample documents you can create. The Publication Types pane on the left provides a list of the various types of publications that you can create with Publisher, while the center pane shows a list of the most popular types of publications. When you click on a type of publication in the Publication Types pane, the center pane changes to show a list of thumbnail images that show you what the various publications of that particular type will look like. (In other words, the list of available templates changes with the type of publication you choose in the Publication Types pane.)

In effect, storyboarding is what the templates do when they create a publication for you. When you create a document by using the Publisher templates, the result is a dummy of the document you're creating. Figure 1-3 shows a four-panel brochure created with one of the Brochures templates. The template helps generate a sample document with a headline, graphics blocks, and text frames with sample text. Each element on the page can be modified, but the document's overall look comes from using a particular Publisher template. Your dummies, or mock-ups, should show similar use of text, graphics, and overall design.

Try moving away from your design and looking at it from afar. (This trick works well for many people.) Better yet, try zooming out so that you can see the overall layout but cannot read the text. Choose View↪Zoom from the main menu and choose 33% or 25% from the submenu that appears. Determine whether its purpose is obvious or whether clutter is obscuring its purpose. If you have too many page elements, try eliminating some.

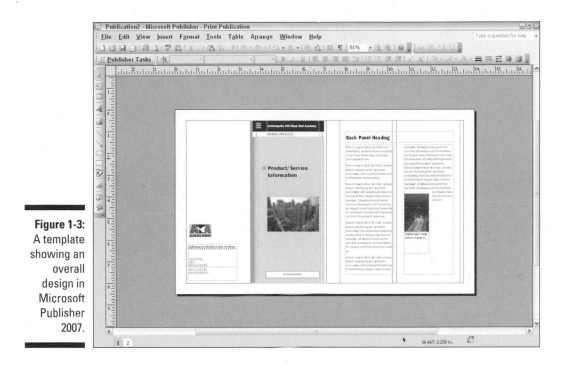

Figure 1-3: A template showing an overall design in Microsoft Publisher 2007.

Assembling a page

After you block out a page design, you can replace the dummy text, pictures, and other frames with the data you want to include on the page. This is the assembly stage of page composition. Depending on the type of object frame (Publisher-speak for a text box or picture frame) or tool selected, you can apply one of the Edit or Insert menu commands to bring the data into Publisher. The basics of importing text are covered in Chapter 6. You can find the related topic of importing tabular data also in Chapter 6. For details on bringing graphics into your publication, see Chapter 10.

Chances are great that after you compose and fill all the frames with real data, the page will require more tweaking. Publisher contains a number of specialized tools for repositioning, resizing, and fitting objects on a page. Chapter 12 details the final steps in the assembly process. You also find information about preparing a publication for output to an outside printer in Chapter 13.

Don't be surprised if the assembly process is largely composed of the tweaking phase of the project. Leave enough time to get this tweaking done the way you want it. (Think of the builder who says that the house is 90 percent done when only 50 percent of the allotted time is spent.)

Printing a page

After your page is composed the way you want it, you're ready to print. You can choose to print files to local printers and select from any of the print drivers that came with Windows XP or Windows Vista. Printing to a local printer is no different in Publisher than it is in most other Windows applications: You simply choose File➪Print.

If you intend to have your publication printed by a commercial printer, you will probably want to send the entire Publisher file to the printer. The printer then has the most flexibility to print your publication correctly. If your commercial printer doesn't have Publisher, you can send your publication as a PDF file. The commercial printer can then extract and modify images but cannot make many other types of changes or corrections. See Chapter 13 for details on having close encounters with printers of the third kind (human ones, that is).

Getting Out of the Gate with Publisher

You start Microsoft Publisher 2007 in one of two ways:

- Double-click the icon for the program on the Windows desktop.
- Choose Start➪Programs➪Microsoft Office➪Microsoft Office Publisher 2007, as shown in Figure 1-4. (Easy!)

Whichever way you start Publisher, you're greeted by the handy Catalog window you see in Figure 1-5. Your first glimpse of the Catalog window shows templates for the most popular publication types — business cards, brochures, and postcards, for example — but you can change the view by choosing other categories from the Publication Types pane, on the left. (Anyone for paper folding projects?)

If you're familiar with earlier versions of Microsoft Publisher, you may be wondering what happened to its wizards. They have been replaced by Publisher templates and the new Publisher Tasks pane.

Using a Publisher template is the easiest way to create a publication in Microsoft Publisher 2007. After you select a publication type and choose a template from the Catalog window, the Publisher Tasks pane appears, presenting you with a set of dialog boxes that leads you through the creation of a project based on selections you make.

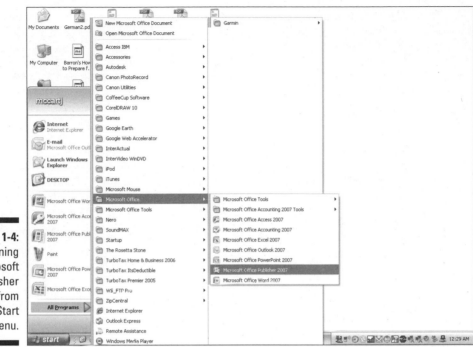

Figure 1-4:
Opening
Microsoft
Publisher
2007 from
the Start
menu.

Figure 1-5:
Microsoft
Publisher
provides
hundreds of
templates in
more than
two dozen
publication
types.

If for some reason Publisher is already open and you're working somewhere else in the program, you can always return to the Catalog window by choosing File➪New from the main menu.

The Catalog window is a *modal* dialog box, which means that you need to make a selection in it or dismiss it before you can go on. You can click and drag the Catalog window's title bar as you would drag any window's title bar.

I just made the assertion that using a Publisher template is the easiest way to create a publication in Microsoft Publisher. The next section is meant to show you just how right I am.

Just the fax, ma'am: Creating a fax cover sheet the quick and easy way

Microsoft Publisher 2007 has hundreds of templates for more than 25 types of publications; if you look back at Figure 1-5, you can see the (rather long) list of available publication types. Some of the more useful publications are in the Business Forms category, where you can find

- ✔ Expense reports
- ✔ Fax covers
- ✔ Inventory lists
- ✔ Invoices
- ✔ Purchase orders
- ✔ Quotes
- ✔ Refunds
- ✔ Statements
- ✔ Time billings
- ✔ Weekly records

The Fax Cover publication type provides a quick example of how to use a Publisher template to quickly create a useful business publication:

1. **In the Publication Types pane (the listing on the left side of the Catalog window), click the Business Forms link.**

The center pane of the Catalog window updates to show the available Business Forms categories.

2. **Scroll down to the Fax Cover section and then select one of the 35 Fax Cover examples.**

   The selected Fax Cover sheet is highlighted, and a larger sample version appears in the top-right portion of the screen.

3. **Click the Create button located in the bottom-right portion of the screen.**

   Publisher creates (surprising, huh?) the Fax Cover for you and presents you with the Publisher Tasks pane visible to the right of the publication, as shown in Figure 1-6.

The Publisher Tasks pane stands ready to help you customize the publication. Its main features include the ones in this list:

✔ **The Page Options tab:** This tab is a bit of a chameleon. It changes depending on the type of publication you are working on. If you are working on a Fax Cover sheet, it might display a business logo that you can click and drag onto your publication. If you are working on a newsletter, it shows a Columns section that lets you change the layout of your publication by changing the number of columns.

✔ **The Options tab:** From this tab, you can quickly and easily select a different template to use and also change the paper size. (The name of this tab changes depending on whichever category you chose; in Figure 1-6, it appears as the Business Form Options tab because I chose the Business Form category.)

✔ **The Font Schemes tab:** Change the font scheme for the entire publication. *Font schemes* are collections of fonts that were created by armies of highly paid design consultants to be pleasing to the eye (the fonts, not the consultants). Selecting a font scheme instantly applies the new fonts to your publication. Of course, you have the option of creating your very own font scheme, too. Who's to say that Old English Text MT and Bauhaus 93 don't go well together?

✔ **The Color Schemes tab:** On this tab, you can change the — you guessed it — color scheme. Just don't go thinking that the same group of highly paid consultants who created the font schemes also created the color schemes. We're talking specialists here. As with the font schemes, you also have the option of creating your own color scheme. Of course, unless you and the person to whom you're sending the fax have one of those newfangled color fax machines, you're probably wasting your time customizing the color scheme on your fax cover.

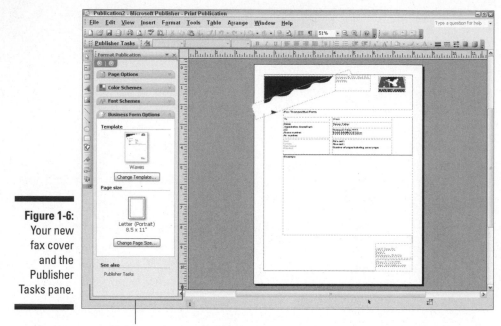

Figure 1-6:
Your new
fax cover
and the
Publisher
Tasks pane.

Tasks pane

Fun facts about Publisher templates and the Publisher Tasks pane

You need to know few important points about the Publisher templates and the Publisher Tasks pane; these tools are used to create new on-screen publications inside Publisher:

✔ **The Print Preview feature lets you see how your document will look when it is printed.** Print Preview shows you your publication without cluttering the screen with all those toolbars, menus, rulers, task panes, etc. It even lets you view multiple pages at once (click the Multiple pages button) or how the publication will look if printed on a monochrome printer (click the Color/Grayscale button). Figure 1-7 shows the fax cover through the "eyes" of Print Preview.

✔ **Publications created with Publisher templates are composed of many individual objects.** If you click any part of a publication, selection handles (little circles on the edges; see Figure 1-8) appear around the selected area. With the help of these little guys, you can manipulate the size, placement, color, and other properties of your publication's parts.

✔ **As handy as templates are, if you're using templates only to create documents in Publisher, you're just scratching the surface of what you can do with the program.** I'm more than happy to present what's under the surface as you read through this book.

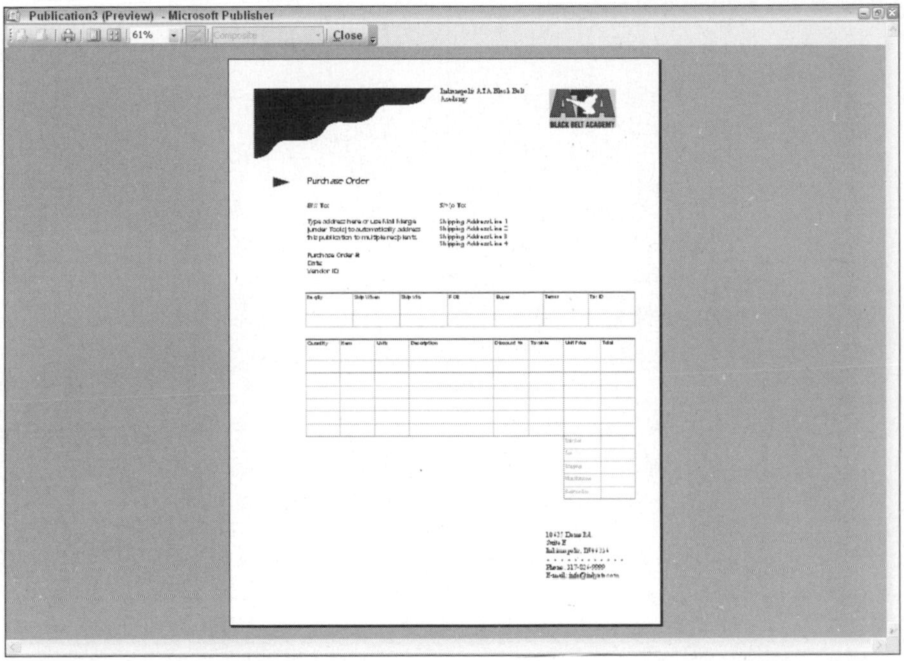

Figure 1-7:
The fax
cover in
Print
Preview
mode.

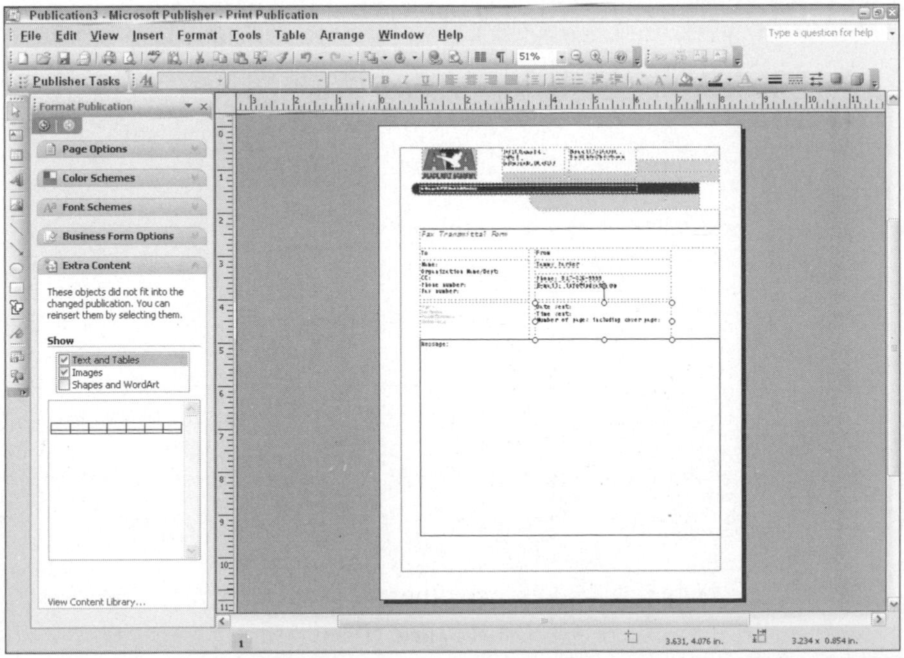

Figure 1-8:
Click an
object, and
selection
handles
appear.

Meet the publication types

Each publication type can generate several versions of publications of the same class, depending on the selections you make. Publisher has 27 publication types (28 if you count the Blank Page Sizes selection):

✔ **Blank Page Sizes:** Use these templates when you want to create a publication from scratch. You can choose the page size you want without Publisher adding any sample pictures or text. You start with a clean slate.

✔ **Advertisements:** Use these templates to create advertisements for your business. Figure 1-9 shows you the style affectionately referred to as The Works.

✔ **Award Certificates:** Choose from 22 different award certificates.

✔ **Banners:** This publication type offers eight types of banners: Informational, Sale, Event, Welcome, Congratulations, Holiday, Romance, and Get Well. You can set a height and width, and you can also decide whether you want to have graphics and borders on your banner.

✔ **Brochures:** Four different brochure styles are offered: Informational, Price List, Event, and Fund-raiser. Figure 1-10 shows previews of some Informational brochures.

✔ **Business Cards:** Choose from more than 50 styles of business cards.

✔ **Business Forms:** You have ten choices: Expense Report, Fax Cover, Inventory List, Invoice, Purchase Order, Quote, Refund, Statement, Time Billing, and Weekly Record. As you click each type of business form in the Publication Types pane, a picture of the default form appears on the right side of the screen. Figure 1-11 shows you an Invoice form that uses the Eclipse style.

✔ **Calendars:** Choose from 46 full-page and 3 wallet-size calendars.

✔ **Catalogs:** Create ten different kinds of catalogs to advertise your wares.

✔ **E-mail:** Use any of these ten e-mail templates to create targeted e-mail marketing campaigns.

✔ **Envelopes:** The Envelopes templates create more than 50 envelope styles that match the Letterheads and Business Cards styles. Publisher remembers the style you used and asks whether you want to base your next envelope on that style.

✔ **Flyers:** This publication type includes styles for Informational, Special Offer, Sale, Event, Fund-raiser, and Announcement.

✔ **Gift Certificates:** Forge — er, I mean, *create* — your own gift certificates! Choose from 35 gift certificate styles.

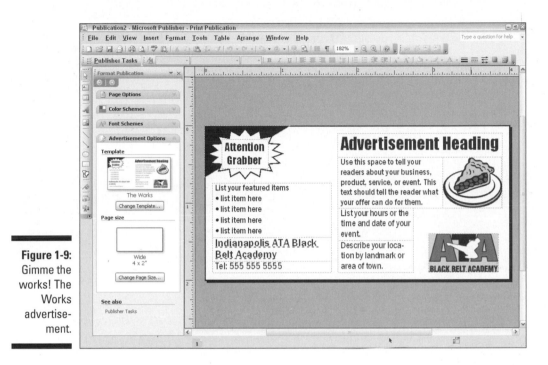

Figure 1-9:
Gimme the
works! The
Works
advertise-
ment.

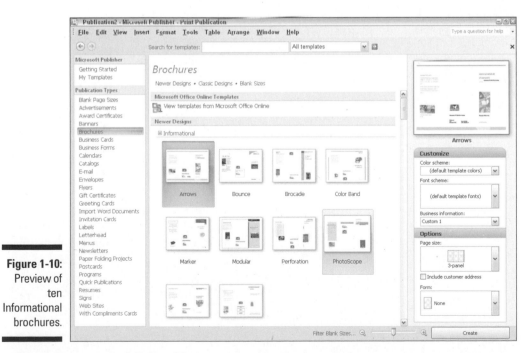

Figure 1-10:
Preview of
ten
Informational
brochures.

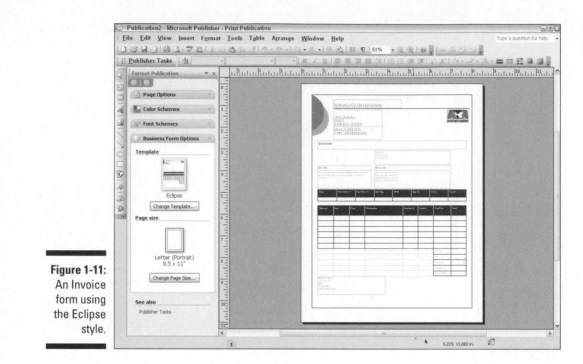

Figure 1-11:
An Invoice
form using
the Eclipse
style.

✔ **Greeting Cards:** Tired of paying $5 for a greeting card? You'll love this publication type. It offers 20 categories of cards. Each of these categories offers you many choices. Figure 1-12 shows you an example of a professional-looking thank-you card that you can create and send to your clients.

✔ **Import Word Documents:** These templates let you gussy up text you created in Microsoft Word 2007. Select from 36 different styles. This is a great tool if you have a Microsoft Word document that you want to update so that it has the look and feel of other publications you have created in Publisher. Have a report that you created in Microsoft Word and you want it to look like that brochure you worked so hard to create? Use the Import Word Documents templates.

✔ **Invitation Cards:** Having a to-do? These templates help you create invitation cards for your party, theme party, holiday party, birthday party, housewarming, shower, event, celebration, or fund-raiser.

✔ **Labels:** You can create labels in any of the following 11 styles: Mailing Address, Shipping, Return Address, Computer Disk, Cassette, CD/DVD, Video, Jar/Product, Binder, Bookplate, and Identification. All these labels match standard Avery labels. The Avery number is provided after the label name.

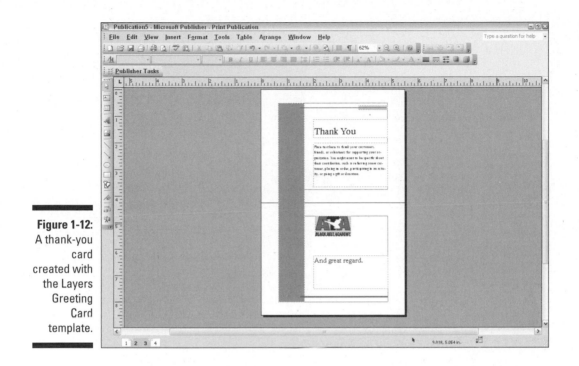

Figure 1-12:
A thank-you
card
created with
the Layers
Greeting
Card
template.

- ✔ **Letterhead:** The Letterhead templates offer you more than 50 styles of letterhead that you can print. Figure 1-13 shows an example of a letterhead using the Modular style. After you create a letterhead for your business or personal use, Publisher remembers the style you used and asks whether you want to base your next letterhead on that style.

- ✔ **Menus:** If you have your own restaurant, the Menus templates let you create Regular, Take-Out, Daily Special, and Wine/Dessert menus in a variety of styles.

- ✔ **Newsletters:** Create almost 70 different styles of newsletters in a variety of sizes and layouts.

- ✔ **Paper Folding Projects:** Build your own paper tiger air force! Afraid to fly? Create origami (the Japanese art of creating paper figures). The four types range from easy to create (the Boat) to difficult (the Parrot). Still, these items are fun to give, and they're pretty when printed from a color printer or on colored paper.

- ✔ **Postcards:** These templates create 13 categories of postcards: Informational, Special Offer, Sale, Event, Invitation, Holiday Party Invitation, Holiday Greeting, Holiday Thank You, Thank You, We've Moved, Announcement, Reminder, and Tent Fold. Each category offers several types of postcards.

- ✔ **Programs:** Create Music, Religious Service, and Theater programs with a few clicks of the mouse.

- ✔ **Quick Publications:** Use these templates when you want to create single-page publications with a professional design and layout.

- ✔ **Resumes:** Choose from Entry Level, Chronological, or Curriculum Vitae résumés with style!

- ✔ **Signs:** Create 40 single-page signs — everything from Authorized Personnel Only to Lemonade for Sale to Wheelchair Access.

- ✔ **Web Sites:** Use these templates to create over 70 different multiple-page Web sites quickly and easily.

- ✔ **With Compliments Cards:** Choose from 35 styles of With Compliments cards. The cards come in handy when you have product samples and freebies to give away and you want to make sure that the recipient knows where they came from. Figure 1-14 shows a With Compliments card in the Marquee style.

You aren't limited to accepting whatever the templates give you. You can replace one font with another, one picture with another, or one border with another, for example. And, you can always use the Publisher Tasks pane to make changes to the design of your publication. If the Publisher Tasks pane is not visible, click the Publisher Tasks button on the Publisher Tasks toolbar to display it. Knowing Publisher well helps you quickly modify these templates' output and makes the result a document that you're proud to show to others.

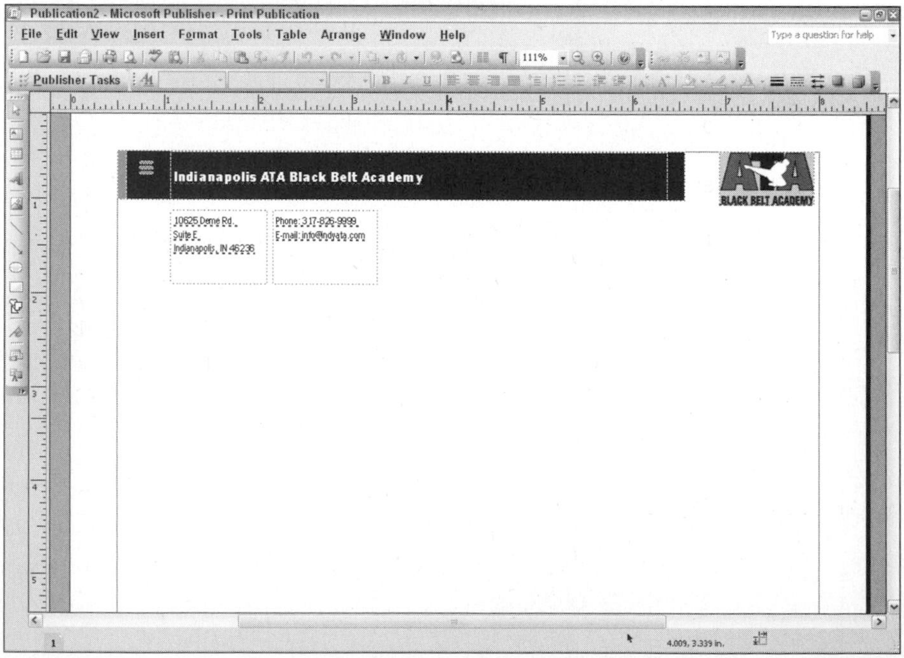

Figure 1-13:
A sample
Letterhead
style.

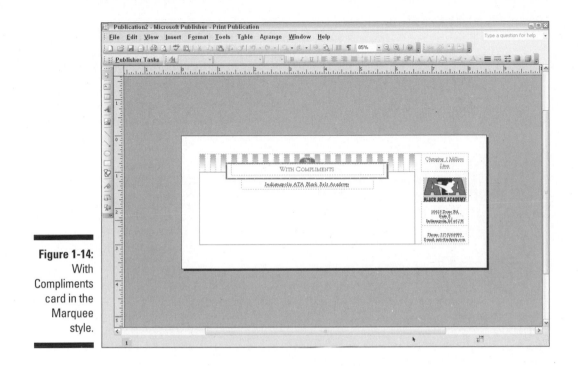

Figure 1-14:
With
Compliments
card in the
Marquee
style.

Create your own templates

If the hundreds of templates the preceding section introduces aren't enough for you, don't despair. You can always create templates of your very own. How do you perform such feats of wonder, you ask? Okay, maybe you didn't ask, but this stuff is handy, and I tell you how anyway. If you really don't want to know, please press the Pause button — now!

To create a template of your own, follow these steps:

1. **Start by creating a publication.**

   You can create one from scratch or start with an existing template and customize it to your tastes.

2. **Choose File⇨Save As from the main menu.**

   The Save As dialog box appears, as shown in Figure 1-15.

3. **Type a name for your new template in the File Name text box.**

4. **In the Save As Type drop-down list box, select Publisher Template (*.pub).**

   Notice that Publisher automatically changes the Save In location to the Templates folder.

5. **Click Save.**

Your template is now available for use. Click the My Templates link — right there in the upper-left corner of the Catalog window — to see the list of templates you've created. Figure 1-16 shows the My Templates pane with two templates I created.

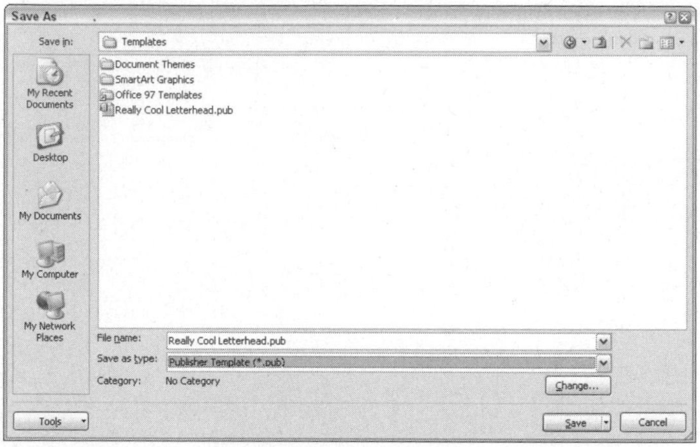

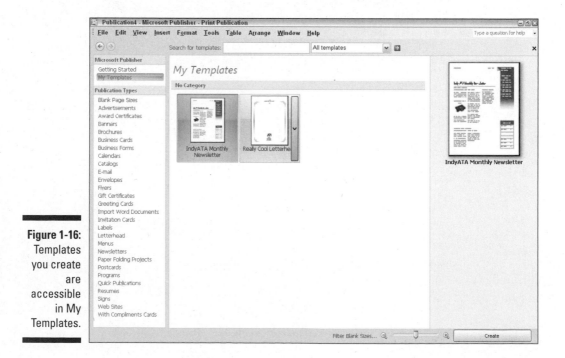

Figure 1-15:
The Save
As dialog
box.

Figure 1-16:
Templates
you create
are
accessible
in My
Templates.

Chapter 2

Success by Design

*W*e live in a fast age. Before, you had time to read the occasional ad or brochure that appeared in your mailbox; now, you may receive dozens of mailings every day. We're bombarded with so much stuff that we tend to ignore most of it.

So here's the deal. Your publication has five seconds to get someone's attention. (Some design gurus claim that most pieces get about two seconds of review before being tossed.) If your published piece doesn't have something that interests your audience and makes people want to explore it further — poof! — it's gone.

If you have only five seconds, you had better make sure that your primary message is the first thing a reader sees. You have little room for error on this score. Consider any design device that you can use to repeat — and build on — the primary message.

This chapter shows you the design basics necessary to do your work in Microsoft Publisher 2007 quickly and well.

Know Your Audience

The first step to creating a successful project is figuring out who your audience is and how they will interact with your work. Knowing your audience helps you refine your publication's look and feel. In addition, it helps you determine your writing style, which is essential for good communication.

You can learn a lot about successful design by studying the work of marketing gurus, particularly those who work in advertising. Advertising combines a creative art form with statistically measured results based on large populations of target markets. One of my favorite books on this topic is *Design for Response: Creative Direct Marketing That Works,* by Leslie Sherr and David J. Katz (published by Rockport Publishers).

While you're designing your publication, show it to prospective members of your target audience so that you can figure out what they need. If your target audience is college students, for example, you might show your publication to several college students and solicit their feedback before you go to the trouble and expense of having it printed.

When you know your audience, you can create a publication that has the correct "voice" or "tone" for that group. For example, a typeface that looks like lettering on a ransom note is inappropriate for business correspondence but may be perfect for birthday party invitations. Publisher has thousands of professionally designed templates, 50 font *schemes* (collections of fonts that look good together in a publication), and more than 90 coordinated color schemes. Finding one that's appropriate to your audience shouldn't be too difficult.

If you're picky and you don't like any of the hundreds of fonts that come with Publisher, you can always buy more. Some vendors sell type in packages designed for specific uses. Their catalogs (which are works of art in themselves) describe the best uses for many typefaces and also suggest typefaces that work well together.

Where Others Have Gone Before

When I start the design phase of a publishing project, I try to collect the best examples of work in that area. I look at the overall design of any piece I collect and look for style elements that I can use as a springboard to creating my own style. Keep file folders of ads you like, marketing pieces you get in the mail, and other publications. Then, when you're ready to create a piece, you can sit down and peruse your samples. Invariably, you'll find an idea or two to get you started. If you don't find anything that strikes your fancy, try one of the many templates that Publisher provides.

Any artwork, images, templates, or designs you find in Publisher and its Design Gallery are there for your use. The following list specifies, according to the Microsoft Software License Terms (MSLT), what you *cannot* do with the media elements (photos, clip art, fonts, and images, for example) in Publisher:

✔ Sell, license or distribute copies of the media elements on a stand-alone basis or as part of any collection, product, or service where the primary value of the product or service is the media element

✔ Use or distribute any of the media elements that include representations of identifiable individuals, governments, logos, initials, emblems, trademarks, or entities for any commercial purposes or to express or imply any endorsement or association with any product, service, entity, or activity

✔ Create obscene or scandalous works, as defined by federal law at the time the work is created, using the media elements

✔ Permit third parties to distribute copies of the media elements except as part of your product or service

Also, according to the terms of the license, you must

✔ Indemnify, hold harmless, and defend Microsoft from and against any claims or lawsuits, including attorneys' fees, that arise from or result from the use or distribution of the media elements as modified by you

✔ Include a valid copyright notice on your products and services that include copies of the media elements

You cannot and should not copy an entire design or image from someone else. That's illegal. Most designs are copyrighted by their authors. When you use other people's work, you can, however, adapt the designs you collect, borrowing an idea here and an idea there.

Sometimes a fine line exists between adapting an idea and copying one. You need to use good judgment. Note that the law in this area is volatile and subject to change. I recommend *The Desktop Publisher's Legal Handbook,* by Daniel Sitarz (Nova Publishing Company) as a good place to start learning about these issues.

Another resource to use when beginning the design phase is a study of before-and-after makeovers. You can find case studies in the design makeover columns in desktop publishing magazines and in some specialized books on desktop publishing. The following resources take this approach:

✔ **Books:**

• *Looking Good in Print,* 4th Edition, by Roger C. Parker and Patrick Berry (published by Coriolis Group Books.)

✔ **Magazines:**

• *Before & After* (www.bamagazine.com), an online magazine that tells you "how to design cool stuff"

• *Communication Arts* (www.commarts.com), the world's largest "magazine on creativity for graphic designers, art directors, copywriters, photographers, illustrators and multimedia designers."

The Keys to Design Success

Most design gurus agree that you can apply certain principles to your designs to make them easier to understand and more attractive to the reader. Although the exact terminology for these principles may vary, the set of principles is nearly always the same.

When you begin to design a publication, you may not always analyze your work in terms of these principles, but you should at least keep them in mind:

✔ **Be consistent.** Elements on a page should be repeated in appropriate places. Consistency is particularly important in longer publications, such as books. The more structured your design, the easier it is to produce the piece.

The best way to enforce consistent design is to create a meaningful style sheet for your publication. A *style sheet* is a collection of styles that allows you to keep your publication consistent and make quick changes. Publisher can help you apply styles or formats to text, objects, tables, and other page elements. Just as word processing documents can have style sheets, Publisher can import or create text styles. You can put together your Publisher project more quickly and more consistently if you use a well-developed style sheet and template rather than simply develop on the fly.

Keep in mind that using one of thousands of templates that Publisher offers is a good way to ensure consistency. For example, you can create a letterhead starting with a Publisher template and then customize the letterhead to your liking. After you're satisfied with the look of the letterhead, you can click the Change Template button in the Publisher Tasks pane and select Envelope to create an envelope with the same "look and feel" as the letterhead.

✔ **Put things where people tend to see them.** People have a tendency to view a page in a diagonal direction, from the upper left to the lower right. Elements in the center of the page get the most attention; elements in the upper-left and lower-right areas get the least attention.

Your design should treat a two-page spread as though it were a single page because the entire two-page spread is the unit of design that readers see.

✔ **Keep your message simple.** To make your reader focus on your content, follow these guidelines:

  • *Use white space.* Many well-designed pieces have a white space content of 50 percent.

- *Limit yourself to no more than two fonts on a page.* You may have noticed that all font schemes in Publisher consist of two fonts.

- *Be judicious with color — apply it as highlighting.* You want to use color to enhance, not distract from, the message you're trying to get across.

✔ **Keep related or similar information on a page.** Keep related information close together or aligned.

You can create a block of related elements by separating them from other elements on the page with rules (lines), frames (boxes), or white space. Likewise, if a graphical image relates to a story, the image should appear close to the story. Any caption for the image should appear close to it — just like the graphics in this book.

✔ **Align everything on a page with something.** Create a grid and place your page elements on that grid, as described in Chapter 4. Creating this type of *page grid* for a layout is similar to creating an outline for a written document.

The same page grid can produce order on pages *without* producing pages that look alike. For example, three- and four-column newspapers and newsletters are common because you can produce many looks within those formats. You can have blocks in the grid that aren't filled in, for example, and graphics that span multiple blocks. Figure 2-1 shows a four-column grid with three rows. This layout generates 12 blocks and offers a lot of flexibility. Figures 2-2 through 2-4 show you three examples that use this grid layout.

✔ **Provide contrast to enliven your work.** Balance consistency by doing the unexpected.

✔ **Use a page hierarchy.** If you use a large headline, readers will probably start reading the page there. You can use smaller headlines to divide a page into sections. You can also use vertical and horizontal rules to break your page into blocks and provide contrast. Emphasize important information by making it look different, but don't emphasize parts of your page that have less importance.

The columns in your page grid don't *have* to be the same width, and the pages in a two-page spread don't *have* to be balanced or symmetrical. Balanced pages seem boring. I tend to vary the size and placement of graphics across columns. I also favor the use of sidebars, pull-quotes (short statements that summarize information on a page), large initial capitals, and column shadings to break up the page.

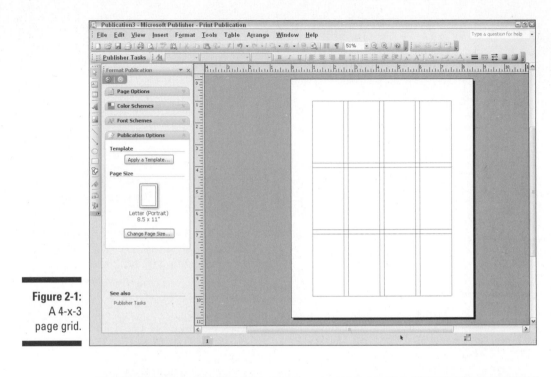

Figure 2-1:
A 4-x-3
page grid.

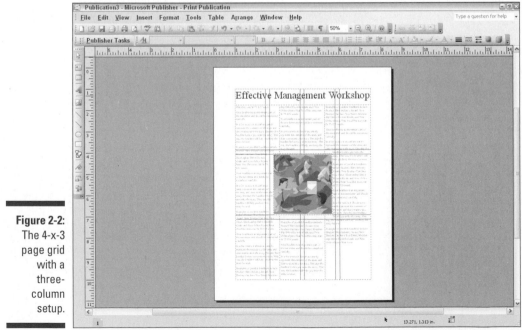

Figure 2-2:
The 4-x-3
page grid
with a
three-
column
setup.

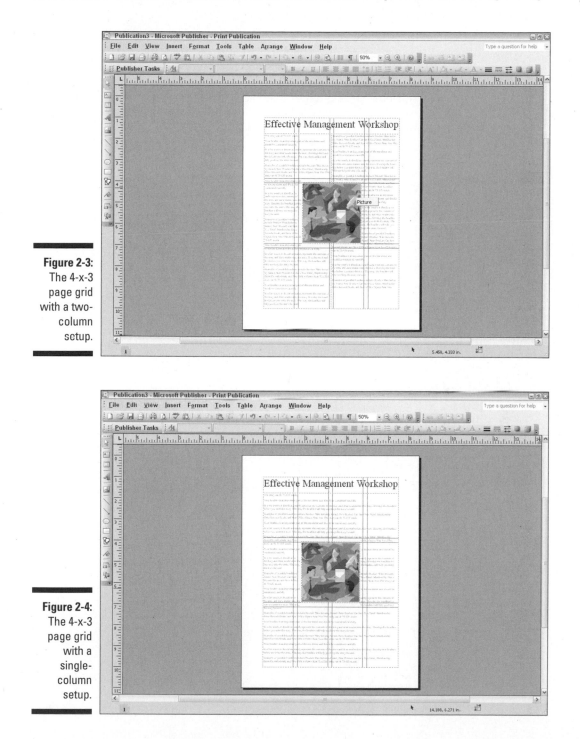

Figure 2-3:
The 4-x-3
page grid
with a two-
column
setup.

Figure 2-4:
The 4-x-3
page grid
with a
single-
column
setup.

Desktop Style Resources

Desktop publishing has turned millions of people into typographers and typesetters. Using type and working with typography aren't skills that come naturally to most people, however. The many rules and guidelines specific to page layout don't pertain to typewritten text or text prepared in word processors. The resources in this section can help you make the transition from text documents to desktop publications.

Two of the most accepted style guides for clear writing in the United States for the English language are

- *The Elements of Style,* 4th Edition, by William Strunk, Jr., and E. B. White (published by Longman)

- *The Chicago Manual of Style,* 15th Edition (published by University of Chicago Press)

A number of texts specialize in the handling of type. In addition to *The Chicago Manual of Style,* the following books are type-worthy additions to your library:

- *Words into Type,* 3rd Edition, by Marjorie Skillin and Robert Malcom Gay (published by Prentice Hall)

- *New Hart's Rules: The Handbook of Style for Writers and Editors,* by R. M. Ritter, ed. (published by Oxford University Press)

- *Pocket Pal: The Handy Little Book of Graphic Arts Production,* 19th Edition, by Michael Bruno (published by International Paper Company)

The following two small texts are noteworthy for beginning users because they deal with typographical issues in a friendly way:

- *The PC Is Not a Typewriter,* by Robin Williams (published by Peachpit Press)

- *The Desktop Style Guide,* by James Felici (published by Random House Information Group)

Desktop publishing has its own language. Each typography reference work mentioned in this section helps you keep your picas separate from your points, your en dashes from your em dashes, and your verso from your recto.

Everything Costs Money

Your budget can play a prominent role in the design of your publication. You don't want to merrily design something only to be shocked by the sticker price when you arrive at the printer. A good designer always asks up front "How much were you intending to spend?" because it helps to ground the project in reality. Perhaps good designers ask the question also because it helps them set their pay scale.

Just because a project has a limited budget doesn't mean that the publication has to be poorly designed. Publisher was created with the idea that you can create professional-looking publications without busting your budget. You must simply rely on techniques that not only enhance your work but also stay within your budget. I have seen creative, effective, and attractive pieces produced on limited budgets, and I have seen expensively designed pieces that belong in the Desktop Publishing Hall of Shame. It takes experience and good judgment to get the most out of what you have to spend.

Keep in mind that *simpler* usually translates into "less expensive." Monochrome printed on plain bond paper generally costs less than four-color printed on specialty paper. The fancier you get, the more you're likely to spend. Talk to the friendly folks at the print shop you plan to use. They can provide guidance on cost versus quality. Sometimes you get lucky, and they can offer a premium-quality paper for a reduced cost because someone else canceled an order.

Establish a good working relationship with the staff at your print shop. They can help you in the early design phase by suggesting paper and color selections. Inquire about their price breaks for quantity printing. They can also supply you with the correct printer driver to install so that your design is only formatted correctly on your screen but also prints correctly to their printer.

Chapter 3

Basic Training

· ·

· ·

I named this chapter "Basic Training" because I discuss things that you need to know to get on with your work in Microsoft Publisher 2007. If you make a mess, this chapter also tells you how to clean up after yourself,

If you know how to create, open, find, close, and save files, you can probably get by without reading this chapter. Still, Microsoft Publisher 2007 offers you new ways to perform these tasks. Chances are that by reading this chapter, you'll discover methods you didn't know about. A few seconds saved here, a few seconds saved there, and before you know it, you have time to do all sorts of things. This chapter should repay your reading time with improved productivity.

Launch Time

When you install Publisher on your computer, the Installer creates an entry on the Programs submenu of the Start menu. Although using the menus is probably the easiest way to *launch,* or start, Publisher, the following list contains other methods you might want to know about:

✔ In Windows XP, choose Start⇨All Programs⇨Microsoft Office⇨Microsoft Office Publisher 2007, as shown in Figure 3-1.

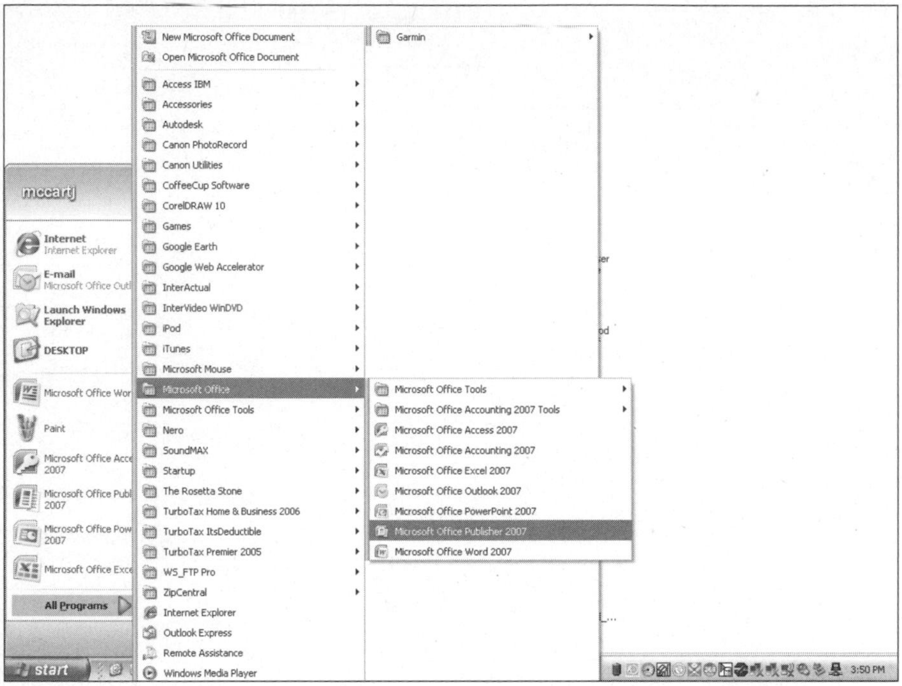

Figure 3-1:
Starting
Publisher
from the
Start menu.

✔ Locate the program icon, shown in the margin, and double-click it.

The program itself was installed in the Office 12 folder, located inside the Microsoft Office folder, which in turn is located in the Program Files folder, which you can navigate to by using Windows Desktop or Windows Explorer.

✔ Double-click the icon for the Publisher file you want to open. (It has a .pub extension.) Publisher launches, with the Publisher file you double-clicked open on the screen.

What's All This on the Screen?

In this section, I show you the names and uses of all the buttons, bars, and bows within Publisher. I don't give you fine details here about all the interface elements that are standard fare for Windows XP and/or Windows Vista. I assume that you already know how to use the menu bar; title bar; scroll bars; Minimize, Maximize, and Restore buttons; and mouse pointer. If you aren't familiar with standard Windows XP/Vista features, please refer to a beginning text on Windows, such as *Windows XP For Dummies, or Windows Vista For Dummies,* both written by Andy Rathbone (published by Wiley Publishing).

If you purchased Publisher as part of one of the many incarnations of Microsoft Office 2007, notice the absence of the newfangled Office Ribbon. (It may be a curse or a blessing, depending on your view of the Office Ribbon.) The bottom line is that you just have to put up with the "old-fashioned" menus and toolbars for now. (My gut tells me that Microsoft will update Publisher to the new interface in the next version.)

Time to start the tour! First and foremost, squirrel away the fact that Publisher uses the term *workspace* to refer to the Microsoft Publisher 2007 window and its customization options. Figure 3-2 shows a blank Publisher publication within its workspace, with all the interface elements handily labeled.

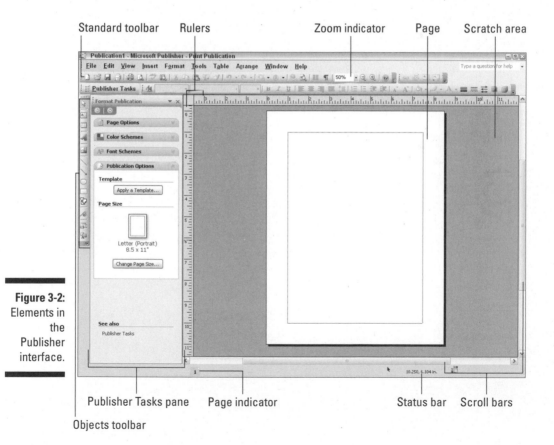

Figure 3-2: Elements in the Publisher interface.

Publisher places the following interface elements on your screen:

✔ **Standard toolbar:** The toolbar, as shown in Figure 3-3, contains icons that duplicate menu commands. When you move your pointer over each button, a ScreenTip appears, to tell you which command the button represents. Depending on the program's status, some buttons might be disabled.

If you select an object on your layout, you might see, below the Standard toolbar (which is always on your screen) an additional Formatting toolbar for that object. For example, when you select a picture, you see the Picture toolbar, which lets you format the picture and controls the way it's displayed in your publication.

If ScreenTips are distracting or you just plain don't like them (I find them helpful), you can easily turn them off in the Toolbar Options dialog box. Choose View➪Toolbars➪Customize to open the Customize dialog box, and then click the Options tab. Click to deselect the Show ScreenTips on Toolbars check box. You can also show (or hide) ScreenTips for objects and show shortcut keys in ScreenTips. Choose Tools➪Options to open the Options dialog box, and then click the User Assistance tab.

You can customize the toolbars and rulers you see by choosing the appropriate commands from the View menu. I talk about these commands in the following section.

✔ **The Objects toolbar:** The 14 buttons in the Objects toolbar (down the left side in Figure 3-2) let you create objects or insert objects from other sources. These buttons also display ScreenTips. The Pointer tool lets you select objects on a page. When you create an object on your layout, that object and the Pointer tool are automatically selected so that you can work with your new object. (By the way, for those counting, the right-pointing arrow at the bottom is Button # 14 — that's the Toolbar Options button.)

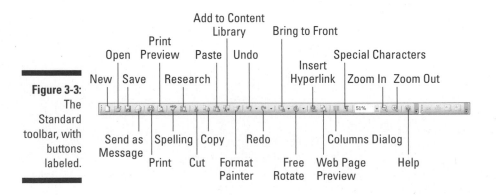

Figure 3-3: The Standard toolbar, with buttons labeled.

Here's a good Objects toolbar trick: If you plan to use the same tool repeatedly, double-click the tool. That tool stays selected until you click another one.

✔ **The rulers:** The horizontal and vertical rulers help position objects on your screen. You can move the zero point of the rulers by clicking and dragging the intersection button or the ruler.

A *guide* is a dotted line that runs the length or width of your page and is used to position objects on your page. To create a guide, hold down the Ctrl key when you click and drag a ruler.

Guides are useful on their own, but an even more useful benefit is that you can set the Snap to Guides feature by choosing Arrange⇨Snap⇨To Guides (or Ctrl+Shift+W). Objects you create close to the guide automatically move to align with the guide. You can also choose Arrange⇨Snap⇨To Ruler Marks or Arrange⇨Snap⇨To Objects for corresponding kinds of alignment. In Chapter 4, I have much more to say about the rulers, guides, and methods you can use for accurately positioning objects on a layout.

✔ **The page-navigation controls:** The page-navigation controls are located at the bottom of the screen, on the status bar. The pages in your publication are represented by little page icons with numbers. The highlighted page shows the current page. To move to any given page in your publication, just click its icon. If you're viewing your publication in Two-Page Spread view, two page icons are highlighted.

You can also use the page navigation controls to rearrange pages within your publication. Simply drag and drop any page icon to the place you want it to appear.

✔ **The Zoom indicator:** The Zoom indicator is on the Standard toolbar. The indicator's text box shows the current magnification. You can click the down arrow to open a drop-down list that lets you change your magnification. You can also use the Zoom In (+) and Zoom Out (–) buttons next to the text box to change your view.

✔ **The scroll bars:** Click the arrows at the ends of the scroll bars to move incrementally; click the scroll bar itself to move a screenful; or click and drag the button (some folks call it the *elevator*) on the scroll bar to move your window view as much as you want.

✔ **The status bar:** Below the horizontal scroll bar, the status bar contains information that changes along with your changing activities on-screen. For example, if you select a layout object, the Current Position box shows the object's on-screen position; the Object Size box shows the object's dimensions. If you haven't selected anything, the Current Position box tracks your mouse pointer's position on-screen, and the Object Size box indicates the size of any area you dragged around (a selection rectangle). Keep an eye on the status bar as you move. It features other helpful messages and is a most useful positioning aid.

Right-click anywhere on the vertical scrollbar to access a context menu that lets you quickly scroll one page up or down or to the top or bottom of your publication. Right-click the horizontal scrollbar to quickly scroll to the left or right edge or one page to the left or right.

The dimensions you see on the ruler and the status bar are shown in inches by default. You can set other units for dimensions and other program preferences by making selections from the Options dialog box. You open this dialog box by choosing Tools➪Options.

✔ **The page:** The white area where your page design appears is the page, sometimes referred to as the *printable area*. Margins appear as blue dotted lines. The stuff that appears outside the margin box is the *nonprintable area*. (It makes sense to me.)

✔ **The work (or scratch) area:** Although the gray area surrounding your page looks dead and useless, it isn't. The work area is a pasteboard that you can use to position objects you want to use later or to modify objects without having to disrupt your layout. You can think of the pasteboard as your scratch area, and you can use it for any purpose that comes to mind (well, almost).

✔ **The Help system:** I have some good news or some bad news. (It's good news if you found the Office Assistants annoying and distracting. It's bad news if Rocky the dog reminded you of the puppy you had as a child.) Microsoft scrapped the whole Office Assistant initiative for a more traditional dialog box.

Publisher offers several sources of help. You can get help from the Help files on your computer that are installed when you install Microsoft Office 2007 or Microsoft Publisher 2007. You can also get help from Microsoft Office Online, Microsoft Office's home on the Web. If you see the words `Connected to Office Online` in the lower-right corner of the Help window, as shown in Figure 3-4, you're searching the Help files located on the Microsoft Online Web site. If, instead, you see `Offline`, you're searching your local Help files.

How do you tell Publisher where you want to search for help? I was hoping you would ask. First, choose Help➪Microsoft Office Publisher Help from the Standard toolbar or press the F1 key. If you see `Connected to Office Online` in the lower-right corner of the screen, any help you receive comes from the Microsoft Office Online Web site. If you would rather not go online for help, click the `Connected to Office Online` text to display the Connection Status menu and then choose Show Content Only from This Computer. The Connection Status menu changes to Offline. You can now search for help on your local computer.

Type the word or phrase for which you want to receive help and then click Search. Do you like to take the scenic route? Take a stroll through the table of contents and click the topic you're interested in. *Drill down,* or refine, your search by clicking subtopics.

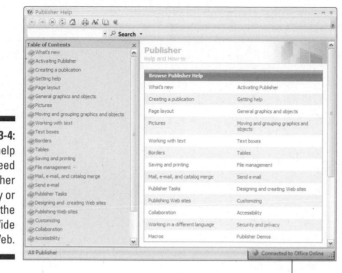

You are connected to
Microsoft's online
Help Center.

Publisher's excellent online documentation leads you to discussions on topics by using keywords. As you navigate tasks, the How Tos Help system screens give you step-by-step directions. Microsoft now uses this technique to "write down" its manuals (and save trees).

The Help system has a number of features you might want to check out, including Publisher Tutorials, keyboard shortcuts, technical support information, a connection to the Microsoft Publisher 2007 Web site, and even an Office Diagnostics feature, which attempts to fix Publisher if it starts misbehaving.

Some Publisher features help people with low vision, fine motor control issues, and other disabilities more easily use the program. Use one of the methods just mentioned to open the Help window and search for the word *accessibility*. Alternatively, you can browse for the Accessibility topic in the Help window table of contents.

For more information on the Help system, check out the "Help Yourself" section, later in this chapter.

Options and More Options

I like to have things my way (just ask my wife), so I like to mess around with the way my programs work. I used to think that it was because I had too much time on my hands. But now I have no extra time on my hands, and I recognize that spending a lot of time playing with a program's options, although sometimes entertaining, can be a real time waster.

Be that as it may, Publisher offers options you can set to change the way the program works. You make your choices on the five tabs in the Options dialog box, which you open by choosing Tools➪Options. The General tab, shown in Figure 3-5, is the first of these tabs. (After you take a peek at all the tabs, I highlight a few of the more helpful options you can set.)

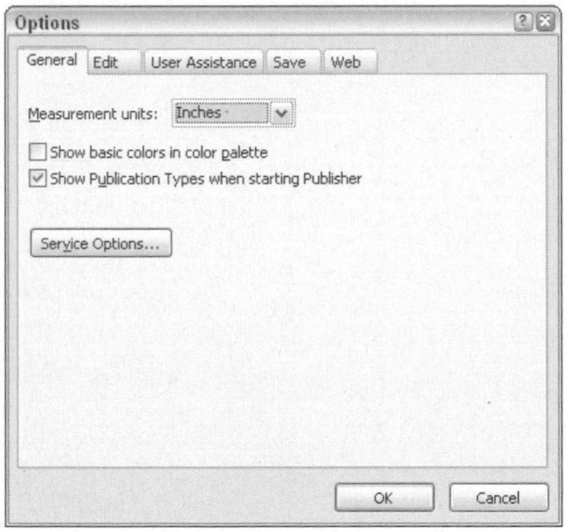

Figure 3-5:
The General
tab of the
Options
dialog box.

When you click the Edit tab and the User Assistance tabs in the Options dialog box, you get to see the dialog boxes shown in Figures 3-6 and 3-7, respectively.

Clicking the Save tab in the Options dialog box brings forth the dialog box shown in Figure 3-8. Figure 3-9 shows the Web tab, which gives you control over the way Publisher handles Web sites you create.

I refer to the selections in the Options dialog box throughout this book whenever I discuss their related features. You can see a quick explanation of any option by right-clicking the option and choosing What's This? from the pop-up menu. Alternatively, you can click the Help (?) button on the right end of the dialog box's title bar and then click a feature name to see the same explanation (which is standard Windows behavior).

This list describes some of the more useful options that you might want to reset in the Options dialog box:

✔ **Measurement Units:** On the General tab, choose inches (the default), centimeters, picas, points, or pixels.

Inches and centimeters are probably familiar measurements. If you've never worked with type, the Points, Picas, and Pixels options might be unfamiliar:

- *Point:* The smallest unit of measure in typesetting. An inch consists of 72 points; to demonstrate, draw a 1-inch line on-screen and change the Measurement Units option to Points. Then you can read the object's new size on the status bar.

  The use of points has a practical application in the design of computer monitors. Most computer monitors create pixels at approximately 72 dots per inch so that type is represented well on-screen.

- *Pica:* Equal to 12 points, or approximately ⅙ of an inch. Specifically, a pica measures 0.166 inch, making 30 picas equal to 4.98 inches. Most page layout programs ignore this small differential, however, and set the pica to exactly ⅙ of an inch, as is the case with Publisher. (Be grateful that Publisher doesn't trouble you with ciceros, didots, and other arcane typographical measurements.)

- *Pixels:* Short for *pic*ture *el*ements, the little dots that comprise the image on your screen. Pixels are the smallest element your monitor can display. Setting the Measurement Units option to Pixels gives you very fine control over the objects in your publication.

✔ **Show Publication Types When Starting Publisher:** Turn off this option (it's on the General tab) if you want Publisher to start with a blank publication every time you launch the program.

✔ **Arrow Keys Nudge Objects By:** You can specify, on the Edit tab, how far Publisher moves a selected object when you press an arrow key.

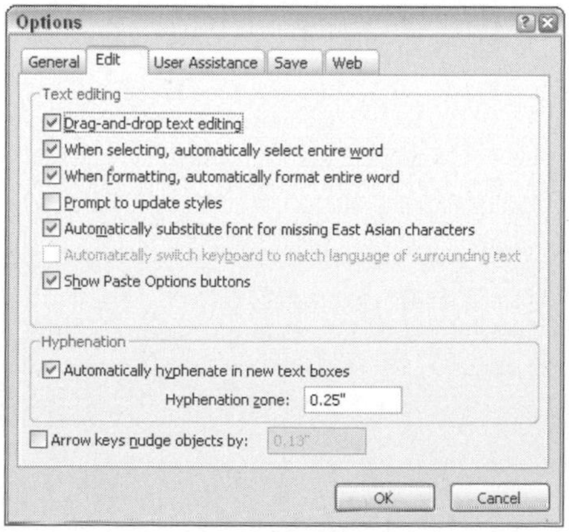

Figure 3-6:
The Edit tab in the Options dialog box.

✔ **Show Tippages:** Located on the User Assistance tab, tippages are a set of helpful hints and message boxes that can help you use Publisher more effectively. Whenever you do something that Publisher thinks you might be able to do more efficiently, it pops up one of these tippages.

For example, if you draw a straight line manually, a Publisher message box tells you that you can constrain lines to the horizontal and vertical directions by holding down the Shift key. To reset tips so that they show up again when you're using a feature you've already used, click the Reset Tips button.

✔ **Show ScreenTips on Objects:** Whenever you place the mouse pointer on an object and this option is enabled (on the User Assistance tab), a ScreenTip appears and tells you which object you're pointing at.

✔ **Save Autorecovery Info Every X Minutes:** You'll love this option the first time your laptop battery runs out in the middle of creating a publication. This option, found on the Save tab, automatically backs up your publication every few minutes (10 by default).

✔ **Organize Supporting Files in a Folder:** Located on the Web tab, this option puts into a single folder all the files you need when you create a Web page so that you don't have to go looking for them.

✔ **Send Entire Publication Page As a Single JPEG Image:** This option, which is on the Web tab, is quite handy when you need to send a publication to someone who doesn't have Publisher. Just keep in mind that the JPEG image can be quite large and that many e-mail servers limit the size of attachments. Note that this feature sends only the currently selected page of your publication. If you need to send a multiple page publication, this option won't help you.

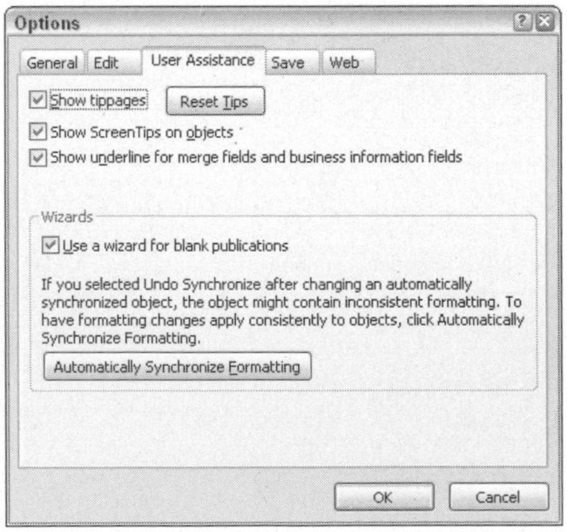

Figure 3-7:
The User Assistance tab in the Options dialog box.

Other helpful options are on the Options tab in the Customize dialog box: Choose Tools⇨Customize and click the Options tab. Here are a couple of options that I find useful:

- ✔ **Show Standard and Formatting Toolbars on Two Rows:** I like to leave this option unchecked, to save some screen real estate.

- ✔ **Large Icons:** Leave this option unchecked unless you suffer from low vision.

- ✔ **Menu animations:** This option lets you select the way menus appear and disappear. Fade is my favorite.

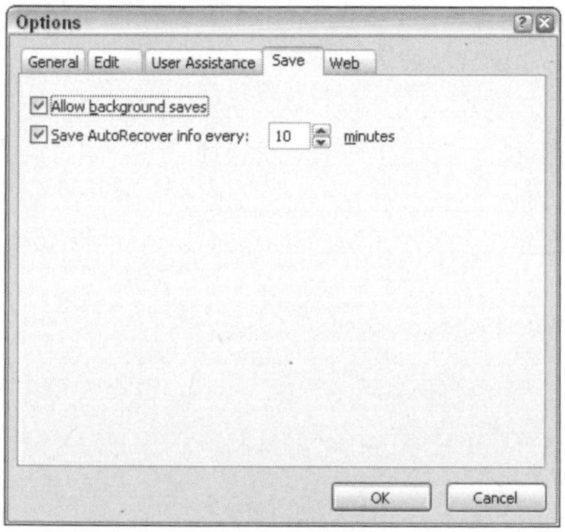

Figure 3-8:
The Save
tab in the
Options
dialog box.

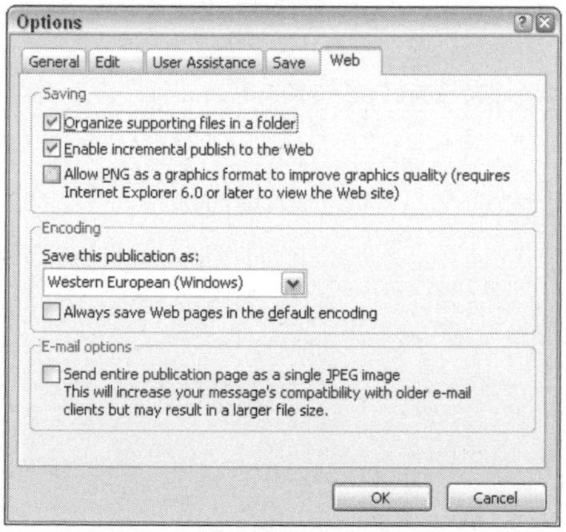

Figure 3-9:
The Web
tab in the
Options
dialog box.

Help Yourself

If you ask Microsoft what happened to the Office Assistants that lurked in Microsoft Publisher 2003, you get a terse answer: "The online Help feature in the 2007 Microsoft Office system has been completely redesigned, and the new design doesn't include the Microsoft Office Assistant." (I heard a rumor that the assistants were spotted at a theme park in central Florida. Personally, I suspect foul play.)

So, you have no cute little animated characters to tell you how to do stuff. Are you stuck? Not by a long shot.

To display the Help system, use any of these methods:

✔ Press F1.

✔ Type a word or phrase in the Search box, located to the right of the main menu bar tool, and then press Enter.

✔ Choose Help⇨Microsoft Office Publisher Help.

The Help system window consists of two panes (see Figure 3-10). You can use the pane on the left, labeled Table of Contents, to search for a topic of interest. Use the pane on the right, the Topics pane, to read what Publisher has to say about the topic.

Figure 3-10:
The Help system opens and displays the Table of Contents pane and the Topics pane.

You can manipulate the Help system, which shows up in its own window, just like any other window, by resizing or moving it to your heart's desire. After the information you're looking for is displayed in the right pane, you can choose to hide the left pane by clicking the Close button in the Table of Contents pane or by clicking the Hide Table of Contents button (it looks like an open book) on the Help window's toolbar. Use the Back and Forward buttons — the left- and right-pointing arrows, respectively — to retrace the steps of your journey through Help Land. The button that looks like a printer prints the contents of the right pane. (I bet you already knew that!) The last button (the one that looks like a push pin) forces the Help windows to remain on top of the Publisher window. Click the button a second time to turn off the feature.

The Table of Contents pane lists a series of "books" containing information about various topics. Click a book to open it and reveal its contents. Books contain pages (no surprise there) and other books. Continue opening books until you see the page that describes the subject you want help with. Click the page to have its contents displayed in the Topics pane, on the right.

The Search box, located right above the Table of Contents pane, works just as you would expect: Simply type your question in the Search text box and click Search. In the list of results that appears to the right of the Table of Contents pane, click the topic that most closely describes the task you need help with. The Help information is then displayed in the Topics pane, on the right, replacing the list of results. Click the down arrow next to the Search text box to repeat a previous search.

The Help system isn't context sensitive. That is, when the Help window opens, you don't simply jump to a topic of interest based on the program's current status or a selected feature. You can tell Publisher to jump to Help on a specific topic, however, by either

✔ Selecting a topic in the Table of Contents pane

✔ Typing a word or phrase in the Search box, to the right of the menu bar, and pressing Enter

Click the drop-down arrow on the Search button to tell Publisher exactly where you want to search for the answer to your question. Your online options, as shown in Figure 3-11, are described in this list:

✔ **All Publisher:** Search all Microsoft Publisher 2007 online resources.

✔ **Publisher Help:** Search the Publisher online Help files.

✔ **Publisher Templates:** Search only in the online Publisher templates.

✔ **Publisher Training:** Search only in the Microsoft Publisher 2007 training resources online.

✔ **Developer Reference:** Gain access to online information about developing Visual Basic Applications (VBA) for Microsoft Publisher 2007.

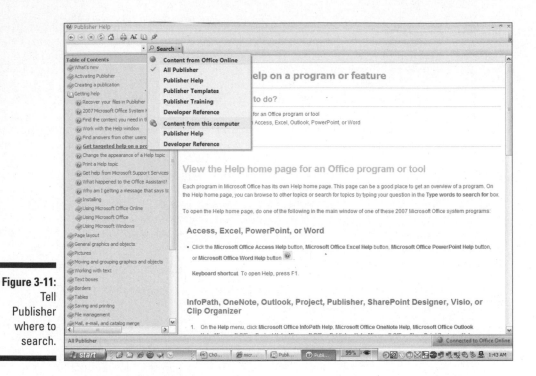

Figure 3-11:
Tell
Publisher
where to
search.

When you aren't connected to the Internet, or when you have chosen to search only on your local computer, your choices are

- **Publisher Help:** Search only the Microsoft Publisher 2007 help files on your local computer.

- **Developer Reference:** Gain access to information about developing Visual Basic Applications (VBA) for Microsoft Publisher 2007.

As you move from task to task in the Help window, the Help system remembers the path you take. To return to a previous Help topic, click the Back button, which appears on the toolbar just above the Search box. By doing so, you retrace your steps in reverse order.

Finding a topic

The Help system works just like an Internet search engine. Type a word in the Search text box and click the Search button or press Enter. The Help system displays one or more results in the Topics pane. Click the link that most closely matches the topic you're looking for.

Notice that, under each link representing the results of your query, the Help system shows the path you can follow in the table of contents to find your answer. If you search for the term *WordArt,* for example, the first result displayed in the Topics pane is Add, Change, or Delete WordArt. Click the link to display the topic you want. Under that link is the path Help⇨General Graphics and Objects⇨Adding or Deleting Graphics or Objects. From the Help system's Table of Contents pane, you can select General Graphics and Objects and then select the Adding or Deleting Graphics or Objects subtopic to reach the same WordArt entry.

Try a synonym to find related instructions and explanations.

When you click anywhere outside the Publisher Help window, the Help window disappears. Click the Publisher Help button on the Windows taskbar to bring back the window. When you're finished with the Help window, click its Close button.

Inch by inch; step by step

When you click a topic in the Table of Contents pane of the Help window, the Topics pane displays either a list of related topics or, sometimes, a list of numbered steps to achieve your goal. Figure 3-12 shows an example of step-by-step instructions.

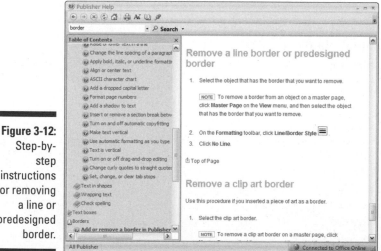

Figure 3-12: Step-by-step instructions for removing a line or predesigned border.

The Topics pane can also display blue text, which Publisher underlines when you point the mouse at it. Place the mouse pointer over the blue, underlined text, and the pointer turns into a hand. The hand pointer indicates that you're pointing at a hyperlink. Click it to view information that's relevant to the current Help topic.

Things You Can Do with Files

You use files to store your work or your data in a computer. I like to look at my work, so I spend a lot of time staring at the Windows Explorer window. Publisher files, or *publications,* have the .pub file extension. You can create files, open and close files, modify files, and save the changes you make to your files. You need to do most such file tasks from within Publisher, but you can do some general housecleaning tasks on your files (tasks you probably know about already just because you own a computer) from outside the program. The following sections cover the "innie and outie" ways of dealing with Publisher files.

Playing with files on the outside

The following short list describes the tasks you can do outside Publisher:

✔ **Select a file (or files):** Click the file on the Windows desktop or in Windows Explorer, or click and drag a selection rectangle around a set of contiguous files. You can also hold down the Shift key and click additional files to extend or reduce your range of selected files.

✔ **Move a file:** On the Windows desktop or in Windows Explorer, click and drag the file to a new location.

✔ **Copy a file:** On the Windows desktop or in Windows Explorer, press Ctrl and click and drag the file to a new location.

Okay, I realize that you can accomplish this task inside Publisher by using the Save As command to copy a file, but this method is much, much faster in the Windows interface.

✔ **Create a shortcut file:** On the Windows desktop or in Windows Explorer, click and drag the file to a new location by using the right mouse button. Choose the Create Shortcuts Here command from the context-sensitive menu that appears. (If you aren't sure what a context-sensitive menu looks like, check out Figure 3-13. Notice that you can also use this menu to copy and move files.)

✔ **Delete a file:** On the Windows desktop or in Windows Explorer, click the file to select it and then press Delete on your keyboard. Or, click and drag the file to the Recycle Bin.

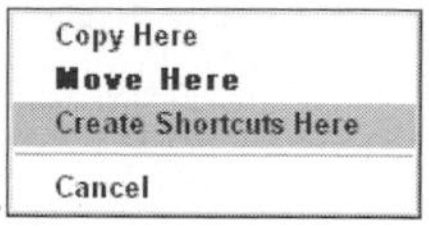

Figure 3-13:
This context-sensitive menu has a Create Shortcut option.

Copy Here
Move Here
Create Shortcuts Here
Cancel

One thing I love about Windows is that these actions are recoverable. If you think that you made a mistake, you can choose Edit➪Undo or press Ctrl+Z in your current Desktop folder or Windows Explorer, and the action is reversed. Cool! If you make a mistake and delete a file that you didn't intend to delete, all is not (necessarily) lost. Open the Recycle Bin folder, select that file in the list, and choose File➪Restore. Your file jumps back to its original location.

Your deleted file isn't really in jeopardy until you give the Empty Recycle Bin command or until the Recycle Bin fills up and needs the space. In that case, the files are deleted by date (first in, first out — or *FIFO*). If the deletion was made by using the menu command and not because of disk space requirements, you still might be able to recover your file: Restart your computer in MS-DOS mode and use the Recover command to try to get your file back. Or, buy a file utility program, such as Norton Utilities, that has the recovery function. The most important thing you can do if you empty the Recycle Bin and need to recover a file is to refrain from performing any other file operations in the meantime. That way, the file system is less likely to overwrite the disk sectors that contain the information from the deleted file.

Always keep adequate copies and save your files by using the Backup option described later in this chapter. You should never need to recover a publication from the Recycle Bin.

Now that I've briefly described the things you can do with files outside Publisher, I turn my attention to the operations you can do inside Publisher.

Starting a publication

Publisher prompts you to create a publication every time you start a session (that is, launch the program). The first thing you notice is the Getting Started with Microsoft Publisher 2007 window, which is divided into three main sections. The Microsoft Publisher Publication Types pane is displayed on the left side of the screen and lists all the different kinds of publications template available — if you haven't turned off that option. The center of the screen initially displays the Popular Publication Types pane. After you select a

Publication Type from the list in the left pane, this center pane will show thumbnails (little pictures) of the various styles of the selected Publication Type. On the right side of the screen you see the Recent Publications pane.

If you're already in a Publisher session, you can get to the Getting Started with Microsoft Office Publisher 2007 screen (shown in Figure 3-14) by choosing File⇨New.

In the Publication Types pane, Publisher shows the list of publication types it can help you create. From the Publication Types list, click the type of publication you want to create, select a design from the center pane, and then click the Create button that appears in the lower-right part of the screen.

After you make your selections, the new publication opens in the window on-screen with the title Publication1 – Microsoft Publisher – Print Publication on the title bar.

You can also open any Publisher publication and choose File⇨Save As to create a new publication. Now you can safely modify the new publication to your heart's content without altering the original.

Don't forget to choose either the Save or Save As command to save your new publication to disk; otherwise, it might exist only in your memory.

Figure 3-14:
The Getting Started with Microsoft Office Publisher 2007 window.

Opening remarks

When you launch Publisher, the program opens the Getting Started with Microsoft Office Publisher 2007 screen so that you can create a new file. If you really want an existing publication, though, follow these steps:

1. **Choose File⇨Open from the main menu.**

   The Open Publication dialog box appears, as shown in Figure 3-15.

2. **Click to select the publication of interest. (You might need to use the Look In drop-down list to navigate to the correct folder for your file.)**

   You can look over the Publication Preview (a thumbnail image of the first page of your publication) in the right pane of the Open dialog box by clicking the down arrow on the Views button and selecting Preview. (Refer to Figure 3-15.)

3. **Click Open to open the publication.**

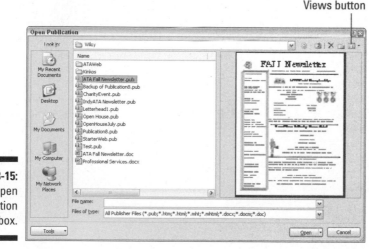

Views button

Figure 3-15: The Open Publication dialog box.

After you're in a Publisher session, choose File⇨New to see the Getting Started with Microsoft Office Publisher 2007 screen again. (Are you smiling yet? What could be friendlier than this?)

The Open Publication dialog box is a standard Windows interface element, only slightly altered to accommodate the capabilities that Publisher offers. You locate files in the file hierarchy by clicking the Look In drop-down list or the Up One Level button. The List button and Details button let you change the way the list box displays the file contents for your current folder.

You can filter your view of the File list box contents by choosing the appropriate filter from the Files of Type drop-down list. You can also click the down arrow on the Open button and select Open Read-Only to open the publication in read-only mode. You can then view a file, but you can't make any changes.

Feel free to open multiple publications simultaneously. After you open one, just repeat the process to open additional publications. As for switching among several open publications, you have these choices:

✔ Click the Windows Taskbar icon representing the publication you want (the easiest method).

✔ Click the Window menu in Publisher, and then select the name of the publication you want to see.

✔ Hold down the Alt key and press the Tab key until the publication you want is highlighted. Then release both keys.

In some cases, having multiple publications open on your screen can be useful. Because Publisher is drag-and-drop–enabled, you can click an object or a frame and drag it to another publication to create a copy of that object.

Finding files

If you know you have a publication on your machine but aren't sure where it is, you can use Windows Desktop Search to look for it. Choose Tools⇨Search to see the Windows Desktop Search dialog box, shown in Figure 3-16. This dialog box lets you search for Publisher files on any drive your computer can see. Select a drive or folder to search by clicking the ellipsis (...) next to the Folder text box. In the search text box, type ***.pub** and then click the Desktop button. (The * is a wild card character that Windows interprets to mean "any file name.") Double-click a file in the Results pane to open it.

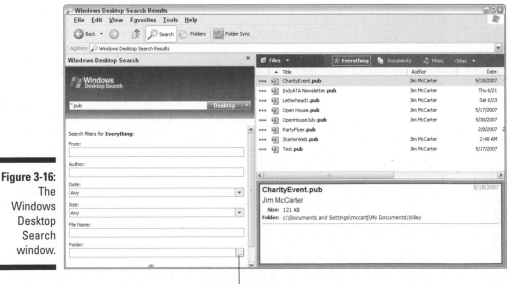

Figure 3-16: The Windows Desktop Search window.

Use this button to set a search location.

Saving your files means never having to say you're sorry

Publisher lets you save two kinds of files: Microsoft Publisher publication (.pub) files and various forms of text files. For the most part, when you work with page layout in Publisher, you're interested in saving publication files. Because you can create text in Publisher in the form of stories or stand-alone text frames, Publisher lets you save your text in a number of formats: plain text, interchange formats such as the rich text format (RTF), and any one of several word processor formats. This feature lets you move your text back and forth with agility between Publisher and any standard word processor.

File-saving formats

A .pub file is the proprietary Publisher format for saving layout information. Other page layout programs may save to .pub files — but they aren't Microsoft Publisher 2007 .pub files. To use a .pub file inside Publisher 2007, you have to save a page layout file in another program as a Microsoft Publisher 2007 .pub file. And, if you decide to open in another program a .pub file created in Microsoft Publisher 2007, you need to save the file in a format that the other program can read or you need a mechanism to convert the Microsoft Publisher 2007 .pub file format during the file opening process. Generally speaking, you can't work with .pub files between Microsoft Publisher 2007 and other programs, such as Quark XPress or PageMaker, because page layout programs implement their page formatting in very different ways.

If you plan to share your publications with someone who has an earlier version of Microsoft Publisher (Microsoft Publisher 2000 or Microsoft Publisher 98, for example) you can do so, but you have to save your publications in the appropriate format.

Publications (well, *all* computer files) are quite unwilling to share their names with another file in the same folder. Multiple files with the same name can exist in different locations among your computer's disks, however. If you try to save a publication to a folder in which a publication of that same name already exists, Publisher opens a dialog box to warn you of the impending duel to the death. Click the Yes button in this dialog box to overwrite the first file with your new one. Click the No button to return to your publication, where you can come up with a new name that doesn't inspire such territorial disputes.

Working with text is an entirely different matter. There's a way of getting text into and out of just about any word processor you want to work in. You can save text to any one of these text formats:

✔ **Plain text:** This format saves text only as lower ASCII characters in a .txt file — which means you get just plain text, with alphanumeric characters and a few common symbols. All formatting and font information, in other words, is lost. Any word processor worth its salt can open .txt files. Saving in this format, the lowest common denominator, doesn't preserve all your work.

- **Rich Text Format:** The .rtf format is an *interchange* format developed by Microsoft to let programs exchange text files that contain formatting information. In the files, instructions on how to format specific characters and paragraphs are contained in directions given as plain text characters. Most word processors support opening and saving .rtf files.

- **Word Processor Filters:** Publisher contains filters to save text to specific file formats, including Word 2007, Word 97–2003, Word 6.0/95, Word 97 and 6.0/95 RTF, and Word 2.*x* for Windows; Works 3.0 and 4.0 for Windows; Windows Write; and WordPerfect 5.*x*, WordPerfect 5.1 for DOS, WordPerfect 5.*x* for Windows, WordPerfect 5.1 or 5.2 Secondary File, and WordPerfect 5.0 Secondary File. Microsoft Publisher 2007 can also save to several Microsoft Word for Apple Macintosh formats.

Saving a Publisher document to one of the text formats mentioned above saves only the text. The pictures and the layout of the document do not get saved.

Publisher can open and import from most file formats to which it can save text; that is, it can bring text files from these other formats into your Publisher layout. I say more about this topic in Chapter 6. For the sake of completeness, though, here's the list of formats that Publisher can use to import text files: Microsoft Excel Worksheet; Plain Text and Plain Text (DOS); Recover Text from Any File; Rich Text Format; Windows Write; Word 6.0/95 for Windows and Macintosh; Word (Asian versions) 6.0/95; Word 97; Word 2.*x* for Windows; WordPerfect 5.*x* and 6.*x*; and Works 3.0 and 4.0 for Windows.

I must say that if you can't get your word processing files into and out of Publisher by using this list of formats, it's time to replace your word processor. Every word processor I know of can convert at least one of these formats.

File-saving mechanics

Here's the deal about saving your files:

- Anything you see on your screen belongs to your computer.

- Anything you save to disk belongs to you.

    It's really that simple. If you forget to save your work and the power goes out, your work is lost. On the Save tab of the Options dialog box, check the Save AutoRecover Information Every *x* Minutes check box and enter a time period in the text box. Publisher opens a dialog box telling you that it's time to save your work every so often (anywhere from 1 to 120 minutes). Get in the habit of clicking Yes.

Save early and often. When you create a new publication, it doesn't really exist until you save it to disk.

To save your file, choose one of these methods:

🔲 ✔ Choose the File⇨Save (or Ctrl+S) or the File⇨Save As command.

✔ Click the Save button (shown in the margin) on the Standard toolbar.

For a new publication, the Save command is identical to the Save As command. If you choose either command, the standard Save As dialog box (shown in Figure 3-17) appears. The dialog box prompts you to choose a Save In location and to specify a filename. After you save the file once, any subsequent Save command saves your changes without displaying the Save As dialog box again. The Save As command enables you to create a new file or overwrite your old one.

If you want to locate a folder in the file system, you can click the Up One Level button (or press Alt+2) to move up the hierarchy or click the Save In drop-down list box to move about any distance. If you want to create a new folder, go to the folder where you want to store the new folder, click the New Folder button (or press Alt+4), and enter a new folder name in place of the highlighted name New Folder that's in the text box.

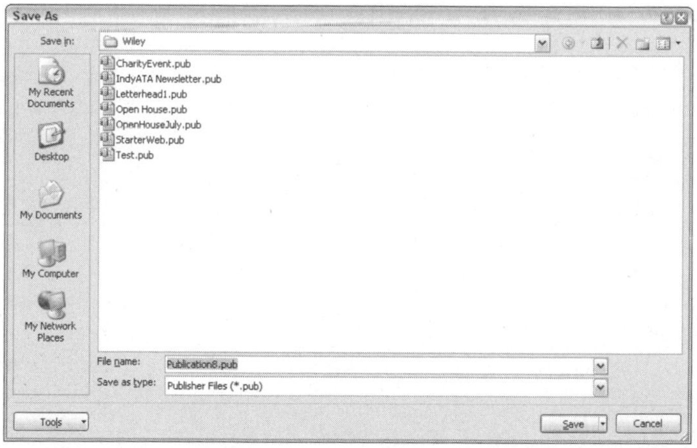

Figure 3-17:
The Save As
dialog box in
List view.

You can change how files look in the file list box by clicking the Views button located in the top-right of the Save As dialog box. Figure 3-18 shows you the Save As dialog box in Details view, for example.

As you create a publication, save multiple copies of it as you progress. Then, if you decide that you like the publication better in a previous state, you can return to it. You can never be too thin, have too much RAM, or have too many backups.

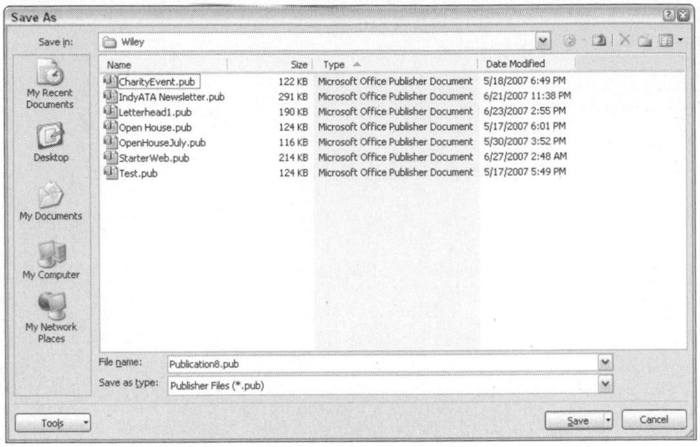

Figure 3-18:
The Save As
dialog box in
Details
view.

Insurance, please

I can't always count on a hard drive working, so I back up to another hard drive, a CD, or a USB memory drive. And, I assume that my first backup will fail, so I back up anything important again. (Have I told you that I'm paranoid? Well, just because I am doesn't mean that they aren't out to get me!)

If you click the down arrow on the Save button in the Save As dialog box, you see a Save with Backup option that does two things for you:

✔ Allows you to return (or *revert,* as it's known in other programs) to the last previously saved state of the file

✔ Protects you from file corruption by providing a backup to revert to. Publications can become large and complex, which makes them more susceptible to corruption than smaller files. (This statement is also true of files that are used frequently, such as font files.)

Backup files don't contain any changes you made to your publication since you last saved the file. That is, if you save a publication three times during a session, the backup publication contains the file in the state it was in after two saves.

You can recover from a computer disaster by reverting to a *backup* copy of a publication, one that contains the words Backup of in front of the file name. You don't see these files on the Recent Publications tab, so you will have to open them from the Open dialog box. You can search for backup files by using the phrase *backup of* * in the Find This File text box in the Find File dialog box. (See the section Finding Files earlier in this chapter.) Double-click the backup file of interest. It opens, and you can work in that copy and save it out to a new file with a name of your choosing. From then on, the backup file is one of your choices in the Existing Publications tab.

A backup file takes the same name as your original publication but uses the .bak extension. The only drawback to using the Backup option is that it doubles your disk space requirements.

Unless you're hurting for space on your hard drive, hedge your bet and always select the Backup option.

If you create backups, you can safely tell the dealer, "Hit me."

Canning templates

You can think of a template as a piece of stationery containing all the content and formatting that was in it when you saved the file as a template. Templates provide a convenient starting place for your work and capture details that you want to make sure not to change. Template files are stored as .pub files.

If you view a template's properties, you see that a template is a file with the Archive bit or file attribute set to On. Different programs use this setting for different purposes. You're probably familiar with the use of the Archive bit to determine whether a file has been backed up. A backup program starts by turning off all Archive settings and then turns them on individually as it performs a backup on that file. Publisher uses the Archive bit to decide whether the file is a template and cannot be overwritten (changed) by a Save command.

From a practical standpoint, a template lets you create a publication based on that template. That file opens as an *unsaved publication,* without any name. When you use a template, the program prompts you to use the Save As command to create a new file. The new file then behaves like any other publication. If you try to save the file to the same location and with the same name, Publisher opens a dialog box like the one shown in Figure 3-19. This dialog box warns that a publication already exists and that you will overwrite the existing file. You can overwrite the file with another template or with a normal publication file.

Figure 3-19:
The
Overwrite
File alert
box.

Microsoft Office Publisher

⚠ The file Publication8.pub already exists. Do you want to replace the existing file?

Yes   No

Nag me

Many programs automatically save *(autosave)* changes for you every so often. Page layout programs, because they involve artistic endeavors, do not, as a rule, perform autosaves. You must manually save your file along with any changes you make to it that you want to retain. Publisher (because it's a do-bee, for those of you who remember *Romper Room*) saves your work from time to time automatically.

You can change this behavior by disabling the option or changing the frequency with which the program autosaves files. Choose Tools➪Options, and then click the Save tab in the Options dialog box. At the bottom of this dialog box, deselect the Save AutoRecover Info Every X Minutes check box or enter a new number in the Minutes text box. The number you type must be at least 1 and no more than 120. This setting specifies the number of minutes that you work inside Publisher before it autosaves your publication.

Another check box you might want to select on the User Assistance tab of the Options dialog box is Show Tippages. This option posts a helpful message box the first time you perform a particular operation and also when it detects an operation that's causing you difficulty.

Close calls

If you have no changes to save in a file, you can close your publication without bother by choosing the File➪Close command. If you made changes, Publisher opens a dialog box (shown in Figure 3-20) asking you if you want to save your changes first before closing the file. Click Yes to save your changes (the default), No to discard them, or Cancel to abort the Close operation and continue working in your publication.

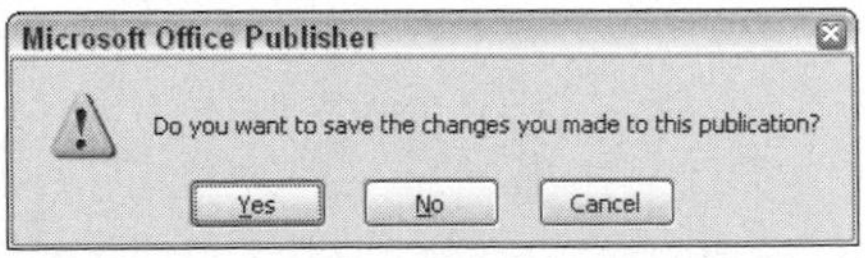

Figure 3-20: You want to save that?

> **Microsoft Office Publisher**
>
> ⚠ Do you want to save the changes you made to this publication?
>
> [Yes]   [No]   [Cancel]

I know of only four methods for closing a publication:

- ✔ Choose the aforementioned File➪Close command.
- ✔ Click the Close box in the Microsoft Publisher 2007 window, on the far right side of the title bar.
- ✔ Press Alt+F4.
- ✔ Choose File➪Exit to close the program.

Shut Down without Crash-Landing

You should close Publisher whenever you finish using the program or you finish your session and want to shut down your computer: Choose File⇨Exit. If you try to close Publisher without saving changes made to a file, a dialog box asks whether you want to save your changes. If you have no changes to save, the program closes directly, and the memory (RAM) used to store the program is released for use by other programs.

To close Publisher, choose the File⇨Exit command or press Alt+F4. Also, you can automatically close various programs when you use the Shut Down command from the Windows Start menu.

So far, so good. Keep in mind, though, that you might not always be able to close Publisher correctly — if a program freezes your computer or the power goes out, for example. In either case, *all your changes are lost.* Your file saved to disk is unaffected by the power outage. (Oh, did I mention that you should save your work early and often?)

Part II
Mark This Page

The 5th Wave   By Rich Tennant

"Okay, technically this should work. Judy, type the word 'Goodyear,' all caps, boldface, at 700 point type size."

In this part . . .

This part shows you how to work with pages and objects in ways that make your page layout both faster and more precise. You also see how your selected printer affects your design.

Microsoft Publisher 2007 has many aids to help you design pages carefully, and many different page designs are already built into the program for you. This part also discusses frames and text boxes, which are the containers for the various objects and elements you place on a page.

Chapter 4

Working with Pages

*W*hen you start a publication, Publisher determines the publication's basic settings for you — the number of pages, the page size, and some margin guides, for example. This default feature is all well and good if you like the decisions Publisher makes, but what if you want to change a setting? You may need to change the margins, for example, to accommodate your design and the capabilities of your printer.

This chapter describes your publication's basic element — the page — and how to change your publication's basic structure, from tasks as minor as adjusting margins to more complex tasks, such as converting a three-fold brochure into a 15-foot banner.

In the Beginning: The Page

The most basic element of a Publisher publication is the individual page. A *page* in the computer world isn't much different from a page in the real world — it's just a chunk of words and pictures that, when printed, all fit on a single piece of paper.

Pages are designed singly or as part of a multipage spread. Publisher makes it easy for you to move between pages, look at pages in different views and magnifications, and add or delete pages as needed to fit your goals.

Moving from page to page

The *current page* is the active page — the page on which your cursor is located. At any time, only one page in your document is the current page, even when you're viewing more than one page at a time. The current page is indicated in the page-navigation controls, located in the lower-left corner of the Publisher window. The current page is the one represented by the buff-colored page. All other pages are white. Figure 4-1 shows the page-navigation controls.

Figure 4-1:
The page-navigation controls with Page 3 as the current page.

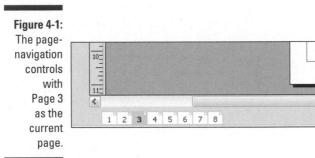

After you have more than one page in your publication, you can move to another page in several ways:

- ✔ Choose Edit➪Go To Page from the main menu, and then type the number of the page you want to work on in the Go To Page dialog box, shown in Figure 4-2.

- ✔ Press F5 to open the Go To Page dialog box; Ctrl+PgDn to move to the next page; and Ctrl+PgUp to move to the previous page.

- ✔ Press Ctrl+G to display the Go To Page dialog box.

- ✔ Click the page you want to go to in the page-navigation controls.

Figure 4-2:
The Go To Page dialog box.

Go To Page

Go to page 3

Your publication has 8 pages, numbered 1 through 8.

OK   Cancel

Scrolling within a page

You use the scroll bars, arrows, and boxes along the right side and at the bottom of your screen to view different parts of the current page. Here's what you can do with the various scroll bar parts:

- ✔ **Scroll arrows:** Click a scroll arrow to slide your view a little bit in the direction of that arrow. If you press and hold down the mouse button, the publication continues to scroll.

- ✔ **Scroll boxes:** Drag the scroll box (it slides like an elevator in a shaft) to slide your view any amount in that same direction.

- ✔ **Scroll bar:** Click above or below the scroll box in the horizontal or vertical scroll bar (the elevator shaft) to slide your view up or down a screenful at a time.

These techniques affect only your view of the current page and do not move between pages. They're standard Windows interface techniques that work in any Windows window.

In addition to using the scroll bars to move your view of a page in the window, you can use these keyboard shortcuts:

- ✔ Press PgDn (Page Down) to move your view down one screenful.

- ✔ Press PgUp (Page Up) to move your view up one screenful.

- ✔ Press Ctrl+right arrow to scroll to the right.

- ✔ Press Ctrl+left arrow to scroll to the left.

By using the last two shortcuts on the list, you scroll an amount that varies, depending on your current magnification and view.

If all this makes Publisher seem like a game of *Motocross Madness* or *Microsoft Combat Flight Simulator,* that's all good. These keystrokes save you a lot of time.

Changing What You See On-Screen

In precise page layout work, you want to move quickly between different views and magnifications. The idea here is that you should be able to work with a detail on your layout and then jump to a view that lets you get an overview of your document to see how the change looks in context.

If you're familiar with all the different views you find in a word processor — for example, the Normal, Outline, and Page Layout views available in Microsoft Word — you may be surprised to find that Publisher offers only one kind of view: a *live,* or editable, page preview. Why does it offer just one mode? Because the purpose of a page layout program is to create and display a page the way it will look when you print it.

Even so, Publisher gives you ways to change how your page looks on-screen. Most of these ways reside within the View menu. You can choose to see a single page or two-page spread, and you can change the magnification of the page or pages you're viewing.

Two-page spreads

Many publications, including this very book, are designed with pairs of pages that form facing pages. *Facing pages,* also known as a *two-page spread,* are what your readers see — and what you, as a designer, design for.

If you're looking at a single page and want to see your layout as a two-page spread (to see two facing pages side by side), choose View⇨Two-Page Spread from the main menu. Odd-numbered pages (1, 3, 5, and so on) are displayed on the right side of the Publisher screen, whereas even-numbered pages (2, 4, 6, and so on) are displayed on the left side.

The standard setup for professional publications, such as this book, starts the text on a right-hand page. Therefore, if your publication has an even number of pages, the first page of the publication is displayed by itself in the middle of the screen, and the last page is displayed by itself in the middle of the screen. If your publication has only one page, that page is displayed by itself in the middle of the Publisher screen.

After you choose the Two-Page Spread command, a check mark appears next to the command on the View menu. Clicking the Two-Page Spread command a second time returns you to the Single Page view at the current magnification.

Your publication doesn't *have* to be a facing-page publication to take advantage of Two-Page Spread view. Use this view at your convenience.

Whole Page and Page Width views

In addition to switching between one- and two-page views, you can view whole pages at one time or view pages in the largest magnification that still shows the entire width of the page or the two-page spread. Choose one of these methods:

✔ Choose View➪Zoom➪Whole Page or press Ctrl+Shift+L to resize the current page or two-page spread so that it appears at the largest possible magnification to fill your screen. This view gives you an overview of your layout.

✔ Choose View➪Zoom➪Page Width to switch to a view of your document that fills the screen horizontally, whether you're in Single Page view or Two-Page Spread view. In this view, you probably have to scroll vertically to see the entire document, but you don't have to scroll horizontally.

Press the F9 key to toggle back and forth between the current view and the actual size (100 percent) of your document.

If you select one or more objects before choosing the View➪Zoom command, you see a new option on the Zoom submenu: Selected Objects. When you choose this option, Publisher resizes your page to the largest magnification that still shows the selected objects.

Figure 4-3 shows a single-page document in Whole Page view. Figure 4-4 shows the same document in Page Width view.

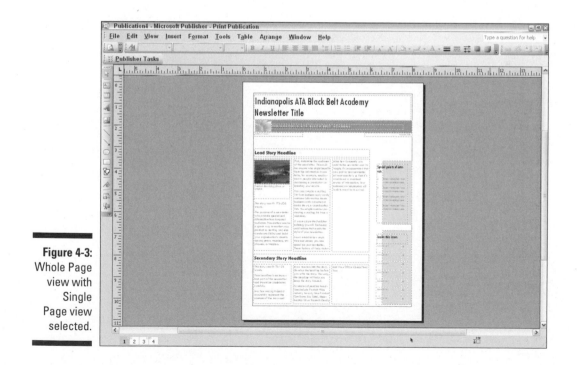

Figure 4-3:
Whole Page view with Single Page view selected.

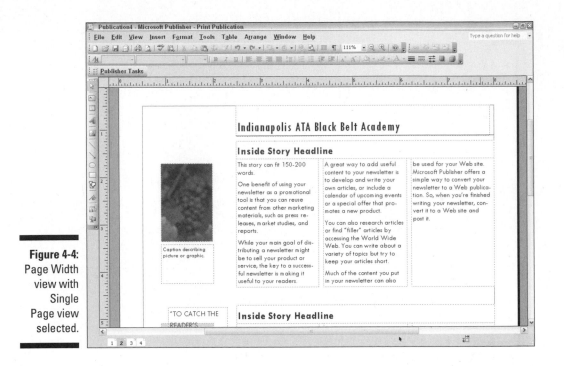

Figure 4-4:
Page Width
view with
Single
Page view
selected.

Zooming around

The Zoom box, located on the Standard toolbar, indicates the current magnification percentage; 100 percent is the actual size. To enlarge or reduce the on-screen size of your publications — much as though you were holding one end of a telescope to your eye while looking at the screen and then switching to look through the telescope's other end — click the down arrow in the Zoom box to reveal the drop-down list, shown in Figure 4-5. If you have used the Zoom feature in other Microsoft Office programs, you should feel very comfortable with this feature in Publisher because it works the same way.

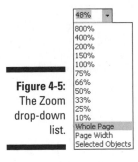

Figure 4-5:
The Zoom
drop-down
list.

If you can't find the Zoom box, it's probably because Publisher is displaying both the Standard and Formatting toolbars on one line. To make Publisher display the Standard and Formatting toolbars on two rows (and thus enable you to see the Zoom box), choose Tools⇔Customize from the main menu. Click the Options tab and check the Show Standard and Formatting Toolbars on Two Rows check box.

Some things to keep in mind when doing your zooming:

✔ The selections on the Zoom drop-down list are the same ones you see when you choose View⇔Zoom from the main menu.

✔ You see the Selected Objects command on the Zoom drop-down list only when you have an object selected on the layout. This command magnifies the layout to the largest view that still contains the object, and centers the object on your screen.

✔ If you right-click anywhere on the layout, you see a context menu. This menu contains the Zoom command which, when chosen, displays the Whole Page, Page Width, and Selected Objects commands.

Lining Things Up

No matter how comfortable you are with your mouse, aligning things freehand is tough work. I know because I have a cordless, optical, laser-precision mouse, and I *still* have trouble getting things to line up without some help. Fortunately, the Publisher electronic guidance devices can help to steady your trembling hands so that objects fall into perfect place with ease. (Don't confuse the Publisher electronic guidance devices with those used in so-called "smart bombs" developed for the military.) This section looks at layout guides and ruler guides and then shows you how to activate the powerful Snap To commands to get everything to line up neatly.

Margin and grid guides

Layout guides are an excellent way to determine where to place various objects on each page. Layout guides don't appear on your printout. On-screen, however, these blue or pink lines provide visual references on every page. Using the Publisher Snap To feature, you can almost magically align objects with these blue or pink lines.

Publisher provides three types of layout guides:

- ✔ **Margin guides** define the boundary of your printable area.
- ✔ **Grid guides** let you set up a grid to make it easier to design your publication.
- ✔ **Baseline guides** help you align text across the columns of a multi-column publication.

Margin guides appear automatically in every publication. Margin guides generally indicate where you should and shouldn't plop objects; they also help you align objects along the perimeter of each page. You're free to put objects anywhere you want, regardless of the margins, however. (Whether those objects look good there and whether they actually print are other matters altogether.)

Grid guides, like the lines on graph paper, are excellent tools for aligning any and all objects that you don't want to align to the margin guides. For example, you may want to set a graphic in the direct center of the page. Grid guides can help you do this.

Baseline guides help you align text in between text boxes in columns even though the text boxes aren't linked. (When text boxes are _linked,_ text from one text box automatically flows to the next text box when the first box fills up.)

If you don't want your text to be aligned across columns, turn off the feature. Choose Format➪Paragraph (for this to work, you must have text in a text box selected). Then, on the Indents and Spacing tab, deselect the Align Text to Baseline Guides check box.

Professional designers — whether they work on a computer or on paper — generally lay out pages according to grids. For example, when creating a three-fold brochure, they use a three-part grid to visually separate the three panels of each page where that brochure eventually will be folded. Or, they may divide nonfolding pages into a grid of rows and columns to see how different parts of the page visually relate to each other and to the page as a whole. In this way, designers can ensure that their pages are readable, are not crowded, and are visually appealing with appropriate spacing and correct alignment.

When you use templates to begin a publication, Publisher sets up grid guides automatically to save you the trouble of doing it yourself. Of course, you can always change them, if you like. To set up or change layout guides, choose Arrange➪Layout Guides. The Layout Guides dialog box, shown in Figure 4-6, appears.

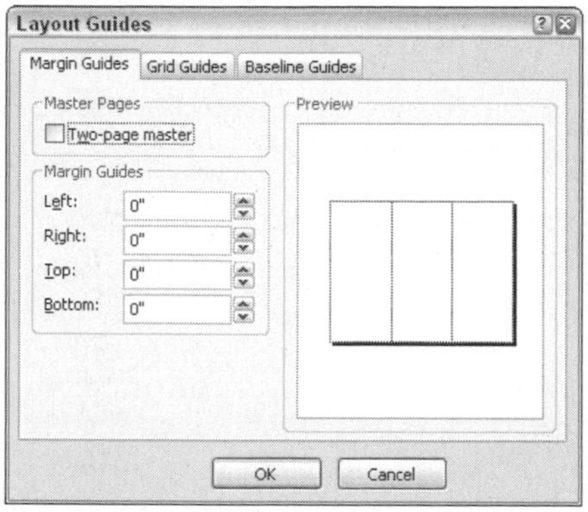

Figure 4-6:
The Layout
Guides
dialog box
for a three-
column
brochure.

You set the margins for your printed page on the Margin Guides tab of the Layout Guides dialog box. Different printers require different margin settings. If you set margins narrower than your printer will print, your page doesn't print properly. Text and figures are cut off at the margins. (I discuss printing in depth in Chapter 13.)

In the gutter

If you want different margin guides for left-facing pages than for right-facing pages, be sure to select the Two-Page Master check box on the Margin Guides tab of the Layout Guides dialog box. This option is important for facing-page publications that will be bound, such as books. When you select this option, the Left and Right text boxes in the Margin Guides area change to Inside and Outside text boxes. Any change you make to the Inside setting affects the right (inside) margin of left-facing pages. The Inside setting also affects the left (inside) margin of right-facing pages. The Outside setting adjusts the outside margins — right margins on right-facing pages and left margins on left-facing pages.

Facing pages typically have different internal margins (gutters), to accommodate the publication's binding. If you're preparing facing pages that will be bound, be sure to specify different numbers in the Inside and Outside text boxes. Generally, the inside should be larger than the outside margins by the amount that the binding will consume. The person who will bind the publication should provide you with this measurement.

With this setup, you can easily create the extra room necessary on each page to accommodate the room that's lost because of the binding. Without this extra room, your pages can look lopsided, and objects on those pages can get buried in the gutter.

When your gutters are properly set, you can spread objects across facing pages. Depending on the target printer's capabilities (how close to the edge of the paper it's capable of printing, for example), the object might not print completely. For objects for which the cutoff doesn't matter (patterns, spot color, and fills), this technique is valuable.

On the Grid Guides tab of the Layout Guides dialog box, enter the number of columns and rows you want. Grid guides evenly divide the space contained by the margin guides. If you want to change the amount of space between the columns or rows, use the arrows next to the respective Spacing boxes.

If you can't see your layout guides after setting them, check the View menu to see whether the View Boundaries and Guides command is hiding your guides. If the View Boundaries and Guides command appears on the menu without a check mark next to it, choose that command or press Ctrl+Shift+O. To hide the guides again, reapply the View Boundaries and Guides command or press Ctrl+Shift+O again. If you still can't see your guides, they may be covered by other objects, such as lines or a frame boundary.

Ruler guides

In addition to setting layout guides, you can set *ruler guides* anywhere on your page. Ruler guides let you arrange elements on your page at any horizontal or vertical position you want. You can create as many ruler guides as you need. This list describes how to work with ruler guides:

- **To create a vertical guide:** Position the mouse cursor over the vertical ruler until the cursor changes to a double-headed arrow. Then click and drag from the vertical ruler right to the desired position on your layout. A green dotted line appears and remains when you release the mouse button.

- **To create a horizontal guide:** Position the mouse cursor over the horizontal ruler. Then click and drag from the horizontal ruler down to the desired position on your layout.

- **To place a vertical guide in the exact center of your view:** Choose Arrange⇨Ruler Guides⇨Add Vertical Ruler Guide. Publisher places a vertical guide in the exact center of the page.

- **To place a horizontal guide in the exact center of your view:** Choose Arrange⇨Ruler Guides⇨Add Horizontal Ruler Guide. Publisher places a horizontal guide across the center of the page.

- **To move a ruler guide:** Just click and drag it.

- **To remove a ruler guide:** Click and drag the ruler off the page.

- **To remove all ruler guides:** Choose the Arrange⇨Ruler Guides⇨ Clear All Ruler Guides command.

Snap to it!

Guides would be interesting visual aids but not generally worth the bother if you couldn't automatically align objects to them. Publisher (like most layout and drawing programs) has a Snap to Guides feature, which directly aligns objects you place close to a guide.

The Snap To commands make it appear as though the guides magnetically tug at your objects as those objects draw near, just as Magneto might use his magnetic powers to snatch the glasses from Cyclops' head. With these "magnetic" forces in place, you can be sure that any objects you draw or drag near a guide automatically align with that guide and with each other. You can also make objects snap to the nearest ruler mark (increment), if you like. You can even make objects snap to other objects.

Here's how to toggle the Snap To commands on and off:

- ✔ Choose Arrange➪Snap➪To Ruler Marks to align with your ruler marks.

- ✔ Choose Arrange➪Snap➪To Guides (or press Ctrl+Shift+W) to align with your layout guides.

- ✔ Choose Arrange➪Snap➪To Objects to align with selected objects on-screen. See Chapter 5 for more about objects.

A check mark next to the command name means that the option is turned on; click it to turn it off. The absence of a check mark means that the option is turned off; click it to turn it on. For some reason, the Snap➪To Objects command has no check mark. When this command is turned on, you see a colored background on the icon next to the command. When the Snap➪To Objects command is turned off, the colored background goes away.

In my experience, the Snap➪To Guides command is *so* much more useful than snapping to ruler marks. That's why it gets the special Ctrl+Shift+W shortcut. I find this command more helpful, in part because you can set up your own guides (whereas you can't control the ruler marks) and in part because those rulers have so darned many marks.

Publisher offers other commands that help you precisely place objects on your layout. (I discuss these commands in Chapter 5.) In particular, you may want to explore the use of the Align or Distribute commands to precisely align objects to your page. Publisher also has Nudge commands that let you use your arrow keys on the keyboard to move your objects a very small amount at a time in any direction. To set up the Nudge commands, choose Tools➪Options from the main menu to open the Options dialog box, and select the Edit tab. Then select the Arrow Keys Nudge Objects By check box and type the amount to nudge the selected object by in the adjacent text box. The minimum and maximum amounts you can enter into the Arrow Keys Nudge Objects By text box depend on the selection you make in the Measurement Units text box on the General tab of the Options dialog box.

- ✔ **Centimeters:** Type any number between 0.03 and 5.08. The default is 0.03 centimeters.
- ✔ **Inches:** Type any number between 0.01 and 2. The default is 0.13 inches.
- ✔ **Picas:** Type any number between 0.06 and 12. The default is 0.07 picas.
- ✔ **Points:** Type any number between 0.72 and 144. The default is 0.84 points.
- ✔ **Pixels:** Type any number between 0.096 and 192. The default is 1.12 pixels.

Using Virtual Rulers

You can use the status bar to determine an object's position and size, or you can use the on-screen rulers, located along the top and left edges of the scratch area. The current position of the cursor is indicated by a sliding line that appears on each of your rulers. To do fine measuring with the rulers, you can enlarge them simply by zooming in on the page. As you magnify a page, the rulers also grow larger.

The unit of measurement on each ruler is determined by the Measurement Units setting on the General tab in the Options dialog box, opened by choosing Tools➪Options. (See Chapter 3 for more on the Options dialog box.)

If the rulers aren't shown, you can display them by choosing View➪Rulers. An even more convenient approach is to right-click a blank area of the screen and choose Rulers from the context-sensitive menu that appears.

To move a ruler, Shift+click and drag it to a new location. When you place your mouse pointer over a ruler and hold down the Shift key, the cursor changes to a two-headed arrow that points up and down if you're pointing at the horizontal ruler, or left and right if you're pointing at the vertical ruler. As you drag, an outline of the ruler accompanies your pointer. When you release the mouse button, the ruler appears in its new location. To return a ruler to its original location, just drag it back in place.

You can move both rulers simultaneously by clicking and dragging the Move Both Rulers box at the intersection of the two rulers.

By default, the zero mark on each ruler is set to the upper-left corner of the page or two-page spread. You may find it convenient to *rezero* a ruler: to change the position of its zero mark, as though you were sliding the ruler end to end over a page.

For example, if one object's right edge ends at the 2¼ mark on the horizontal ruler and another object's left edge begins at the 5⁵⁄₁₆ mark, how much space is between those objects? Is this math class? Who knows, and who really cares? Wouldn't it be easier to measure it if the horizontal ruler's zero mark aligned with one of those edges?

To move a ruler's zero mark, simply point to a ruler, press and hold the Shift key, and click the *right* mouse button to drag the zero mark to a new location. The mouse pointer changes, as it does when you move a ruler, to a two-headed arrow, pointing up and down if you're pointing at the horizontal ruler or pointing right and left if you're pointing at the vertical ruler. As you drag, the ruler stays in place but a solid line follows your pointer. When you release the right mouse button, the ruler rezeroes at that line.

To reset a ruler's zero mark, double-click it. To rezero both rulers to the upper-left corner of the page or two-page spread, double-click your left mouse button in that blank box at the intersection of the two rulers.

When you're working inside a text or table frame, a subsection of the horizontal ruler automatically provides a special zero mark for just that frame or current table column. (I discuss text and table frames in Chapter 5.)

Creating Master Pages

When you create a multiple-page publication, you may want certain objects to appear on all or most of the pages. These objects can include the publication's title, your name, page numbers, a company logo or some other image, a plea to send money — whatever. Publisher lets you create a *Master* page that contains objects that appear on each page of your publication.

Master pages benefit you because they

- ✔ Eliminate the boring, repetitive work of placing and managing objects that appear on every page
- ✔ Eliminate a source of bloated file sizes because information that needs to be repeated is entered only once
- ✔ Enforce design consistency

To understand Publisher Master pages, imagine each regular publication *(foreground)* page as a piece of see-through tracing paper laid over a cardboard backing. You can see all the objects on the backing, along with the layer of objects on the tracing paper. As you move from page to page, the tracing paper changes, but the backing remains the same. If you change something on the tracing paper, only the tracing paper changes. If you change something on the backing, however, that change affects the appearance of any tracing paper laid over that backing. The Publisher Master pages work just like that cardboard backing; the foreground pages work like the pieces of tracing paper.

Any objects on a Master page are repeated on foreground pages throughout the publication. Those Master page objects that aren't obscured by objects above them in the foreground print together with any foreground objects present on each foreground page. To work with the Master page or any object on it, you must first move the foreground pages out of the way, just as you would lift tracing paper from a cardboard backing.

Mastering the Master page

To move to the Master page, choose View➪Master Page or press Ctrl+M.

The Ctrl+M shortcut derives from the word *Master*. Most page layout programs let you create master pages.

Rarely does anything radical happen when you move to the Master page. Any on-screen changes usually are very subtle, and the Master page may look like just another blank publication page, sporting the same layout guides as your publication's foreground pages. One way to tell whether you moved to the Master page is to look at the page-navigation controls in the lower-left corner of your screen. If the page-navigation controls are still there, you're in the foreground. If the page-navigation controls have been replaced with one or more Master page buttons that show letters rather than page numbers, it's proof that you successfully moved to the Master page. Perhaps the most obvious clue that you have moved to the Master page is the sudden appearance of the Edit Master Pages toolbar, shown in Figure 4-7.

To return to the foreground pages, click the Close Master View button on the Edit Master Pages toolbar, choose View➪Master Page, or press Ctrl+M. (This command toggles with the View➪Master Page command.) You return to the last foreground page you were on, and the normal page controls return in triumph.

Figure 4-7:
The Edit
Master
Pages
toolbar.

Edit Master Pages ▼
 Close **M**aster View

Working with multiple Master pages

When you start a publication, Publisher creates just one Master page for you. This strategy works fine for many publications, but sometimes you need a little more flexibility. For example, you may want to create a newsletter that has the same Master page elements (such as pictures or WordArt) on the front and back pages but different page elements on the inside pages. For this, you need to have more than one Master page (two, in this case).

To create a second Master page if you have only one, open the Master Page view by choosing View⇨Master Page (or pressing Ctrl+M). The Edit Master Pages task pane, shown in Figure 4-8, lets you create new master pages. It also displays a list of all the master pages that you have already created. Click the New Master Page button, located at the bottom of the Edit Master Pages task pane, and then click OK.

When you create a new background, the new Master page is blank. If you want elements on the existing Master page to appear on the new Master page, you have to put them there yourself.

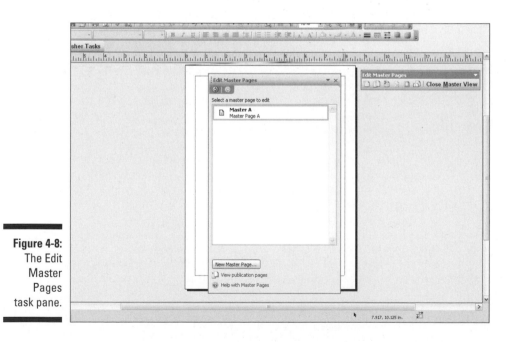

Figure 4-8:
The Edit
Master
Pages
task pane.

If you have more than one Master page and delete one (by selecting it in the Edit Master Pages task pane and clicking the Delete Master Page button on the Edit Master Pages toolbar — refer to Figure 4-7), Publisher permanently deletes all objects on that Master page. (Fortunately, Publisher warns you before deleting the Master page and informs you that it will apply the first Master page to any pages in your publication that were using the deleted Master page.)

If you delete a Master page (and all its objects) and later decide that you really would rather not have done so, you can probably recover it by clicking the down arrow on the Undo button on the Standard toolbar and selecting Delete Master Page from the drop-down list. Of course, if you have saved the publication in the meantime, you're out of luck.

To move between Master pages (if you have more than one of them), choose one of these methods:

- ✔ Choose View➪Master Page from the main menu (or press Ctrl+M) and then select a Master page in the Edit Master Pages task pane. (Refer to Figure 4-8.)
- ✔ Choose View➪Master Page from the main menu (or press Ctrl+M) and click the page-navigation control button (A or B, for example) that represents the Master page you want to view.

After you create your new Master page, you still have to tell Publisher which pages should use it. Go to the page to which you want to apply a different Master page and choose Format➪Apply Master Page. The Apply Master Page task pane, shown in Figure 4-9, appears. In the Apply Master Page task pane, select a Master page from the drop-down list under the page icon.

If you want to apply a Master page to a range of pages in your publication, you can do so easily by using the Apply To section of the Apply Master Page dialog box, shown in Figure 4-10, which appears when you click the Apply to Page Range button in the Apply Master Page task pane.

If you're creating a facing-page publication, such as a book or a newsletter, and you want to have Master pages that mirror each other (that is, a graphical image close to the left margin on the left-facing page should show up close to the right margin on the right-facing page), you don't have to create any additional Master pages. Go to Master Page view (choose View➪ Master Page or Ctrl+M) and place the elements you want on the Master page. This page will become the right-facing Master page. In the Edit Master Pages task pane, click the down arrow next to Master A and select Change to Two-Page. Publisher automatically mirrors to the left-facing page everything you have put on the Master page.

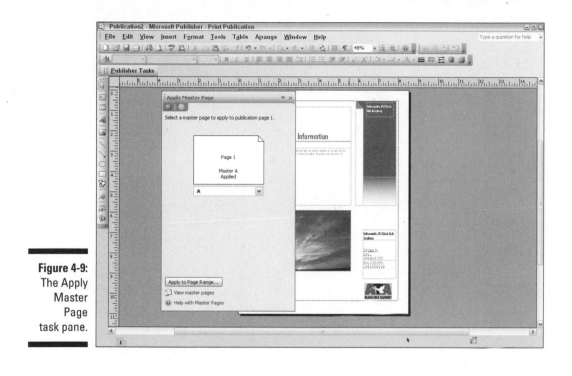

Figure 4-9:
The Apply
Master
Page
task pane.

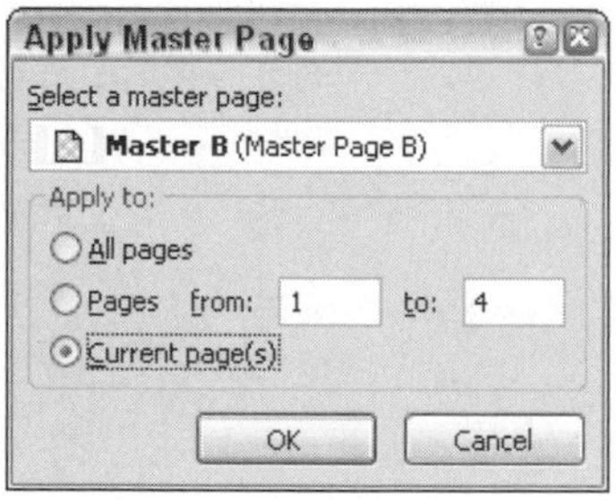

Figure 4-10:
Apply a
Master
page to a
range of
pages in
your
publication.

Adding Master page objects

Adding objects to Master pages is just like adding objects to foreground
pages, which I describe in Chapter 5. Because Master page and foreground
objects must share the final, printed page, however, you should consider a
couple of things before you add a Master page object:

✔ **If you have only one Master page:** Any object you put on it is repeated
on every foreground page.

✔ **If you have two Master pages:** Any object you put on the left Master page is repeated on every left-hand foreground page; any object you put on the right Master page is repeated on every right-hand foreground page; and any object you put on both Master pages is repeated on every left-*and* right-hand foreground page. You can eliminate all Master page objects from specific foreground pages, however, as I explain later in this chapter.

Place Master page objects where they don't interfere with foreground objects. The easiest solution is to keep Master page objects near the margins. If you choose to put an object in the middle of a Master page instead, it might get covered up by a foreground object.

Also, try to add all Master page objects before you begin adding foreground objects. Otherwise, you may need to rearrange the foreground objects to make room for Master page objects.

Creating headers and footers

To Publisher, a *header* consists of stuff — text or graphics or both — that repeats along the top of pages, whereas a *footer* consists of stuff that repeats along the bottom of pages. (You're probably already familiar with this concept from your word processor, and it's the same in Publisher.) Headers and footers usually contain such boring and traditional information as the publication title, current chapter or other division title, author's name, company or publication-specific logo, and page number. Because headers and footers are supposed to repeat on most or all pages, the Master page is the perfect place for them.

To create headers and footers, follow these steps:

1. **Choose View⇨Header and Footer from the main menu.**

   Publisher displays a blinking cursor in the page header along with the Header and Footer toolbar, as shown in Figure 4-11.

2. **Type the text that you want to appear in the header.**

   The text you type appears in your header, at the blinking cursor.

3. **Click the Show Header/Footer button on the Header and Footer toolbar to switch to the footer.**

   Microsoft Publisher displays a blinking cursor in the page footer.

4. **Type the information that you want to appear at the bottom of every page.**

   The text you type appears in your footer, at the blinking cursor.

5. **Click the Close button on the Header and Footer toolbar when you finish adding text to your headers and footers.**

Figure 4-11:
The Header
and Footer
toolbar.

 Here's a way to save yourself some work if you're creating a facing-page publication with similar headers and footers: Set up the headers and footers on
the Master page before changing the Master page to a two-page spread.
Publisher automatically copies your headers and footers to mirrored positions on the new background.

Inserting page numbers

One of the most common uses for headers and footers is to hold page numbers. Publisher is more than happy to number your pages for you. (Nice
program. Good program. Sit. Stay. Have a bone.)

To number pages, all you need to do is add a semisecret page-numbering code
(a *page-number mark*) to a header or footer. If your publication has two Master
pages and you want page numbers to appear on both the left and right pages,
you need to insert a page-number mark to the header or footer on *both* Master
pages.

Follow these steps to add page numbers to a header or footer:

1. **Choose View➪Header and Footer.**

   Publisher displays a blinking cursor in the page header along with the
   Header and Footer toolbar.

2. **(Optional) In the header, type some identifying text at the blinking
   cursor, such as the word *Page*.**

3. **Click the Insert Page Number button on the Header and Footer toolbar or press Alt+Shift+P.**

   The aforementioned semisecret page-numbering code — the *page-
   number mark* — appears on the Master page. Although this mark
   appears to be just a pound sign (#), it changes to the appropriate page
   number on each foreground page. Honest!

4. **(Optional) Select the page-number mark and format it as you would
   format any other text.**

   Formatting text is covered in Chapter 7.

5. **Click the Close button on the Header and Footer toolbar.**

Don't try to be sneaky and just type a pound sign from your keyboard to indicate where you want page numbers to appear. Although it looks just like a page-number mark, it produces only pound signs on your foreground pages.

In the foreground, each page proudly displays its own page number. By default, Publisher uses only Arabic numerals (1, 2, 3, and so on) for page numbering. If you want to number your pages some other way, perhaps with small Roman numerals (i, ii, iii, and so on) for the introductory pages of a book, you have to open the Section dialog box, shown in Figure 4-12. Choose Insert➪Section from the main menu. Then, in the Number Format drop-down list box, select the number format you want to use.

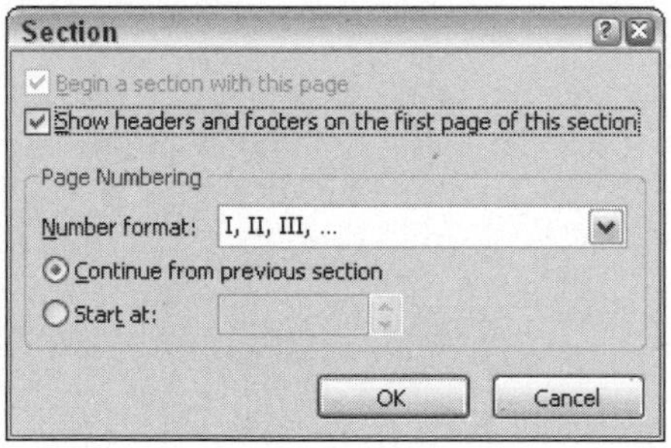

Figure 4-12:
In the Section dialog box, you choose how to format page numbering.

Section	? ×
☑ Begin a section with this page	
☑ Show headers and footers on the first page of this section	
Page Numbering	
Number format: I, II, III, ... ▾	
⦿ Continue from previous section	
○ Start at:	
OK	Cancel

If you're desktop-publishing something that requires separate series of page numbers, such as several report sections that will be printed with other report sections, you don't have to create each section of your publication in a separate file to accommodate those separate series. Use the Section dialog box (refer to Figure 4-12) to define sections. Open the Section dialog box by choosing Insert➪Section from the main menu, and then select the Begin a Section with This Page check box. You can then set the page numbers in each section to continue from the previous section or to start at a number other than 1 by changing the value in the Start At scroll box. You can also format the page numbers in each section independently. In Publisher, you can use any number up to 1,000.

The changes you make in the Section dialog box affect the page numbering only for the current publication.

Getting a date

Placing dates and times in headers and footers isn't much different from putting page numbers there. Follow the procedure described in the preceding section, but click the Insert Date and Insert Time buttons on the Header and Footer toolbar rather than click the Insert Page Number button.

If want to choose a date and time in a format that's different from the default setting, you have to choose Insert➪Date and Time from the main menu. Publisher opens the Date and Time dialog box, as shown in Figure 4-13. Click to select a format, and then select the Update Automatically check box if you want to create a placeholder that updates the date whenever you open or print your publication. The program cleverly uses your computer's date and time. If you leave the Update Automatically check box deselected in the Date and Time dialog box, Publisher simply inserts the current date or time and doesn't update it.

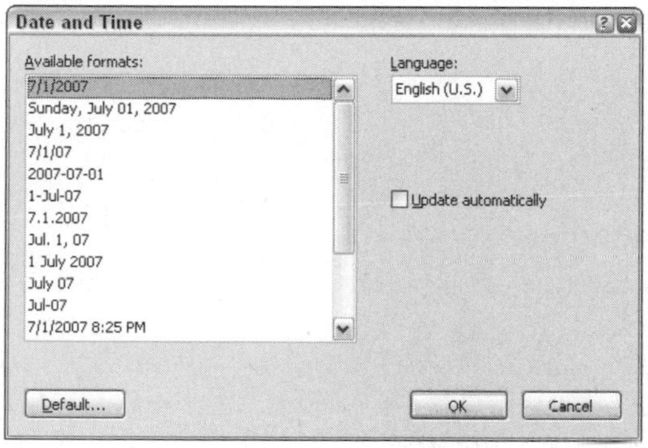

Figure 4-13:
The Date
and Time
dialog box.

Suppressing Master page objects

Traditionally, headers and footers are left off a publication's first page. In larger publications, headers and footers are also usually left off the first page of each chapter or other major division. The headers in this book are a prime example. Go ahead: Flip through this book and you'll see.

To hide *all* background objects, move to the foreground page for which you want to hide Master page objects, and then choose View⇨Ignore Master Page from the main menu.

No ambiguity here — if you're viewing a single page, the Master page objects disappear. When you apply this command to a two-page spread, Publisher opens the Ignore Master Page dialog box, shown in Figure 4-14, to ask you to select which page you want to ignore — left page or right page or both.

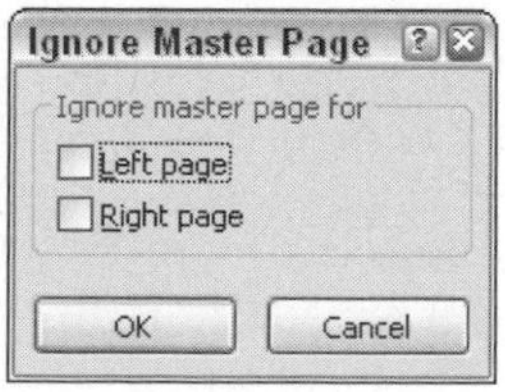

Figure 4-14:
The Ignore
Master
Page
dialog box.

The Ignore Master Page command is one of those toggle commands: Issue it once to turn it on, and issue it again to turn it off. If you're viewing two pages, the Ignore Master Page dialog box appears again. Just select or deselect one or both boxes and then click OK.

Adding and Deleting Pages

Publisher offers you several ways to add pages — perhaps more ways than you will ever need. And, if you end up with *too* many pages, you can, of course, delete them.

Adding pages

When you create a blank publication or use the Quick Publication template, Publisher creates only one page to begin with. (The other templates create a number of pages, depending on the document type.) Regardless of how many pages Publisher creates by default, you can always add more blank pages if you need them.

New pages may not appear entirely blank. They may display the margin and other layout guides that you set up to appear on every page of your publication. They may also display some Master page objects. (I discuss Master pages and objects in greater detail in Chapter 5.)

Publisher provides an easy way to insert a blank page (or two) at the end of your document: Just click the page-navigation control to advance to the last page in your document, and then press Ctrl+Shift+N.

If you're in Single Page view, Publisher inserts one new, blank page and moves you to that page. If you're in Two-Page Spread view, Publisher inserts two new, blank pages and moves your view to those pages.

Oops. If you insert a page accidentally, you can choose Edit➪Undo Insert Page, press Ctrl+Z, or click the Undo button on the Standard toolbar to remove it.

You aren't limited to adding pages to the end of your publication. If you choose Insert➪Page from the main menu, you can insert any number of pages before or after the current page, or, if you're in a two-page spread, between the current pages. You can add blank pages, add pages with a single text frame, or even duplicate the contents of a single page.

Follow these steps to insert a new page or pages into your publication:

1. **Move to the page or spread that you want to immediately precede, follow, or flank your new pages.**

2. **Choose Insert⇨Page.**

   The Insert Page dialog box appears, as shown in Figure 4-15. This dialog box is one of the most useful ones you encounter, and its options for page creation can save you a lot of time.

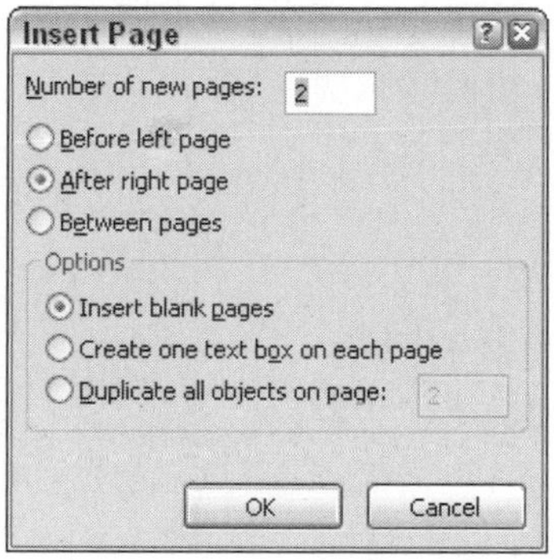

Figure 4-15:
The Insert
Page dialog
box for a
two-page
spread.

Although Ctrl+Shift+N is listed on the Insert menu as a shortcut for the Insert⇨Page command, Ctrl+Shift+N does *not* open the Insert Page dialog box. Instead, it immediately adds one blank page (if you're in Single Page view) or two blank pages (if you're in Two-Page Spread view) after the current page or spread — no questions asked. I object to listing keystrokes that don't exactly issue menu commands, and I think it should be considered a bug. (It quacks like a bug!) The same behavior existed in previous versions of Microsoft Publisher, however.

3. **In the Number of New Pages text box, type the number of pages you want to insert.**

   The default is 1 for Single Page view and 2 for Two-Page Spread view.

   Inserting pages in even numbers is a good idea so that left-hand pages don't become right-hand pages and vice versa. This rule of thumb isn't as important at the initial stages of a publication, but inserting pages in odd numbers can wreak havoc if you insert them after having laid down some objects.

   Because booklet pages print in groups of 4, Publisher displays a dialog box and prompts you to add additional pages so your booklet publication will print properly.

4. **Click the radio button that indicates where you want the new page (or pages) to be inserted.**

   Your choices are Before Left Page, After Right Page, and Between Pages.

5. **In the Options area, click to indicate which kind of pages you want to insert:**

   - *Insert Blank Pages:* Inserts pages that have no objects of their own, just like the pages that are added when you insert pages by using page controls.

   - *Create One Text Box on Each Page:* Places a blank text box on each new page you create. Each text box matches your publication's margin guides. This option is an excellent choice for publications such as books, which have page after page of (primarily) text.

   - *Duplicate All Objects on Page:* Makes a copy of whichever objects already exist on the page number you specify in the text box and places those objects on each of the new pages.

6. **Click OK.**

If you accidentally insert pages, you can remove them by immediately choosing Edit⇨Undo Insert Page from the main menu.

If you want to duplicate objects on your new pages, you have to place the objects on the source page *before* you choose the Insert⇨Page command.

Even though you may be tempted to use the Duplicate option (Insert⇨ Duplicate Page from the main menu) to copy objects that you want on every publication page, such as headers, footers, and page numbers, *don't do it.* Doing so creates larger file sizes. Use Master pages instead. With a Master page, a single instance of an object serves all your printed pages. See the section "Creating Master Pages," earlier in this chapter, for more details.

If you're importing a great deal of text and you don't know how many pages you need to fit that text, you can have Publisher automatically add the necessary number of pages for you, create text frames on those pages, and then fill those frames with the text. Chapter 6 tells you more about this labor-saving feature.

Deleting pages

Deleting a page, especially from Single Page view, can be frighteningly easy — and shouldn't be taken lightly. When you delete a page, it's as though the page you deleted never existed. No mourning. No nothing. No kidding. (Have I mentioned backups recently? Like in the last page or two?)

When you delete a page, all the objects on that page are also deleted. Only objects off the page, on the scratch area, remain untouched. Publisher then automatically renumbers the remaining pages so that you don't end up with a wacky page sequence.

Follow these steps to delete a page:

1. **Move to the page you want to delete.**

2. **Choose Edit⇨Delete Page from the main menu.**

   Note that this command isn't available if you're viewing the Master page of your publication.

3. **Respond to the Publisher prompts asking you to confirm your deletion.**

   You have two main choices:

   - *In Single Page view:* When you choose the Edit⇨Delete Page command, Publisher displays a confirmation box asking whether you really want to delete the page if the selected page contains any objects. Click Yes to delete the page. Click No if you're having second thoughts. Use this command with caution. Press Ctrl+Z if you accidentally delete a page. If the page you select for deletion is blank, you receive no warning before the page is deleted.

   - *In Two-Page Spread view:* Publisher opens the Delete Page dialog box, as shown in Figure 4-16. Click the radio button for the option you want: Both Pages, Left Page Only, or Right Page Only.

4. **Click OK.**

Figure 4-16:
The Delete
Page dialog
box for a
two-page
spread.

Deleting pages, even with an alert box, is dangerous. Pay particular attention to page deletions, because they're an excellent method for losing work.

As with inserting pages, you should delete pages in even numbers so that your left- and right-hand pages don't get fouled up. If you delete just a left- or right-hand page in Two-Page Spread view, Publisher opens a dialog box asking you to consider deleting pages in even numbers instead.

Try as you might, and as much fun as it might be to do it, you cannot delete the only page in a single-page publication. If you try, Publisher simply deletes any objects on that page and leaves the page itself in place. The Master page isn't affected when you try to delete the only page in a single-page publication.

Modifying the Page Layout

Every publication you create, no matter how basic, already has a specific page layout that determines each page's physical size and orientation and whether the paper requires special folding to create the individual publication pages. But just because the page layout is determined the moment you start a publication doesn't mean that you can't change it later by choosing File⇨Page Setup.

Do you get the feeling that there's *nothing* that can't change later in a publication? I don't think there is, but changing things — including page layouts — exacts an increasingly heavier toll as you go along. For example, if you lay down all the text and graphics in a 16-page pamphlet and then change the size of the pages, you may create plenty of extra work to do just to get the text and graphics to fit properly again. Making the correct choices early in your project saves you considerable time later on. The time you spend fixing up your publication is time you don't spend doing the creative work that makes desktop publishing fun.

Always select your target printer, as discussed in Chapter 12, before you spend any time adjusting the page setup.

To change the page setup of a document, choose File⇨Page Setup. The Page Setup dialog box, shown in Figure 4-17, appears.

You use the options in the Page Setup dialog box to change the page size of your publication. If you can't find a page size from the hundreds of choices available, you can even create your own page size.

When the Page Setup dialog box opens, it displays the current design template superimposed on the various page sizes from all the publication types. Your design will fit on some page sizes better than on others. For instance, if you start with a three-panel brochure, you can see from the Page Setup dialog box that the publication will fit better on B4 (Landscape) than it will on any of the business card sizes.

In addition to changing the size of the paper for your publication, you can change the way the publication prints to your printer. Choose File⇨ Print Setup to display the Print Setup dialog box, as shown in Figure 4-18.

You can select these options:

- The printer model
- The paper size the printer will print on

 ✔ The correct paper bin for the selected paper size

 ✔ Portrait or Landscape orientation

The Preview box in the Print Setup dialog box shows how your selections affect the printed job.

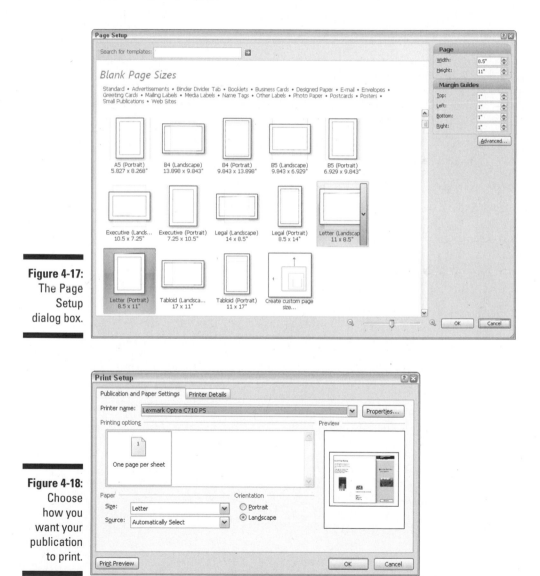

Figure 4-17: The Page Setup dialog box.

Figure 4-18: Choose how you want your publication to print.

Designated drivers

Perhaps the most common design mistake that desktop publishing beginners make is doing page layout with the wrong printer driver. This mistake is easy enough to make, even for experienced desktop publishers who are aware of the problem. A change in printers, the service you're using, or the specifications for the publication itself can result in having to change printer drivers. And, you may not have control over those situations.

If you lay out pages by using the wrong printer driver, many of the page setup options you take for granted might not exist when you send your file to be printed. After all your hard work of carefully nudging objects around the page, you might find that objects are cut off, blurry, or otherwise poorly printed. If your publication is being printed by a printer service, discussing the printer driver before you initiate a design project can save you time. See Chapter 13 for more detailed information about printing your publication.

Make sure that you're designing your page for the correct printer as early in the project as possible.

Chapter 5

Objects and Frames

. . . .

. . . .

*I*n the language of Microsoft Publisher 2007, an *object* represents any publication design element: a text or graphic frame, a line, a circle, or some other item on a page. Objects fall into different categories, and each category has a set of properties. After you know how one object in a category works, you can understand the behaviors and properties of related objects in that category. If you have a good set of objects, you can conquer the world.

Chapter 4 discusses the basic elements of your publication's pages. It's now time to add structure to your pages with frames and drawn objects. In this chapter, I focus on how you use frames and drawn objects to create a design framework into which you can add the content that makes each publication unique.

This chapter focuses on two types of objects: those contained in frames and those that aren't. *Frames* are container objects into which you place the content of your publication. Text and graphics are two common examples of publication elements that require frames. You can also use frames to create tables and special text effects.

Not all objects on a layout use frames, however. Some objects — such as lines, circles, rectangles, ovals, and other shapes that you draw by using the tools in the Publisher toolbox — are complete, in, of, and by themselves. You find out how to create these types of objects in this chapter.

Being Framed Is a Good Thing

As I mention in the introduction to this chapter, frames are *container objects* that hold your publication's content. Frames have *properties* that you can change — they have a size and shape, they can be resized and moved, they can be transparent or opaque, and they can have color or patterns applied to them, for example. (Basically, frames have all the properties you associate with drawn objects.) Frames exist as separate objects, but you can associate frames as a group by using the equivalent of electronic glue.

Frames also have special properties that aren't common to objects in general. For example, text frames can be linked so that the contents of one frame flow into the next frame. This feature is particularly valuable for text in a long document, where you may want an article to begin on one page and continue on another.

Publisher provides four frame types:

- ✔ **Text:** A text frame is a container for text. Text frames can be linked to create Publisher stories. In Publisher-speak, a *story* consists of all the text that's contained in one frame — or that continues to another, linked frame.

  Some text frames are part of a Business Information Set, which contains information about you or your organization. See the section "Adding In Your Business Info," later in this chapter, for details.

- ✔ **Table:** This frame type is a container for (surprise!) tables. It helps you arrange text in tidy rows and columns. Table frames are useful for presenting large amounts of data in a clear, easy-to-understand format.

- ✔ **Picture:** Picture frames have special properties that let you modify the way graphics look in them.

- ✔ **WordArt:** WordArt creates graphical objects based on type — the characters and symbols you make with your keyboard. By using WordArt, you can create many special text effects that are useful in headlines and other places.

Each of the program's four frame types behaves a little differently. In addition to holding different sorts of objects, each type varies in how you create, delete, and otherwise manipulate it.

Creating frames

To create a frame, you select the appropriate tool on the Objects toolbar and click and drag with the tool on your layout. Figure 5-1 shows you where each tool is located on the Object toolbar. The tool you select determines the frame's type, whereas your drawing action determines the frame's size and position in the publication.

After you create a frame, you might notice a slight change in your toolbars. For example, if you click a text box, the Formatting toolbar appears underneath the Microsoft Publisher 2007 Standard toolbar, with buttons that let you change the format of your frame or the objects you put in it. For the most part, these formatting buttons are duplicates of menu commands. Plenty of formatting tools are available for the various frame types, although different commands appear for each specific frame type.

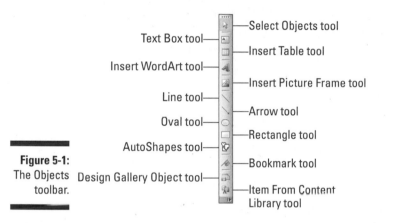

Figure 5-1:
The Objects
toolbar.

Follow these steps to draw a text box or picture frame:

1. **Click the Text Box tool or Picture Frame tool on the Objects toolbar.**

2. **Choose one of these options:**

   • **Picture Frame:** You're treated to a variety of choices. If you choose Clip Art Picture from File or From Scanner or Camera, you need to either navigate to the location of the stored file or select the piece of clip art or graphic that you want to insert. At this point, your job is done, and you can sit back, relax, and admire the artwork that now appears in your project.

   • **Text Box or Picture Frame Using the Empty Picture Frame option:** The cursor changes to a crosshair. Move the crosshair over the publication page or scratch area. The sliding ruler lines and the status bar's position box show your exact position. Click and drag to create the outline of your frame.

   As you drag, the program draws a sample to show you the size and shape of your new frame. The status bar's size box indicates the frame's size.

3. **Release the mouse button to create the frame.**

   Publisher creates your text or picture frame and selects it (makes it *active*) so that you can work with it further.

   Figure 5-2 shows you a selected text box. Picture frames and text boxes look the same except that text boxes can have buttons used to link frames for automatic content flow control.

   To draw a table, the steps are pretty much the same as for creating a text or picture frame. (Okay, you *do* have to pick the Insert Table tool.) Just don't be surprised, after you release the mouse button to create the frame, when Publisher opens the Create Table dialog box, as shown in Figure 5-3.

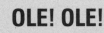

OLE! OLE!

Publisher makes good use of *Object Linking and Embedding,* or *OLE,* a special form of cut-and-paste technology that enables you to incorporate into your layout many kinds of data that the program doesn't directly support or can't directly create. A WordArt frame would be better termed an OLE frame, after the kind of object that fills that frame. Although Publisher incorporates WordArt directly into its package, you can create frames by pasting in designs from any software application that supports OLE.

You implement OLE by choosing Edit⇨Paste Special from the main menu. You can create either embedded OLE objects or linked OLE objects. When you create an *embedded* object, the object is placed and stored (embedded) directly in your publication file, as is the information that enables Publisher to link back to the program used to create the object. With a *linked* object, the only information that's stored in your publication file is the data needed to link back to the original OLE server program.

Whether you create linked or embedded OLE objects, you make any changes to them in the OLE server program rather than in Publisher. You can specify that you want the changed objects to be updated either automatically in your layout or manually, on a case-by-case basis. Also, you can choose to apply changes made to embedded data to the copy of the object that exists only in your publication.

You choose the Insert⇨Object command to select an OLE server program and create an OLE frame. Publisher ships with a picture browser for the Microsoft Clip Gallery. Select the OLE server (such as Microsoft Excel Chart or Microsoft Word Document) from the Object Type list box to choose from any OLE server registered with Windows.

Although OLE is nice to use in other kinds of programs, it's an essential part of working in a page layout program, such as Publisher. If you understand this feature, it can save you time, hard drive space, maintenance, and grief. I revisit OLE throughout this book.

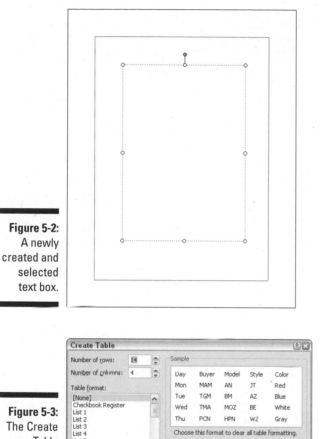

Figure 5-2:
A newly
created and
selected
text box.

Figure 5-3:
The Create
Table
dialog box.

You then need to follow these additional steps:

1. **Select the number of rows and columns you want in your table.**

2. **(Optional) Choose a format for your table.**

   If you're just dying to get a feel for what the table will look like, you can get a sneak preview by taking a peek at the Sample window.

3. **Click the OK button.**

   Your table frame is now complete. A sample table frame is shown in Figure 5-4.

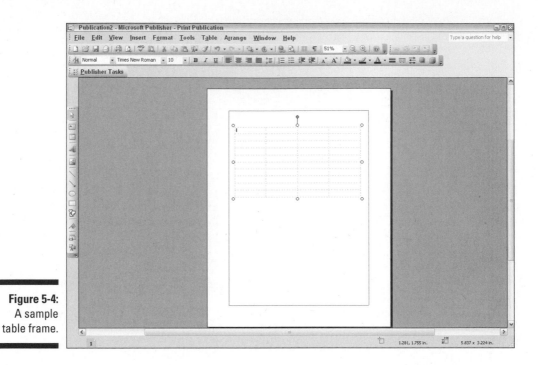

Figure 5-4:
A sample
table frame.

So far, so good. Although all three frames (text, picture, and table) that I discuss in this part of the chapter behave similarly, it turns out that the WordArt
frame is somewhat different. When you draw a frame for that object type, the
WordArt Gallery opens.

1. **Select the WordArt style that appeals to your discerning eye and then
   click OK.**

   The Edit WordArt Text dialog window opens. It looks just like the one
   you see in Figure 5-5.

2. **Type the text of your Word Art and then click OK.**

   If you're feeling extra creative, you can change the font and its attributes
   (size or bold or italics) before clicking the OK button.

3. **(Optional) Continue formatting your WordArt.**

   Because the WordArt graphic is still selected, you notice that the
   WordArt toolbar appears directly on top of your WordArt. You can use
   the toolbar to do lots of cool things to your WordArt; find out more
   about WordArt in Chapter 9. If you're not happy with the words in your
   WordArt, double-click the frame; when you do, the WordArt text box
   opens on your screen, and you can make changes.

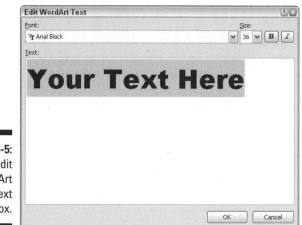

Figure 5-5:
The Edit
WordArt
Text
dialog box.

After you draw a frame, Publisher automatically deselects whichever frame tool you might have been using and then activates the Select Objects tool so that you can manipulate your object. This feature is a pain to use if you want to draw several frames of the same type one right after the other. To make a frame tool stay selected, double-click the tool icon. When you're done drawing frames with that tool, deselect the tool by clicking any tool in the toolbox. This technique works for any tool in the toolbox (for example, the Line, Box, and Circle tools), not just for frame tools.

Selecting frames and objects

Before you can change a frame or an object in Publisher, you have to select it. After you select an element, you can fill it, resize it, move it, delete it, or do whatever your heart desires. You can also select multiple frames or any set of objects on a page, thus enabling you to perform the same operation on a set of frames or objects simultaneously — as long as the operation is legal for the selected elements.

For example, if you select two text boxes, Publisher lets you add borders to both of them at the same time. If you try to paste text from the Clipboard into two selected text boxes simultaneously, however, the program gets confused and creates a third text box with your text.

A frame is automatically selected after you finish drawing it, as shown earlier, in Figure 5-2. You can tell that a frame is selected because it displays eight little circles, or *selection handles,* around its perimeter. Some selected frames display more than just selection handles. For example, a text box may display a Go to Previous Text Box button or a Go to Next Text Box button; you find out how to connect text frames and work with tables in Chapter 6.

If you revisit a frame after creating it, you have to select it again. In Publisher, you use the Select Objects tool to select (or reselect) frames and objects. You can use any of these selection techniques:

- ✔ **To select a single frame:** Just click it. The frame — along with its contents, will be selected.

- ✔ **To select additional frames:** Hold down the Shift or Ctrl key and click the frames.

- ✔ **To deselect one frame from a range of selected objects:** Hold down the Shift or Ctrl key and click the frame.

- ✔ **To select multiple frames that are close to one another:** Click and drag around the frames. As you drag, Publisher shows you a *selection box* — a dotted line that indicates the area you're encompassing. When the selection box surrounds all the frames (or objects) you want to select, release the mouse button.

- ✔ **To select everything on the current publication page (or pages) and the scratch area:** Choose the Edit⇨Select All command or press Ctrl+A. (You don't need to select the Select Objects tool to perform this task.)

These selection techniques work for all types of objects, not just frames.

Figure 5-6 shows you several frames and objects selected on a layout. The selected objects are (clockwise from the upper-left corner) an AutoShape, a text frame, a rectangle, another AutoShape, and a table frame. Notice that although you find a single *bounding box* (the rectangle that encompasses the selected items) around them, each object still has its own set of selection handles. (The rounded-arrow shape isn't selected with this range of objects.)

You can tell that this multiple selection is *ungrouped* because each object retains its own selection handles. In the ungrouped condition, the objects and frames retain their individual identities. (Publisher handles the objects as independent entities unless they're *grouped;* you find out about grouping later in this chapter.) Because a multiple selection isn't a single object, you cannot resize the selection or any individual component, but you can move the selection around and apply other commands, such as formatting. For example, if you apply a border to the multiple selection, each component of · the selection takes on that border format.

Sometimes when you click a frame (or an object), you can't select or modify it. If this happens, check out these possibilities:

- ✔ **The frame or object may be a Master page object.** To select a Master page object, you first have to move to the Master page by choosing View⇨Master Page or pressing Ctrl+M.

✔ **The frame or object is grouped.** Figure 5-7 shows you the same set of objects shown in Figure 5-6, but this time they're grouped together. You can click the Group Objects button to ungroup a group; look for more information about groups later in this chapter.

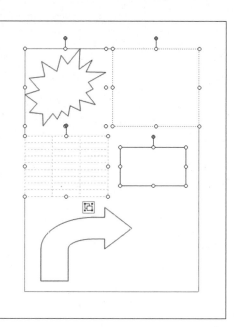

Figure 5-6:
Multiple
objects
and frames
(ungrouped).

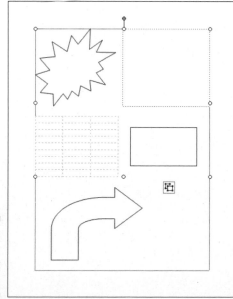

Figure 5-7:
A selected,
grouped set
of objects.

If you can't find the Group Objects button, look for the two small, overlapping boxes. Grouping works as a toggle: Click it the first time, and your selected objects are grouped, and the icon becomes a bit darker; click the button a second time to ungroup the objects — rendering the icon a bit lighter.

After you're done working with a particular frame or set of frames, deselect them so that you don't accidentally delete or change them in some way. Selected frames can be frighteningly easy to delete. Many programs offer a Lock command to freeze objects, to prevent you from accidentally moving or deleting them. But Publisher doesn't have this handy feature, so you must be especially careful.

To deselect frames, click in a blank area of the publication page or scratch area. Or, click a single frame or object to deselect every other frame and select just that one.

Editing frames

Because frames can contain objects, you can make two types of deletions:

- ✔ Delete the entire frame itself, which also deletes all its contents.
- ✔ Delete the contents of the frame by selecting the contents themselves.

To delete a frame, you select the frame and choose Edit➪Delete Object from the main menu. You can also select the frame and press Delete. In the case of a table frame, you have a container with many "drawers"; you can delete the contents of each cell in the table by selecting the contents of that cell and pressing Delete. When you have selected text in a text frame or an insertion point in a cell of a table frame, you can press Ctrl+Shift+X to delete the frame. Using only the Delete key in those cases deletes the selected text or the contents of the current cell in the table.

In the case of text or table frames, you may notice that the commands Delete Text and Delete Object appear on the Edit menu. These Delete commands bypass the Windows Clipboard and simply remove the object from your layout. If you want to make use of the Windows Clipboard, you need to use the Cut, Copy, and Paste commands, which are also on the Edit menu.

The Windows Clipboard is a piece of computer memory (RAM) that can store text, formatted text, graphics, and other objects. It's sort of a temporary holding tank where you can keep data that you want to use again. You can use the Clipboard to work with frames and the contents of frames within Publisher. The operations that I outline in the following bulleted list work with frames and, generally, with objects of other types. When you use the

Clipboard between Windows programs, you can transfer only the contents of the Clipboard that the receiving program understands. For example, you can't paste a Publisher frame into WordPad, but you can move formatted text between the two programs.

The Edit menu's Cut, Copy, and Paste commands work as described in this list:

✔ **Cut:** Choose Edit➪Cut or press Ctrl+X to place the current selection on the Windows Clipboard and remove it from your layout. The previous contents of the Clipboard are lost.

✔ **Copy:** Choose Edit➪Copy or press Ctrl+C to make a copy of your selected element and place it on the Clipboard. The selection remains intact on your layout. The previous contents of the Clipboard are lost.

To quickly copy a selected frame or the selected object, press Ctrl within the frame and drag the frame to a new location. Copying is a great time-saver and an ideal way to make exact duplicates of frames you've already drawn.

✔ **Paste:** Choose Edit➪Paste or press Ctrl+V to place the contents of the Clipboard on your layout at your current position. The previous contents of the Clipboard remain intact. You can apply the Paste command any number of times you want.

Pasted text is placed at the insertion point. If Publisher finds no inser-tion point, it creates a text box in the center of your screen and places the text in it. If a cut or copied text frame is on the Clipboard, the Paste command puts the frame back on the page at the position from which it came.

If an object such as a line is on the Clipboard, Publisher pastes that object at a position that's offset slightly from the originally selected object. If you move to a new page after you place an object on the Clipboard, the object, when pasted, is placed on the new page at the same position in which it appeared on the original page.

When you flush the contents of the Clipboard, by either replacing them (with another Cut or Copy command) or restarting your computer, the contents are gone and cannot be restored.

The Cut, Copy, and Paste commands also show up on the context-sensitive (or *shortcut*) menu that appears when you right-click a frame or an object. Figure 5-8 shows you this menu for a text box. You can select the entire con-tents of a page or publication and cut and paste it to another page or publica-tion. You can also drag and drop text, frames, and other objects between publications if you have two Publisher publications open on your screen.

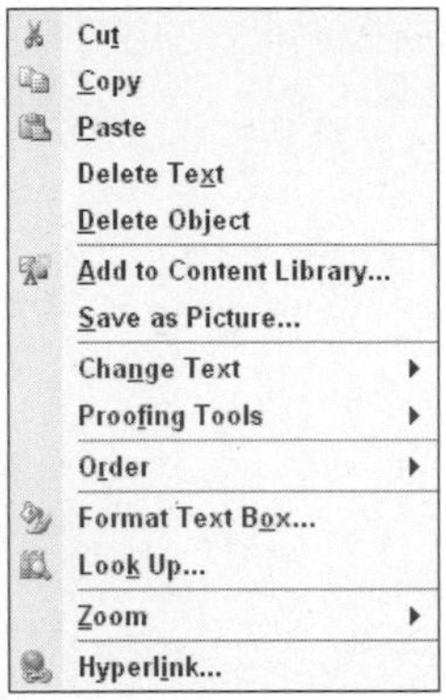

✄	Cu̲t
📋	C̲opy
📋	P̲aste
	Delete Te̲xt
	D̲elete Object
🖼	Add to Content Library...
	Save as Picture...
	Cha̲nge Text ▸
	Proofing Tools ▸
	O̲rder ▸
🔧	Format Text B̲ox...
📖	Loo̲k Up...
	Z̲oom ▸
🌐	Hyperli̲nk...

Figure 5-8:
Context-
sensitive
menu in a
text box.

TIP

You definitely should explore the right-click menus for every frame and object that Publisher creates. They offer many editing and modification commands that provide useful shortcuts.

The Edit menu also offers another Paste command: Paste Special calls up objects that must be managed by outside programs through Object Linking and Embedding, or OLE. Earlier in this chapter, in the "OLE! OLE!" sidebar, I discuss one example of OLE. Publisher can be an OLE client and use the services of any OLE server program that is recognized by Windows for a particular object's file type.

Filling frames

Frames are so important to creating publications that I devote entire chapters in this book to them. Mourn the trees! Chapters 6 and 8 offer more information about text boxes, and Chapter 6 discusses table frames as well. Because WordArt frames create special text objects that are really graphics, I discuss them in Chapter 8, which talks about type and where the lingo flies fast and thick. Chapter 9 covers picture frames.

Moving and resizing frames

For one reason or another, frames don't always end up in the right size or shape or at the place where you want them to be. Nobody's perfect.

To move a frame or an object, move your pointer over the border or the shape itself until the pointer turns into a four-point arrow. Then click and drag the frame or object to a new location.

You can constrain a move to either the vertical or horizontal direction by holding down the Shift key.

As you drag, a dotted outline of the frame follows your pointer. When the outline is where you want your frame to be, release the mouse button.

If you want to move a frame or set of frames to a different page within your publication, drag the frame or set completely off the publication page and onto the scratch area. Then move to the destination page and drag the frame or set from the scratch area to that page.

Perhaps you need to make a graphic bigger or create more room for your text. Rather than delete the frame and any work you've done on it, use the frame's selection handles to resize the existing frame. As you move the cursor over the selection handles, the mouse pointer becomes a double arrow. After the double-arrow pointer appears, you can

- Click and drag a selection handle to resize a frame horizontally, vertically or diagonally.
- Hold the Ctrl key and drag a selection handle to resize both horizontal or both vertical edges at the same time.
- Click and drag a corner selection handle to resize a frame both horizontally and vertically at the same time.
- Hold down the Shift key and drag a corner selection handle to resize a frame along its diagonal and retain the relative proportions of its height versus its width.
- Hold down the Ctrl key and drag a corner selection handle to force the frame's center to retain its position on the page.
- Hold down the Shift and Ctrl keys together as you drag a corner selection handle to maintain a frame's proportion and resize it around its center.
- Click and drag the green circle attached to the frame by a short line to rotate the frame in either direction.

You resize and move objects in the same manner as you do frames, by using the selection handles on each object's bounding box.

Many page layout programs offer features that enable you to resize a frame to a specific dimension or to reduce or enlarge a frame by a percentage. Publisher is no exception. Select a text box and then choose Format⇨Text Box from the main menu. The Format Text Box dialog box appears, as shown in Figure 5-9. Click the Size tab. Using the drop-down lists in the Size and Rotate area, enter a new height and width for the selected text box. (If you want, you can even specify an angle of rotation by using the Rotation drop-down list.) Click the Layout tab of the Format Text box (which you can see later in this chapter, in Figure 5-24) and enter the exact position in the Position on Page area. Specify whether the Horizontal and Vertical options are measured from the upper-left corner, center, or upper-right corner of the page.

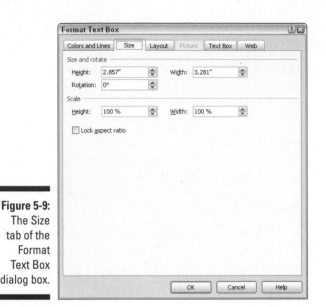

Figure 5-9:
The Size
tab of the
Format
Text Box
dialog box.

To specify the size and location of a picture, choose Format➪Picture from the main menu to open the appropriate dialog box. For an AutoShape, choose Format➪AutoShape. If you want to resize or change the location of a table — yessirree — choose Format➪Table.

Entering a negative number in either the Horizontal or Vertical position box places the left edge of the object in the scratch area.

The way that resizing a frame affects its contents depends on the frame's type. Resizing a picture or WordArt frame changes the size of the picture or WordArt object within that frame. Resizing a text or table frame, however, merely changes the amount of area available for the text within the frame; the text itself doesn't change size but, rather, rearranges itself to fit the new shape of its home. However, if the text box is formatted for Best Fit or Shrink Text on Overflow, the size of your font changes if you change the frame size.

If you want even more control over resizing the frames in your publication, display the Measurement toolbar by choosing View➪Toolbars➪ Measurement. The Measurement toolbar appears, as shown in Figure 5-10. This toolbar isn't particularly user friendly, as you can plainly see. The Measurement toolbar is divided into nine rows. The first two rows control the horizontal and vertical position of the object — its *x* and *y* coordinates. The second two rows control its width and height. The next row controls the object's rotation. The next two rows control text scaling (horizontally) and *tracking,* or the general spacing between characters. The last rows control kerning and line spacing. *Kerning* is the amount of space between pairs of characters, whereas *line spacing* is, well, the space between lines. In addition to resizing frames, you can move a frame as easily as you can slide a brand-new playing card across a freshly waxed table. Swoosh!

In the spirit of giving you more options than you can possibly use, Publisher provides four ways to move frames and objects: dragging, nudging, lining up, and the ubiquitous cutting-and-pasting (discussed earlier in this chapter). I cover the first three options in more detail in later sections of this chapter, after I dispose of the details of working with drawn objects. Each method for moving frames and objects has its own advantages, depending on where you want to move a frame and how adept you are with using the mouse.

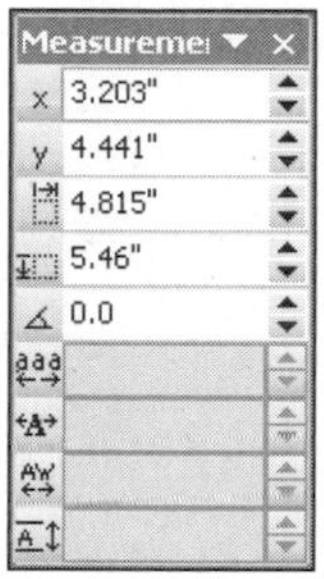

Figure 5-10:
The
Measure-
ment toolbar.

Adding In Your Business Info

After you get the hang of working with frames, you can start to explore some of the time-saving features that Publisher has up its sleeve. A case in point is adding in all your contact information.

To relieve you from the tedium of entering information about yourself, your business, or your organization every time you create a publication, Publisher provides Business Information Sets. Every publication you create has a Business Information Set associated with it, although you don't see the information unless you (or a design template) insert it into the publication. After you create a Business Information Set and associate it with your publication, you can decide exactly *which* tidbits of information — if any — you want to appear in your publication. Publisher lets you create as many Business Information Sets as you like. When you create a publication, Publisher uses for the new publication whichever Business Information Set you used last.

Each Business Information Set contains eight components:

- Individual name
- Job position or title
- Organization name
- Address

    ✔ Tagline or motto

    ✔ Phone and fax numbers and e-mail address

    ✔ Logo

    ✔ Business Information Set name

Switching Business Information Sets

To create a Business Information Set, choose Edit➪Business Information. The Business Information dialog box, shown in Figure 5-11, leaps to the screen. Select one of the Business Information Sets from the Select Business Information Set drop-down list. If you haven't previously ventured into this area, you're treated to the Create New Business Information dialog box. You can enter new information into the selected Business Information Set, change any existing information, and even give the set a snappy new moniker, if you want. Click the Update Publication button to apply your changes and close the Business Information dialog box.

If you made any changes to the components in the selected Business Information Set, be sure to save your publication before switching to a different Business Information Set, or else you lose any changes.

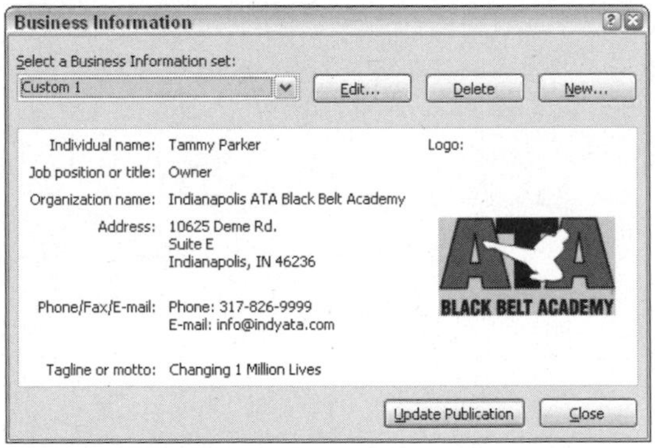

Figure 5-11:
The
Business
Information
dialog box.

Business Information	
Select a Business Information set:	
Custom 1	Edit... Delete New...
Individual name:	Tammy Parker
Job position or title:	Owner
Organization name:	Indianapolis ATA Black Belt Academy
Address:	10625 Deme Rd. Suite E Indianapolis, IN 46236
Phone/Fax/E-mail:	Phone: 317-826-9999 E-mail: info@indyata.com
Tagline or motto:	Changing 1 Million Lives
Logo:	ATA BLACK BELT ACADEMY

Update Publication   Close

Inserting Business Information Set components

Each component of the Business Information Set can be inserted into a publication. Choose Insert➪Business Information from the main menu to display the Business Information task pane, as shown in Figure 5-12. As you pass your mouse over any of the components, a rather large down arrow appears, just to the right of the component. Click the down arrow next to the name of the component you want to insert, and select Insert This Field from the drop-down list. The Business Information Set component is inserted into the publication with little round selection handles around its perimeter. With the exception of the Logo component, Business Information Set components look and behave just like text frames.

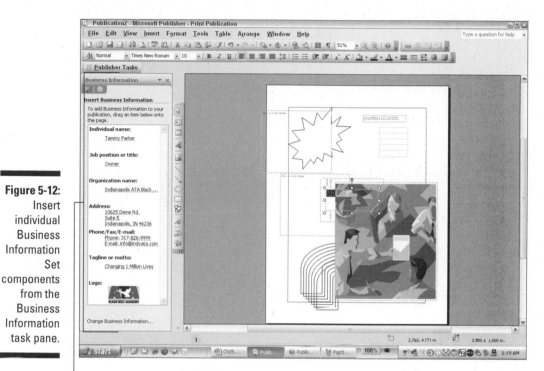

Figure 5-12:
Insert
individual
Business
Information
Set
components
from the
Business
Information
task pane.

Business Information task pane

You can distinguish a plain-old text frame from a Business Information Set component by pointing at the box with the mouse. (Pointing with your finger would just leave smudges on the screen.) A Business Information Set component has a dotted blue underline, and a circle with the lowercase letter i (the international symbol for information) appears above it. This little guy is a Smart Tag button. Clicking the Smart Tag results in a menu that lists the options to edit or update your Business Information set.

Changing Business Information Set components

Publisher makes changing business information in your publication easy. Choose Edit⇨Business Information to open the Business Information dialog box. Select the Business Information Set you want to edit, and then click Edit to open the Edit Business Information Set dialog box. Make changes to the Business Information Set and click Save. As an added bonus, you can click Update Publication in the Business Information dialog box, and your newly improved info magically appears in the current publication. That's all there is to it!

If that method isn't easy enough for you, try this: Edit the Business Information Set component text just as you would edit any text in a text box. Then click the Business Information Smart Tag button and select Save to Business

Information Set from the menu that appears. Presto, change-o — all instances of your Business Information in your current publication then change.

If the Business Information Set component you want to change isn't in the publication, you have to insert it before you can change it.

Removing business information

You can remove business information in two ways:

- **Delete a Business Information Set component from the current publication but leave the Business Information Set unchanged.** Click the component you want to remove and press Ctrl+Shift+X. Poof! The component is gone — but the Business Information is still available for your future endeavors.

  If you change your mind, just press Ctrl+Z to undo the deletion, or choose Insert⇨Business Information, click the down arrow next to the component name, and select Insert This Field to reinsert it into the publication.

- **Clear the information from the Business Information Set.** Choose Edit⇨Business Information to open the Business Information dialog box, select the Business Information Set from which you want to delete information, and click the Edit button.

  When you finish deleting, click Save and then click the Update Publication button. The components you deleted from the Business Information Set are also removed from your publication.

Drawing Isn't Just for Preschoolers

Most Publisher users typically start out by creating frames. As I mention earlier in this chapter, frames are an excellent way to get an idea of what your final layout will look like. Sometimes, however, it becomes a question of which comes first — the frame or the object *inside* the frame. If you've ever used a drawing program, you're probably familiar with basic drawing elements such as ovals, lines, and rectangles. Publisher is nothing more than a fancy drawing program. (Okay, it *is* more than just a fancy drawing program, but work with me here, will ya?)

Earlier sections in this chapter explain how to create frames and then resize them, move them, and delete them. Now comes the fun part — you can either create a frame and plunk a drawing inside the frame, or you can create your drawing without the benefit of a frame.

The drawing tools are located on the bottom half of the Objects toolbar; you can see them labeled in Figure 5-13:

✔ **Line tool:** Creates lines on your layout. Click and drag a line from a starting point (where you click and begin dragging) to an ending point (where you release the mouse button).

✔ **Arrow:** Looks and feels pretty much like a line except it has a pointy head on it!

✔ **Oval tool:** Creates an oval. If you want to create a perfect circle, press the Shift key while you click and drag.

✔ **Rectangle tool:** Create a rectangle. Press the Shift key while you click and drag to create a square.

In the language of *object-oriented,* or *vector,* programs (which is what techies like to call drawing programs when they don't want normal people to understand what they're saying), a basic shape is called a *primitive.* Lines, circles, and squares are primitives. More complex shapes (such as the custom shapes) that can be broken apart into unrelated line segments or that are a grouped set of shapes (such as those you see in the Design Gallery) are shapes you can create for yourself in Publisher. The AutoShapes and Design Gallery libraries exist to make your task in Publisher easier.

✔ **AutoShapes tool:** Creates more complex shapes. I'm fond of this special tool because it lets you easily create interesting shapes that you can use for captions, callouts, product bursts, and many other purposes. Figure 5-14 shows you the Basic Shapes pop-up menu for the AutoShapes Tool. Click to select the shape that you want from the menu and then drag to create your object on the layout.

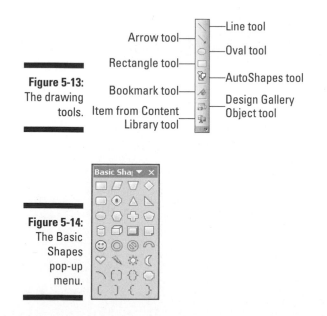

Figure 5-13:
The drawing
tools.

Arrow tool —
Rectangle tool —
Bookmark tool —
Item from Content
Library tool

Line tool
Oval tool
AutoShapes tool
Design Gallery
Object tool

Figure 5-14:
The Basic
Shapes
pop-up
menu.

Basic Shap

✔ **Bookmark:** With so many goodies to choose from, you might find that some of your graphics get lost in the shuffle! Bookmarking a graphic is a quick way to find all instances of the same graphic.

✔ **Design Gallery Object tool:** Lets you select from a library of objects. Click the Design Gallery Object tool to open a window, shown in Figure 5-15, that lets you select from a number of objects in a library and then inserts your selection into your publication.

Objects are organized by category in the Design Gallery. Click Mastheads to see all available masthead styles. Click Tables of Contents to see all available table of contents styles. Click Reply Forms to — well, you get the idea.

You can think of the Design Gallery as a clip art collection of useful objects. Use them as special elements in your publication for pull quotes, captions, and other elements. Most Design Gallery objects are groups of other objects that you can modify for your own use. See Chapter 9 for more detail on this tool.

✔ **Item from Content Library:** The only thing worse than doing something the first time is having to do exactly the same thing again the *next* time. Saving objects to the Content Library allows you to use them repeatedly — which is an excellent way to ensure the consistency of your publications.

Figure 5-15:
The Design
Gallery.

Understanding object properties

Objects have some basic properties that you probably already know about. This is head-banging stuff, but it lets me introduce some terms that are useful in discussions to come. If the italicized words in this section are familiar to you, you're not a pilgrim, and you should mosey on.

Size and shape

The first thing you notice about an object is that it has a *shape*. (Strangely, most people tend to notice that!) A shape is the actual defined area of the object and is indicated in Publisher by its border. When you select a shape, the shape is surrounded by the smallest rectangle that will encompass that object — its *bounding box*. Figure 5-16 shows you a shape with its bounding box. The bounding box has the properties of a frame, and when the encompassed shape has right angles (like a rectangle), the shape's bounding box and border coincide.

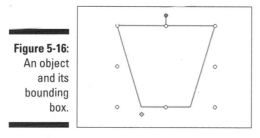

Figure 5-16:
An object
and its
bounding
box.

Use the selection handles on the bounding box to resize a shape or an object. When a shape is irregular, you can see the bounding box and the border separately. If you look closely at Figure 5-16, you notice that the lower-left vertex of the trapezoid (the shape) displays a yellow, diamond-shaped handle. That handle lets you reshape the trapezoid by changing its defining angle.

Borders, colors, and fills

Even if no border is applied to a shape, Publisher draws a dotted line so that you can see the shape and work with it. If you don't like this dotted line, you can apply a border (technically called a *stroke*), to the shape. Publisher lets you define a border thickness between 0 and 22 inches. (Only the author of this book likes to work with invisible shapes and writes and talks to invisible people.)

To apply a border to a shape, click the shape and then choose Format⇨ AutoShape from the main menu. Astute reader that you are, you might be wondering why you're not finding options like Oval and Rectangle on the

Format menu. Publisher simplified things a bit by adding the "one shape fits all" AutoShape item to the menu. Regardless, the Format AutoShape dialog box opens, as shown in Figure 5-17.

You can apply a weight to a shape's line or stroke. *Weight* is a term used by typographical folk to describe the thickness of a line. Usually, line weight is measured in *points,* which is a common unit of measurement used in publishing. Publisher gives you the option to define the thickness of a border in inches, centimeters, picas, points, or pixels.

You can also apply a color and even a pattern to a border stroke. Or, described another way, a stroke can have a fill and a fill effect. Using the term *fill* in this way can be confusing, though, because it's more commonly used to refer to the interior of a shape — the part surrounded by the stroke. Like a stroke, the interior of an object can have a color and a pattern applied to it.

Publisher lets you apply BorderArt to further beautify the borders of your frames and boxes. I tell you more about BorderArt in Chapter 9. Other, more capable programs give you finer control and let you apply to a stroke any attribute that you can apply to an object's fill.

In addition to having fills and fill effects, lines can have arrowheads, in case you're not happy with the basic arrow tool. You open the Line dialog box by choosing Format⇨AutoShape or by clicking the Line/Border Style button on the Formatting toolbar and choosing More Lines from the pop-up menu. This dialog box lets you assign arrowheads, line color, and line widths to a selected line.

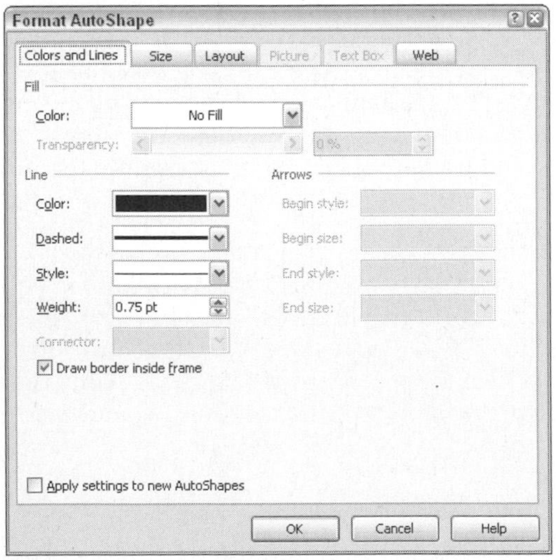

Figure 5-17:
The Format
AutoShape
dialog box.

Color is a broad subject and a very technical one for desktop publishers. I tackle it in detail in Chapter 10. For now, just think of it as a basic property of an object.

To apply a color to the fill of a selected shape, you need to go to the Fill section of the Format AutoShape dialog box. You can do this in two ways:

✔ **Click the down arrow on the Fill Color button on the Formatting toolbar.** On the pop-up selection menu, shown in Figure 5-18, display the Colors dialog box by clicking the More Fill Colors option.

✔ **Choose Format⇨AutoShape from the main menu.** In the Format AutoShape dialog box that opens, on the Colors and Lines tab, select More Colors from the Fill Color drop-down list. The much larger and more capable Colors dialog box, shown in Figure 5-19, appears.

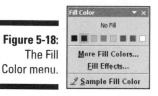

Figure 5-18:
The Fill
Color menu.

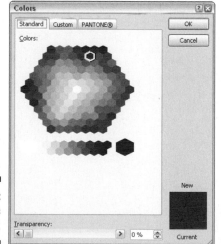

Figure 5-19:
The Colors
dialog box.

To apply a pattern, shading, or gradient to the selected object's fill, follow these steps:

1. **Click the Fill Color button on the Formatting toolbar to reveal the pop-up selection menu. (Refer to Figure 5-18.)**

2. **From this pop-up menu, open the Fill Effects dialog box by clicking the Fill Effects button.**

3. **In the Fill Effects dialog box, click the tab for the fill style you want to use.**

   Figure 5-20 shows the options available when you select the Gradient tab.

4. **Make your selections and then click OK.**

In the vocabulary of color, a tint or shade is a mix of a color with white. Patterns use a base color for the lines or dots and a background color — normally black and white, respectively. Gradients are effects in which the color is varied in some manner and in a specific direction (for example, from dark to light and outward from the center of the object). The effects you can produce with gradients are cool!

Cool-looking gradients can use a lot of computer memory and create challenges for your printer. Make sure that the printer you select can handle these large files. See Chapter 13 for more about printing.

Object transparency

Objects also have the property of being *transparent* (see-through) or *opaque* (not see-through). Many fancy drawing and page layout programs let you control the degree of transparency of an object and even the type of color that shows through. Publisher lets you assign transparency to an object by using a percentage of from 0 to 100. A clear object lets other objects beneath it show through; for most desktop publishing purposes, this option is sufficient. Set the transparency on the Gradient tab of the Fill Effects dialog box.

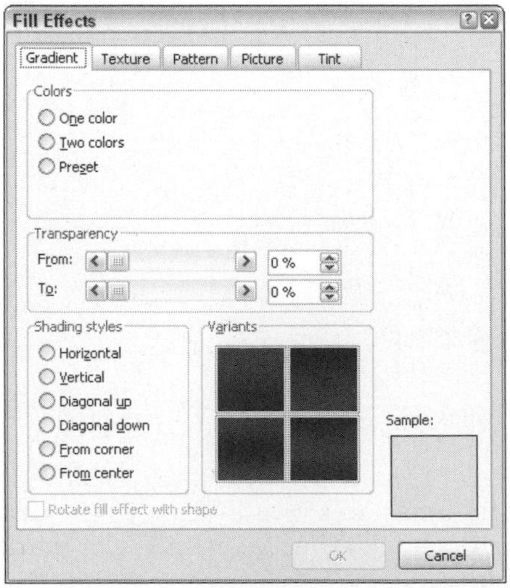

Figure 5-20:
The Fill Effects dialog box.

To make an opaque object or frame completely transparent, press Ctrl+T. Press the keystroke again to make a transparent object or frame opaque — a technique that works less often because not all object types support it.

Relative positions

Another property that objects have in a layout is their position with respect to one another. When you create an object, it's placed on top of all other objects created before it and in strict order, from back to front. You can change this automatic order, often referred to as the *layering order* or *stacking order,* by using a set of commands that I cover later in this chapter. You use these commands to send objects backward or forward in the stacking order. You can also align objects with each other and create groups of objects that behave like a single object. I talk about alignment and grouping later in this chapter, too.

Using the Format Painter

When you set an object's properties "just so," you usually want to lock the object and prevent it from being changed. This important command is, unfortunately, missing in Publisher 2007, which makes it imperative that you delete objects *carefully.* The program offers the Format Painter, however — a "just so" command that lets you apply the same set of formatting from one object to another object. The two objects don't even have to be the same kind of object.

You can copy an object's format by selecting the object whose format you want to copy. Then click the Format Painter button on the Standard toolbar; the button looks like a paintbrush. Finally, click the object you want to format.

If you want the Format Painter's brush to stay "loaded" with your format until you change it, double-click the Format Painter button. Now you can click as many objects as you want, and the same formatting is applied to all of them. Click another toolbar tool or click a blank area of the workspace to turn off the Format Painter.

Aligning and positioning objects

The most natural method for moving an object or frame is to drag it. *Dragging* an object is the electronic equivalent of using your finger to slide a playing card across a table. In Chapter 4, I explain some of the tools used for precisely positioning objects and frames on a layout when you're dragging them into position: position measurements in the status bar, ruler marks, layout and grid guides, and ruler guides.

Ruler marks and guides work with Snap To commands, also covered in Chapter 4, to help you position objects precisely. When you place an object's border or center axis (either horizontal or vertical) close to a ruler mark or guide, it snaps into alignment with the mark or guide.

Three additional sets of commands, found on the Arrange menu, are used for precise positioning or alignment:

- **Align or Distribute:** This command opens the submenu shown in Figure 5-21. Selected objects are aligned horizontally using the Align Left, Align Center, and Align Right menu options. Align your objects vertically by using the Align Top, Align Middle, and Align Bottom menu items. You can set either or both of these alignment (horizontal or vertical) options.

  You can also align objects to the page margin. To have alignment take effect, select the Relative to Margin Guides option, select the object that you want to align and then choose the left or right align button. You can also use the Distribute Horizontally or Vertically options to evenly arrange the objects on the page.

- **Nudge:** Choose Arrange⇨Nudge to access the Nudge feature. *Nudges,* for those of you not in the know (nudge, nudge, wink, wink), are small movements of an object in one direction.

  Most programs give you a nudge. Some programs give you a swift kick in the pants. Publisher gives you a submenu. The traditional way to implement nudges is to select an object and press the arrow keys. Each time you press an arrow key, your object moves slightly in that direction. Earlier versions of Publisher required you to hold down the Alt key and press the arrow keys to perform this action. Now you can simply select the object you want to nudge and press the up, down, left, or right arrow keys.

  You can specify the distance that an object moves each time it's nudged, by changing the Arrow Keys Nudge Object By setting on the Edit tab of the Options dialog box. (Choose Tools⇨Options from the main menu to open the Options dialog box.)

- **Rotate or Flip:** Publisher offers five commands on the Arrange⇨Rotate or Flip submenu for rotating and flipping selected objects: Free Rotate, Rotate Left 90°, Rotate Right 90°, Flip Horizontal, and Flip Vertical.

  The Free Rotate command is interesting. You can place your mouse on Free Rotate handle, which looks like a green dot connected to the object by a short line and drag the object to whatever degree of angle you want. The second and third commands rotate objects 90 degrees counterclockwise and clockwise with each application; the last two commands reflect your selection through a horizontal and vertical mirror plane.

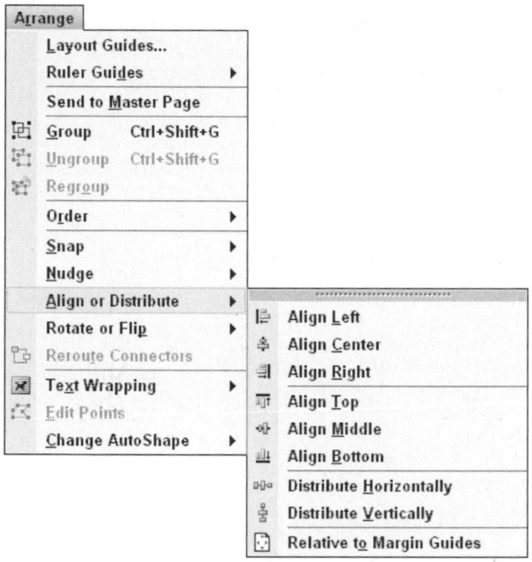

Figure 5-21:
The Align or
Distribute
submenu.

| Arrange |
| Layout Guides... |
| Ruler Guides ▶ |
| Send to Master Page |
| Group Ctrl+Shift+G |
| Ungroup Ctrl+Shift+G |
| Regroup |
| Order ▶ |
| Snap ▶ |
| Nudge ▶ |
| Align or Distribute ▶ |
| Rotate or Flip ▶ |
| Reroute Connectors |
| Text Wrapping ▶ |
| Edit Points |
| Change AutoShape ▶ |

Align Left
Align Center
Align Right
Align Top
Align Middle
Align Bottom
Distribute Horizontally
Distribute Vertically
Relative to Margin Guides

Building layers on top of your layers

The position that an object has on a page is uniquely defined by its layer. In the natural creation order, the first object created is at the back, and the last object created is at the front. It's like football players diving for a fumbled ball: Whoever gets there first ends up on the bottom. Fortunately for your publication, frames don't suffer from broken bones and torn ligaments. Both the Master and foreground pages have separate layer orders, and they can't be mixed.

Grouped objects are considered to be in the same layer — until they're ungrouped. Then they return to their natural relative order, one ungrouped object to another. You can defeat the natural layering by using a set of commands on the Arrange menu. Layers have some important implications. Opaque objects obscure any objects behind them. Text boxes, table frames picture and WordArt frames are transparent by default.

No matter which order you use originally to layer objects, however, you can rearrange these layers any way you want by using the four layering commands on the Arrange⇨Order submenu:

- ✔ **Bring to Front:** Choose Arrange⇨Order⇨Bring to Front, or press Alt+F6 to bring selected objects to the top layer.

- ✔ **Send to Back:** Choose Arrange⇨Order⇨Send to Back, or press Alt+Shift+F6 to send selected frames to the bottom layer.

- ✔ **Bring Forward:** Choose Arrange⇨Order⇨Bring Forward to bring selected frames up one layer.

- ✔ **Send Backward:** Choose Arrange⇨Order⇨Send Backward to send selected frames down one layer.

No matter how far down you send a frame or other object on a foreground page, it always remains on top of any Master page object. And, no matter how far up you bring a frame or other object on a Master page, it always remains below any foreground object.

Layering, or adjusting the layers and transparency of objects so that other objects either show through or are hidden, is one of the most important design techniques you can apply to your publications. By using this technique, you can place text in front of a picture so that it appears to be part of the picture, apply fills and patterns that the object doesn't support by itself, wrap text around a graphic (another layering technique discussed later), and more. Figure 5-22 shows you an example of a layered starburst with a transparent text frame on top.

Wrapping Text around Objects

Take a look at Figure 5-23, which shows you one of the most important types of layering — text wrapping. This special layer effect is created with intelligent frame margins. Notice how the text makes room for the graphic and neatly wraps around it. (Is the text just well behaved, or did the graphic forget to put on its deodorant this morning?)

Creating regular text wraps

In the bad old days of traditional publishing, wrapping text required painstaking hours of cutting, pasting, and rearranging individual lines of text. And pity the poor fool who suggested making a change to the text after the wrapping was complete!

In Publisher, though, wrapping text is amazingly easy. Just place any type of frame — even another text box — on top of a text box, and the text underneath automatically wraps around the frame above it.

Text doesn't wrap if one frame is on a foreground page and the other is on the Master page; both frames have to be on the same page, so to speak.

Although the program tries its best, it can sometimes wrap text too closely or too loosely around a frame. (My wife has had occasion to declare that I am not wrapped too tight.) Closely wrapped text can be difficult to read, whereas loosely wrapped text can waste space and create big gaps on the page. With all frames except table frames, you can easily change the amount of space between the wrapping text and the box it wraps around by changing the margins of the wrapped-around frame.

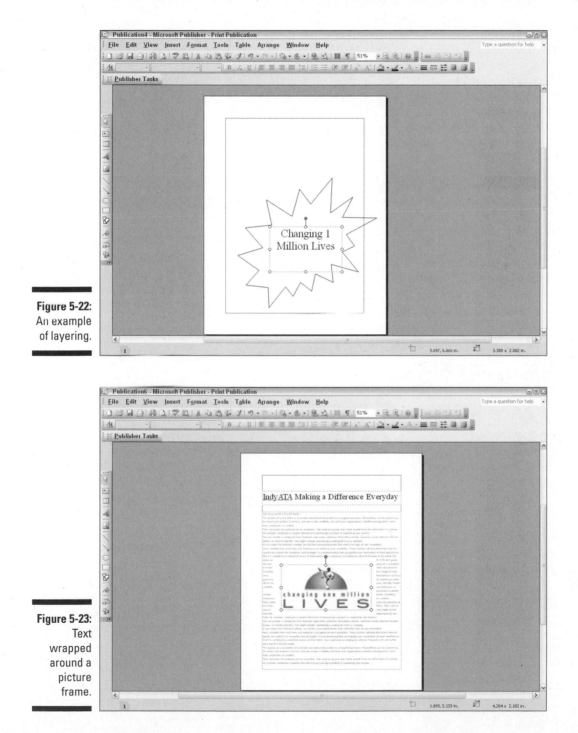

Figure 5-22:
An example
of layering.

Figure 5-23:
Text
wrapped
around a
picture
frame.

To increase the margins of a text box, click the text box and then choose Format⇨Text Box from the main menu. Make your selections from the Layout tab of the Format Text Box dialog box, as shown in Figure 5-24. Turn off text wrap by selecting None in the Wrapping Style area of the Layout tab. The measurements in the Distance from Text area change the amount of space between the text in a text box and the border of the text box.

To change the properties of a picture or WordArt frame, follow these steps:

1. **Select a picture and then choose Format⇨Object from the main menu.**

   If you're formatting WordArt, you choose Format⇨WordArt. If you're a right-clicker, you can also right-click the picture or WordArt and choose Format Object or Format WordArt from the contextual menu.

2. **Make your selections from the Layout tab of the Format Object or WordArt dialog box.**

   It looks amazingly similar to the Layout tab of the Format Text Box dialog box.

3. **Adjust the way text wraps around a graphic or WordArt so that the text wraps around the entire picture frame or just the graphic contained therein.**

   See the example in the Wrapping Style section of the Format dialog box.

By default, Publisher wraps text in a rectangular pattern around the perimeter of a frame. (Refer to Figure 5-23.) If you're working with a picture frame, however, you can have your text wrap to the actual shape of the graphic within that frame by the Tight option in the Wrapping Style section of the Format dialog box. Figure 5-25 shows you an example. Very cool!

Fine-tuning text wraps

Picky, picky, picky. Some folks like their text wrapped around their graphics "just so" — it's very important to them. Depending on the justification you use in your text, Publisher can do a poor job of wrapping text around a graphic to match its shape, particularly when you use justified text. The program wraps text around most of its own clip art because the text boundaries are built in already. But Publisher can become mighty confused about the shapes of "foreign" graphics and can be especially pitiful when it comes to creating text boundaries for WordArt objects.

A couple of tools offer some help in this area. The first tool lets you create and adjust an irregular boundary on your graphic to control how text wraps around it. To create this kind of effect, select the graphic and then choose Arrange⇨Text Wrapping⇨Edit Wrap Points from the main menu. Doing so adds reshape handles for wrapping text to your graphic. Click and drag these handles where you want them. You can also add a handle by holding down the Ctrl key and clicking the point on the outline of the graphic where you want to add a reshape handle. To remove a reshape handle, press Ctrl+Shift while clicking the offending handle.

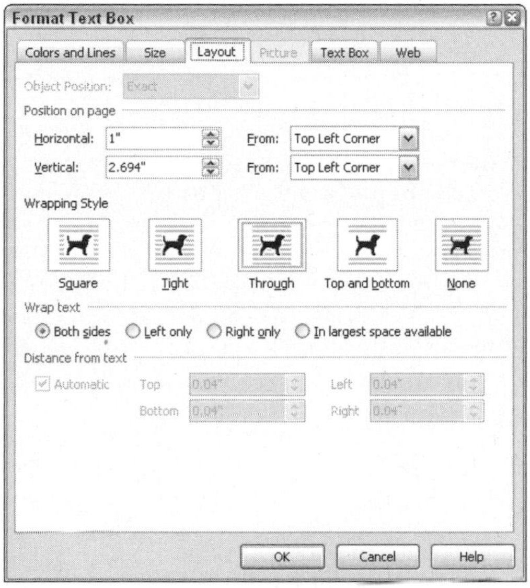

Figure 5-24:
The Layout tab of the Format Text Box dialog box.

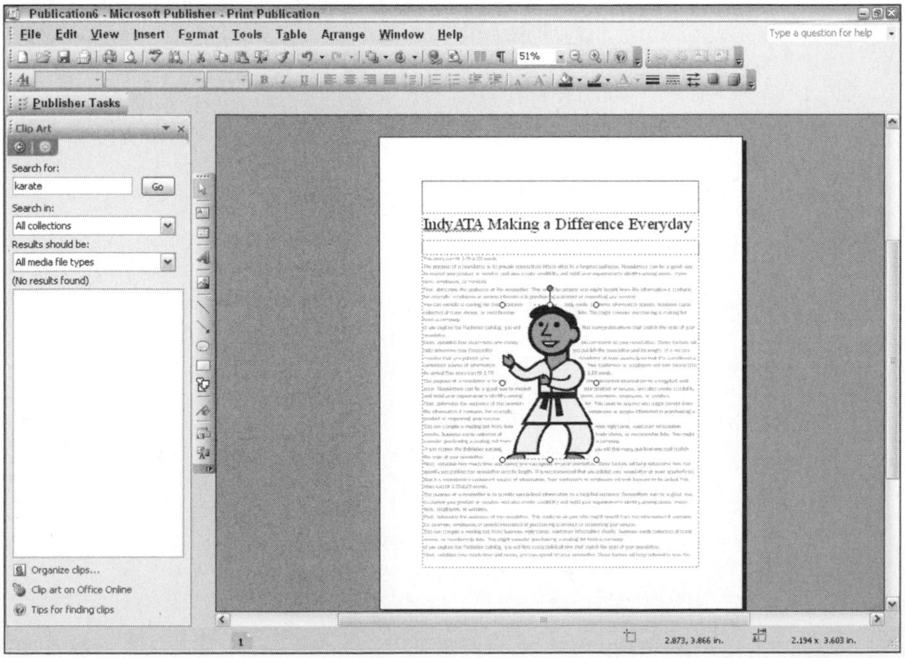

Figure 5-25:
Creating a tight wrap around a graphical image.

Figure 5-26 shows you what Wrap Point handles look like "in the flesh." The topic "Fine-tune how text wraps around a picture" in the Publisher online Help system gives you more information.

Grouping Objects

Some things in "the real world" just seem to go together: peanut butter and jelly, macaroni and cheese, death and taxes. In your publications, too, some things might belong together: several drawn objects that comprise a logo; a graphic and its caption; a table frame and the picture frame you stuck behind it to make text wrap the way you want.

When you want different objects on your layout to stay together and behave as a unit, you can apply some electronic glue to stick them together in a *group.* There, they can share their most personal problems: "Hi, my name is Igor. I'm a picture frame trapped in a table frame's body."

Grouping tells Publisher to treat the collection of objects as a single object. Thus, you can easily move or copy a group while keeping the objects in the same positions relative to each other. You don't have to worry about accidentally leaving behind one line, box, or frame. You can also resize a group while maintaining the same relative size and position of the frames within that group. Trust me: This method is a heck of a lot easier than resizing and adjusting the position of each object in a group individually and getting the same results.

To group two or more objects, use one of these methods:

- ✔ Select the objects that you want to include in your group by holding down the Shift or Ctrl key while clicking each object, and click the Group Objects button, which appears in the lower-right corner of the selection's bounding box. The button changes to resemble locked puzzle pieces. You can even group groups.
- ✔ Select the objects and then choose Arrange➪Group.
- ✔ Select the objects and then press Ctrl+Shift+G.

To ungroup a group of objects, choose one of these methods:

- ✔ Select the group and click the Group Objects button again. You have to click outside the grouping for your change to take effect.
- ✔ Select the group and choose Arrange➪Ungroup from the main menu.
- ✔ Select the group and then press Ctrl+Shift+G.

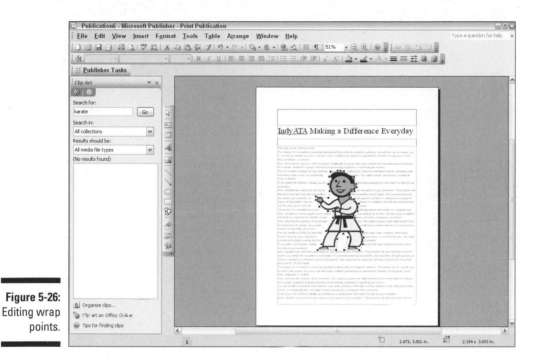

Figure 5-26:
Editing wrap
points.

What you can do to an object in a group depends on that object's capability. Earlier in this chapter, you see how you can apply borders to several shapes at a time in a group. You can also resize a group; if you do, each object resizes proportionally. You can type text in a text or table frame that's part of a group; just click the frame and start typing.

It's possible to modify a single object in a group without ungrouping it from the rest of the group. For example, to change the properties of one of the objects in a group, simply double-click the object's border; in a jiffy, the Properties dialog box opens. Alternatively, you can right-click the object, and again the Properties dialog window comes to life.

Part III
10,000 Words, One Maniac

The 5th Wave   By Rich Tennant

"Of course graphics are important to your project, Eddy, but I think it would've been better to scan a <u>picture</u> of your worm collection."

In this part . . .

Fancy graphics and layouts can draw attention to your publication, but words usually comprise the core of your message. The three chapters in Part III cover working with text in your publication: Where and how do you get text? What do you do to it after you have it? And, how do you select type to convey the feeling of what you're trying to say? I don't tell you what to write — that's up to you. (I do tell you how to get information from other Microsoft Office 2007 programs into Publisher 2007, though.) After reading this part, you'll be able to produce, with less effort, a publication that has better-looking text.

Chapter 6

Getting the Word

· ·

In This Chapter

▶ Getting text into Publisher

▶ Sending text out of Publisher

▶ Forming, reforming, and deforming stories

▶ Working with story text

▶ Inserting Continued notices

▶ Working with table frames

· ·

*I*n this chapter, I help you look closely at two frame types: text boxes and table frames. You use *text boxes* to place and manage text in your publication. Microsoft Publisher 2007 has some special features to help you manage text frames across pages: the capacity to make text *flow* automatically between linked frames, and *stories,* which are just blocks of text managed as a single entity. You can even place Continued notices (Continued on Page and Continued from Page) in your publication to help readers follow a story that begins on one page and continues on another.

In addition to providing regular text boxes, Publisher 2007 has two other types of frames for holding text: table frames and WordArt frames. If you've worked in a spreadsheet program, such as Microsoft Excel, or used a word processor that offers a table feature, such as Microsoft Word, the table frames features in Publisher 2007 should look familiar to you. If not, you can find out what you need to know about table frames at the end of this chapter. You can also create a shape, select it, and start typing. Like magic, your text then appears in the shape.

WordArt frames enable you to create fancy text by using WordArt to manipulate type. I cover WordArt in Chapter 9 because this type of frame is more commonly used for short pieces of decorative text, rather than for the longer text that comprises most people's publications.

Getting Into the Details of Text Boxes

If you're accustomed to creating text in other computer programs, you may find it odd that you can't just begin typing right away in a Publisher publication. You must first create a *text box* to tell the program where to put your text. Not that this is in any way a big deal — Chapter 5 shows you how easy creating a text box is: You simply click the Text tool in the toolbox and then click and drag to create the text box.

After you create a text box, you can fill it in one of three ways:

- ✔ Type text directly into the text box.
- ✔ Paste text from the Clipboard.
- ✔ Import text from your word processor or text file.

The next few sections give you a bit more detail on each technique.

Typing text

Publisher offers a complete environment for creating page layouts, so you soon discover that you can write your text in text boxes with little trouble. Admittedly, Publisher isn't the most capable text creation tool, and it doesn't have all the bells and whistles you would expect to find in your word processor, but it has been updated to integrate more closely with the Microsoft Office suite of applications. The idea is to let you leverage skills acquired from other Microsoft programs, such as Microsoft Word.

If you acquired your copy of Publisher as a part of one of the Microsoft Office 2007 suites, you may notice big changes in the way most of the Microsoft Office 2007 applications look and function. Microsoft replaced the menus and toolbars in some (but not all) of the programs with the Ribbon, which is part of what Microsoft has now named the Microsoft Office Fluent user interface. The idea was to group the tools you use the most in an easily accessible place (the Ribbon). If you have experience in using any of the previous versions of Microsoft Office, I have some good news: Many text editing features in Publisher 2007 will look familiar to you:

- ✔ **Menus and toolbars:** You may recognize the File, Edit, View, Insert, Format, Tools, and Help menus on the menu bar. Also, the New, Open, Save, Print, Cut, Copy, Paste, Format Painter, Undo, Redo, Show/Hide ¶, and Microsoft Publisher Help (it's Microsoft Word Help in Word) buttons from, say, Word 2003 should all seem familiar.

✔ **AutoCorrect:** This feature lets you automatically fix some common errors, such as correcting two initial capitals or automatically capitalizing the names of days.

✔ **Spell Check:** This feature automatically checks spelling as you type; it flags any misspelled or repeated words by underlining them.

If you're used to typing on a typewriter or in a word processor, you may be used to doing some things that you shouldn't do in Publisher — or in any page layout program — when you enter text.

Here's a list of things *not* to do when you're entering text:

✔ **Don't press Enter to force a line ending.** Pressing Enter tells the program that you've reached the end of a paragraph. If you press Enter at the end of every line, you cannot format the lines of your paragraph as a unit, which can be a bad thing. When you get to the end of a line of text, let Publisher word-wrap the text to the next line for you (which it does automatically). Press Enter only to end a paragraph or a short, independent line of text (such as a line in an address).

Note: If you need to force a line break without creating a new paragraph, press Shift+Enter. This keystroke creates a *soft carriage return* (↩) and places the symbol at the end of the line.

✔ **Don't press Enter to create blank lines between paragraphs.** Publisher 2007 has a much better way to create spaces before and after paragraphs: Choose Format➪Paragraph from the main menu and then adjust the Line Spacing settings in the Paragraph dialog box that appears.

✔ **Don't insert two spaces between sentences.** Use just one. It makes your text easier to read.

✔ **Don't press the Tab key or spacebar to indent the first lines of paragraphs.** Instead, use the paragraph indent controls, explained in Chapter 7. These controls offer much more flexibility than tabs.

✔ **Don't try to edit or format your text as you go.** It's much more efficient to complete all your typing first, your editing second, and your formatting last.

In addition to all these don'ts, I want to add a definite do: Do turn on the Show Special Characters command. Special characters are symbols that represent elements such as spaces, tabs, and line endings. These symbols help you figure out why your text appears the way it does. To turn on this feature, choose View➪Special Characters or press Ctrl+Shift+Y. Better yet, click the Show Special Characters button (the one that looks like a backward *P*) on the Standard toolbar. Figure 6-1 shows a text block with special characters turned on.

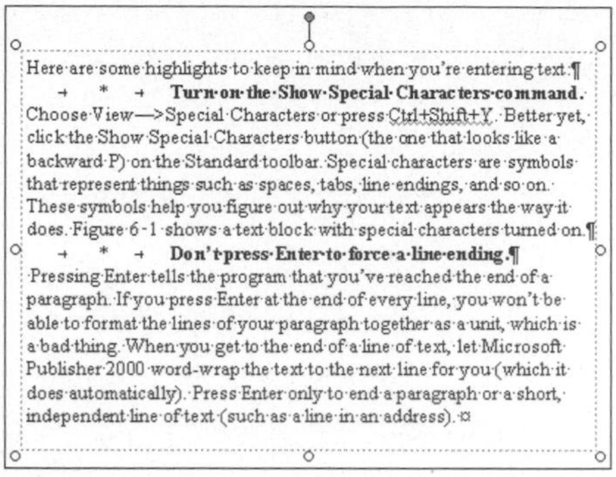

Here are some highlights to keep in mind when you're entering text. ¶
→   *   →   **Turn on the Show Special Characters command.**
Choose View —> Special Characters or press Ctrl+Shift+Y. Better yet,
click the Show Special Characters button (the one that looks like a
backward P) on the Standard toolbar. Special characters are symbols
that represent things such as spaces, tabs, line endings, and so on.
These symbols help you figure out why your text appears the way it
does. Figure 6-1 shows a text block with special characters turned on. ¶
→   *   →   **Don't press Enter to force a line ending.** ¶
Pressing Enter tells the program that you've reached the end of a
paragraph. If you press Enter at the end of every line, you won't be
able to format the lines of your paragraph together as a unit, which is
a bad thing. When you get to the end of a line of text, let Microsoft
Publisher 2000 word-wrap the text to the next line for you (which it
does automatically). Press Enter only to end a paragraph or a short,
independent line of text (such as a line in an address). ✺

Figure 6-1:
Special
characters
in text
boxes help
you follow
what's
going on.

If any of the suggestions in this section seem new to you, I recommend that
you check out one of the typographical style books mentioned near the end of
Chapter 2, in the section about desktop style resources. I'm especially fond
of *The PC Is Not a Typewriter,* by Robin Williams (Peachpit Press). If you're
working in a specific word processing program, you may also want to pick
up the *For Dummies* book on that program.

As you type, your text begins filling the text box from left to right and from top
to bottom. If the text box isn't large enough to accommodate all your text, you
eventually reach the bottom of the text box. When you type more text than
can fit into a text box, the extra text moves into the invisible *overflow area.*
You can type blindly in that overflow area; the program keeps track of everything you type. If you're like most people, though, you probably want to see
what you're typing as you type it.

The Text in Overflow indicator alerts you when you type more text than can
fit into the current text box. The indicator is located in the lower-right corner
of the text box. (Figure 6-2 shows you a text box with the Text in Overflow
indicator doing its thing.) If you see the indicator at the bottom of a text
frame, you know that the text box isn't large enough to contain the text.

"Good enough," you might say, but what can you do to be able to see what
you type again? You have several options, although the most straightforward
method is to simply enlarge the text box by clicking the text box to select it,
placing your mouse pointer on one of the round selection handles, and dragging the cursor to enlarge the text box. (If you're still confused, Chapter 5
explains this process in even more detail.) With a larger text box, the text in
the overflow area has room to spread out (and automatically appears). You
can also use the Create Text Box Link button to link text boxes for autoflowing, as described later in this chapter, in the section "Autoflowing text."

The first thing you may notice about text in a text box is that, in most views
that provide an overview of your publication, the text is much too small to
read. Do yourself a favor and press F9 to zoom in to view your text as you
type it into your text frame. Pressing F9 toggles the view between the current
magnification and 100 percent magnification.

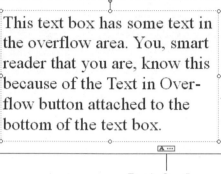

This text box has some text in the overflow area. You, smart reader that you are, know this because of the Text in Over-flow button attached to the bottom of the text box.

Text in Overflow
indicator

Pasting text from the Clipboard

You can paste text into a Publisher publication by using the Windows Clipboard. Here's how to do it:

1. **In Publisher, select the Text Box tool on the Objects toolbar and draw a text box on the page (if you don't have a text box created).**

2. **Highlight the text in the program containing the text that you want to use.**

3. **Choose Edit⇨Copy or press Ctrl+C.**

4. **In your Publisher publication, click the Select Objects tool on the Objects toolbar, and click in a text box to set the insertion point at the position where you want your text to be pasted.**

   Feel free to flip over to Chapter 5 to find out how to create text boxes.

5. **Choose Edit⇨Paste or press Ctrl+V.**

   If you didn't set an insertion point in Step 4 or didn't have a text box selected, Publisher creates a new text box and imports the copied text into that text box. In most cases, the text box that Publisher creates isn't the size and shape you want, and it isn't in the place you want it to be. Save yourself some time by creating the text box before you paste.

If you can copy formatted text successfully to the Windows Clipboard, the text should be pasted correctly into your text box. For more information about using the Windows Clipboard, see Chapter 5.

If the text on the Clipboard can't fit in the text box you selected, the program performs an autoflow operation. First, it displays a dialog box informing you that the inserted text doesn't fit into the selected text box and asks whether you want to use autoflow. I talk about autoflow in more depth later in this chapter, in the section "Autoflowing text."

Importing text

As an alternative to using the Windows Clipboard to import text into a text box, you can choose Insert⇨Text File to move text between your word processor and Publisher. (The process is rather more complicated than my description here lets on — the text does a bit of a two-step, in that it first gets converted to an intervening text file and is then brought into Publisher.)

If you haven't typed your document in Microsoft Word yet, save yourself a few steps and use Word to type and edit your text *inside* Publisher. I explain this particular bit of magic a little later in this chapter, in the section "Using Word to edit your text."

Before you choose Insert⇨Text File, you must save your text to a file by using a format that Publisher can read. Fortunately, Publisher accepts many different file formats, including the ones in this list:

✔ All Publisher files (No surprise here!)

✔ Plain text (ASCII) or plain formatted text (RTF)

Although most programs should at least be able to save text as plain, or *ASCII,* text, ASCII should be your last resort because ASCII text uses no formatting. If you save a text file in ASCII format, the file loses all formatting (such as bold, italic, or underlining). Try to avoid this option.

✔ Single File Web Page (*.htm, *.html)

✔ Rich Text Format, or RTF: In RTF (the Microsoft text-based, formatted text interchange format), ASCII characters are saved in your file, along with special commands to indicate formatting information — such as bold, italic, or underlining. You don't need to concern yourself with these formatting commands; you need to know only that the RTF text format saves formatting on text.

✔ Microsoft Word 2007 (and other versions for Windows or the Macintosh)

✔ Recover Text from Any File

✔ WordPerfect 5.*x* and 6.*x*

✔ Microsoft Works

If your word processor doesn't save to one of these file formats automatically, check to see whether it offers an Export command, which can translate your word processor file into a form that Publisher understands.

Okay, you save whatever you want to import into your Publisher publication to a file using an acceptable format. Now what? To import the text file into Publisher, follow these steps:

1. **Locate the text box into which you want to import the text, and then position the insertion point inside the box where you want the text to appear.**

2. **Choose Insert⇨Text File.**

   The Insert Text dialog box, shown in Figure 6-3, appears.

3. **Locate the file you want, highlight it, and then click OK.**

   After a moment, the text appears in the selected text box.

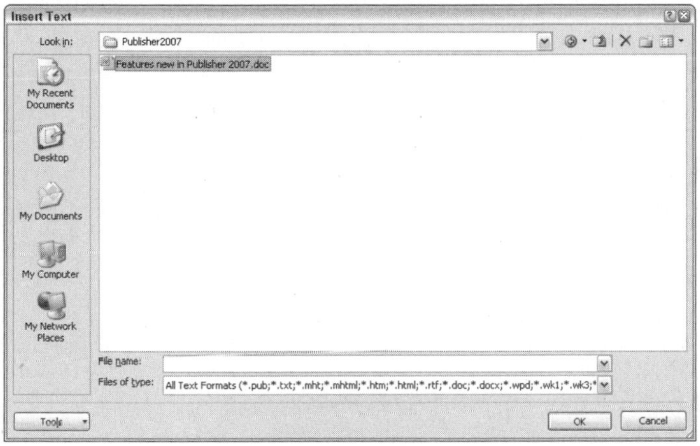

Figure 6-3:
The Insert Text dialog box displays a selected DOC file.

Here are some tips for using the Insert Text dialog box:

- ✔ If you can't find your text file, make sure that you selected the correct import filter from the Files of Type drop-down list.

- ✔ To see all files in a folder, select All Text Formats in the Files of Type drop-down list.

- ✔ If the file still doesn't appear, you're looking in the wrong place. Use the Look In drop-down list, at the top of the dialog box, to switch to another location.

- ✔ If not all the imported text can fit in the selected text box, the program opens a dialog box asking whether you want to autoflow the rest of your text into other text boxes. (I present more information on autoflowing text later in this chapter, in the section "Autoflowing text.")

You can view the contents of a text file without importing the file into your publication. Choose File⇨Open (or press Ctrl+O) to access the Open dialog box, click the down arrow next to the Files of Type text box, and select All Text Formats. Find the file you want and click Open. Publisher opens the text or word processor file as a full-page publication that offers the requisite number of pages filled with full-page text boxes. Keep in mind that, depending on your computer and the size of the document you're opening, this process can take a while to complete.

 As an alternative to using the menu commands, you can display context-sensitive menus (see Figure 6-4) by right-clicking a text box. On the context menu, select Change Text and then select Text File. The Insert Text dialog box opens. You may find that using the context-sensitive menu for the Insert Text task is easier than moving the mouse cursor to the top of the screen. (To me, it's six of one and half a dozen of the other.)

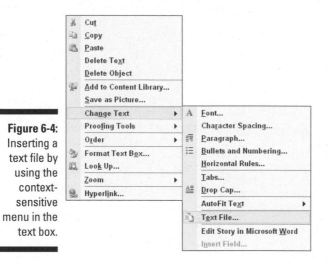

Figure 6-4: Inserting a text file by using the context-sensitive menu in the text box.

Exporting text

Hey, here's something you already know how to do! Just as easily as you can transfer text that's created elsewhere into Publisher, you can also send text out of the program so that other computer programs can use the text. (Isn't it nice when programs share? I feel like I'm back in kindergarten.) Just as bringing text into Publisher is called *importing*, sending text out is called *exporting*.

Publisher provides two ways to export text:

- ✔ **Choose Edit⇨Copy to copy selected text from Publisher to the Windows Clipboard, and then switch to another Windows program and choose Edit⇨Paste to paste it directly into that program.** If the program you're pasting text into uses the Ribbon, choose Paste on the Clipboard group of the Home tab.

> ✔ **Choose File➪Save As to send all text in a publication to a text file or word processor file in one of the formats listed in the preceding section.** Publisher opens a dialog box informing you that the file type you selected supports only text. Click OK to save it anyway.

It's probably unfortunate that Publisher (still!) doesn't have an Export command on its File menu, as other desktop publishing programs do. Then I could make believe that there's more to know about exporting text from the program than there really is. It's almost too easy.

Word up

In the past, the folks at Microsoft went to a lot of trouble to make typing and editing text in Publisher as easy as typing and editing text in Microsoft Word. One way they did that was by maintaining a remarkable similarity between the toolbars in Publisher and in the available versions of Word.

My, how times have changed. Microsoft Word 2007 was released with its new Ribbon feature, and now we have to unlearn the old way of doing things in Word and learn the new ways. If you went to the trouble of learning them, you may want to stick with Word 2007 when you want to create and edit text, rather than create and edit text within Publisher. I do. Let's face it: Publisher is an excellent publication design and layout program, but a word processor it isn't.

Inserting a Word document

If you have an existing Microsoft Word document that you want to include in your publication, follow these steps:

1. **Locate the text box into which you want to import the Word file, and then position the insertion point inside the box where you want the text to appear.**

2. **Choose Insert➪Text File.**

   The Insert Text dialog box appears. (Refer to Figure 6-3.)

3. **Select All Text Formats from the Files of Type drop-down list.**

4. **Locate your Word document, highlight it, and click OK.**

   After a moment, the text from your Word document appears in the selected text box. Breathe a sigh of relief as you realize that you don't have to reformat all that text. Your Word document retains its formatting when you import it into Publisher.

Using Word to edit your text

If, after bringing your Word document into Publisher, you need to make changes, you don't have to launch Word, open the Word document, save your changes, close Word, and import the document all over again. And, you don't have to edit the text in Publisher, either. Just tell Publisher that you want to use Word to edit the text contained in the current text box:

1. **Click inside the text frame that contains the text you want to edit.**

2. **Choose Edit⇨Edit Story in Microsoft Word.**

   Word leaps (or crawls, depending on your computer) onto the screen, replete with your Publisher text.

3. **Edit the text to your heart's content.**

4. **Choose File⇨Close & Return To <your publication name>.**

   If you're lucky enough to have Word 2007 installed on your computer, you may have noticed by now that it has no File menu. Just click the Office Button, in the upper-right corner of the Word window. You see the Close & Return To <your publication name> menu choice at the bottom of the menu.

   Word wanders off to whatever hiding place it occupies when you aren't using it, and your publication, including the edits made in Word, returns to the screen. (Try to refrain from doing a victory dance if anyone is watching.)

Using part of a Word document

The technique of inserting a text file works well for bringing an entire Microsoft Word document into a publication, but what do you do if you want to use only part of a Word document? You copy and paste, of course! Follow these steps:

1. **Launch Word and open the document that contains the text you want to place into your publication.**

2. **Use your favorite text selection technique to highlight some text.**

3. **Choose Edit⇨Copy, press Ctrl+C, or click the Copy button on the Standard toolbar.**

   If you use Word 2007, you can just click the Copy button in the Clipboard section of the Home tab.

4. **Switch to the Microsoft Publisher 2007 window by clicking its button on the Windows taskbar.**

   If the Windows taskbar isn't visible, you can switch applications by pressing Alt+Tab. Hold down the Alt key and press Tab until the Microsoft Publisher 2007 icon is highlighted in the Cool Switch box that appears. Release both keys.

5. **Click in the text box at the location where you want to insert the text from the Word document.**

    If the text box is empty, click anywhere inside the text box.

6. **Choose Edit➪Paste, press Ctrl+V, or click the Paste button on the Standard toolbar.**

    The text from the Word document appears in the selected text box as if by magic. (Gotta love that copy-and-paste operation.)

Let Me Tell You a Story

In its simplest form, a Publisher *story* is a block of text that exists in a single, self-contained text box. When you add large amounts of text to a publication, you often have text that doesn't fit in a single text box. In these cases, the traditional publishing solution is to *jump* (continue) each story to other pages. Jumps are extremely common in newspapers and magazines: How often each day do you see lines that read "Continued on page 3" or "Continued from page 1"?

The capability to jump a particular story between text boxes and pages is one of the best arguments for using Publisher rather than a word processing program. Although most word processing programs deal with all the text in a file as one big story, Publisher excels at juggling multiple stories within a single publication. For example, you can begin four stories on page 1 and then jump half those stories to page 2 and the other half to page 3. At the same time, you can begin separate stories on pages 2 and 3 and jump each of those stories to any other page. If there's not enough room on a page to finish a story that you already jumped from another page, you can jump the story to another page and then another and another. The sky (or maybe the forest) is the limit.

Forming, reforming, and deforming stories

To enable a story to jump across and flow through a series, or *chain,* of several text boxes, you connect those text boxes to each other in the order that you want the story to jump and flow. A chain of connected text boxes can exist on a single page or across multiple pages. You can even connect text boxes that are in the *scratch area* (the gray work area surrounding your page) and then later move those text boxes to your publication pages.

Although you can use side-by-side connected text boxes on a single page to create *snaking* columns, where text ends at the bottom of one column and continues again at the top of the next (as you find in a newspaper or magazine), you may find it easier to set multiple columns within a single text box on a page.

How and when you connect text boxes depends on your situation:

✔ **If you haven't yet typed or imported text:** You can manually connect empty text boxes to serve as a series of ready-made containers for that text. When you then type or import your text, it automatically jumps and flows between text boxes, like water jumps and flows between the separate compartments in a plastic ice-cube tray. (Just remember not to put your Publisher files in the freezer.)

✔ **If you're typing text in Publisher and don't know how much text you'll have:** You can manually connect to new text boxes as you run out of room in each current text box.

✔ **If you're importing text and there's not enough room to fit it in the current text box:** You can use the program's autoflow feature to help connect your text boxes. You can even have Publisher draw new text boxes and insert new pages as needed to fit all the text.

The next few sections show you how to best handle each of these situations.

Connecting text boxes

When you select a text box, you may see one of several items attached to the top or bottom of the text box. The Text in Overflow indicator (refer to Figure 6-2) lets you know that the text doesn't fit in the text box and has, well, overflowed. The appearance of either the Go to Next Text Box button or the Go to Previous Text Box button is an indication that the selected text box is already connected to at least one other text box. Clicking one of these buttons moves the insertion point to the next or previous connected text box in the chain.

Here's how to connect a text box to another text box:

1. **The easiest way to create linked text boxes is to create a series of text boxes first. Select the Text Box tool on the Objects toolbar and draw text boxes of the number and size that you estimate you need.**

   You might need to modify the number or sizes of text boxes later, but it's helpful to begin with a series already created.

2. **Click a text box to select it.**

   The Connect Text Boxes toolbar appears next to the Standard toolbar.

   If the Connect Text Boxes toolbar is being stubborn and doesn't show up when you click a text box, you can force the toolbar to appear by choosing View➪Toolbars➪Connect Text Boxes from the main menu.

3. **Click the Create Text Box Link button on the Connect Text Boxes toolbar.**

   The Text Box Link Button looks exactly like three links in a chain.

   The mouse pointer changes from a standard arrow pointer to a cute little pitcher pointer, bearing a downward-pointing arrow. As you move over an empty text box, the pitcher tilts, and the arrow points to the right. The metaphor that Publisher is using is that you're pouring text from one text box to another. (It could be worse. In earlier days, programs often used a loaded-gun icon.)

   By the way, anytime you accidentally click the Create Text Box Link button, you can press the Esc key or just click away from a text box to get rid of the pitcher pointer.

4. **After clicking the Create Text Box Link button in Step 2, click the empty text box to which you want to connect the first text box. The text "pours" into the text box, filling it until it overflows.**

5. **To link additional text boxes, click the Create Text Box Link button again, and then click the next empty text box (even one on another page) to which you want to connect in the sequence.**

   The pitcher pointer tips sideways, drains its text, and reverts to a normal pointer.

The two text boxes are now connected; any text in the first text box's overflow area appears in the second text box. Also, as you type or enter additional text into the first text box, it pushes extra text into the second text box. To create a chain of more than two linked text boxes, repeat the preceding steps. If a chain is empty, you can link another chain to its first text box to create the combination of the two chains.

As you might guess, you can connect only text boxes. If you select a table frame or a picture frame, you don't see the Connect Text Boxes toolbar. Also, you can't connect a text box that's already connected to some other text box or a text box that has some text in it already. If you try to do this, Publisher displays a message box informing you that the text box must be empty.

After you connect text boxes, extra buttons appear at the top and/or bottom of each text box when the text box is selected. Figure 6-5 shows examples of three connected text boxes on a page and in sequence. Notice that when the middle text box is selected, two buttons are attached to it: the Go to Previous Text Box button on top and the Go to Next Text Box button on the bottom. Think of the text boxes in Figure 6-5 as three separate figures, though: If you try to select all three text boxes at the same time on your screen, you see the text boxes selected as a group with only a single Group Objects button.

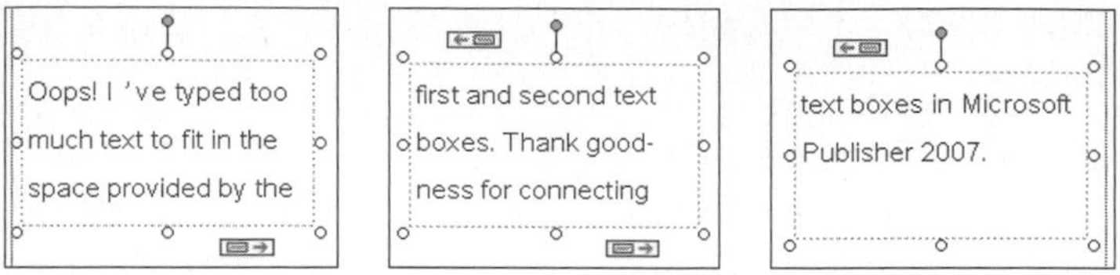

Figure 6-5:
Three
connected
text boxes.

Don't worry too much about connecting text boxes in the proper order the first time around. After you connect text boxes, you can disconnect and rearrange them quite easily. Later in this chapter, the "Rearranging chains" section tells you how.

Moving among the story's frames

One of the first issues to consider when you work with multiple-text-box story text is how best to move among the story's text boxes — and how to know which text box follows which! You can move easily and reliably between connected text boxes by using either the mouse or the keyboard. Both methods are easy.

Use one of these two methods to move between connected frames by using the mouse:

 ✔ **To move backward in the sequence:** Click the Go to Previous Text Box button.

 ✔ **To move forward in the sequence:** Click the Go to Next Text Box button.

These two buttons are shown in Figure 6-5. The arrow button at the top of the text box is the Go to Previous Text Box button; the arrow button at the bottom is the Go to Next Text Box button. The first text box in a chain has no Go to Previous Text Box button, whereas the last text box has no Go to Next Text Box button.

You can also use the Go to Previous Text Box and Go to Next Text Box buttons on the Connect Text Boxes toolbar. They're the second-to-last and last buttons on the toolbar, respectively. Figure 6-6 shows the Connect Text Boxes toolbar.

Use one of these methods to move between connected text boxes by using the keyboard:

 ✔ **To move to and select the chain's next text box:** Press Ctrl+Tab from a connected text box (that's selected).

 ✔ **To move to and select the chain's previous text box:** Press Ctrl+Shift+Tab from a connected text box (that's selected).

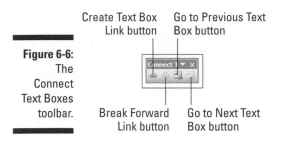

Create Text Box
Link button

Go to Previous Text
Box button

Figure 6-6:
The
Connect
Text Boxes
toolbar.

Break Forward
Link button

Go to Next Text
Box button

If your connected text boxes are full of text, you can also use many of the keyboard shortcuts for navigating text (listed in Chapter 7) to move between connected text boxes. If your insertion point is on the last line of text in a connected text box, for example, you can press the down-arrow key to move to (and select) the chain's next text box.

Autoflowing text

Publisher uses an *autoflow* feature to help you fit long text documents into a series of linked text boxes. This feature is handy for automatically managing the flow of text among pages of your publication. To autoflow text into a set of linked text boxes, you select the first text box in the chain. When you insert (or copy) text into the text box, Publisher fills the connected text boxes, beginning with the text box you selected, with the inserted text. If the inserted text fits in the selected text box or chain of text boxes, you're done.

If not all the text fits into the first text box or the set of linked text boxes, Publisher displays the message box shown in Figure 6-7. Click Yes to autoflow your text, or click No to put the text into the overflow area of the first text box. Publisher then proceeds to the next text box in the sequence and again asks your permission to autoflow text to that text box. Publisher continues posting this message box with every additional text box it requires.

Figure 6-7:
Publisher
asks
whether
to use
autoflow.

Microsoft Office Publisher

The inserted text doesn't fit in this box. Do you want to use autoflow?

To have Publisher automatically flow text throughout your publication, asking for confirmation before it flows into existing boxes, click Yes. To connect boxes yourself, click No. For information on connecting text boxes, press F1.

Yes   No

If you don't have enough linked text boxes to take care of the incoming text, the autoflow process continues: Publisher autoflows the extra text into the first empty or unconnected text box it can find or, failing that, the first text box of any empty, connected series of text boxes that exist in your publication. At each new text box, the program asks your permission to use that text box.

Wait — there's more! If no empty text boxes are available, Publisher displays a third message box that asks whether you want to create additional pages at the end of your publication and fill those pages with full-page text boxes until the imported text has been placed. If you click Yes, Publisher 2007 continues flowing the story to the end, creating new pages and full-page text boxes as required. At the end of this process, the program displays a dialog box that tells you the number of new pages created and your current page location, as shown in Figure 6-8.

Figure 6-8:
Publisher
tells you
how many
pages it
created.

Microsoft Office Publisher

Publisher has inserted 1 new page(s) for your text. You are now on page 2.

OK

Publisher looks for text boxes from top to bottom, and then from left to right and, finally, from page to page. The program even suggests empty text boxes that it finds in the scratch area. If you want Publisher to connect text frames in a different order, forget autoflow and instead connect the frames manually.

The autoflow process is a lot more complex to explain than it is to do. I find it natural, efficient, and well thought out; I doubt that it will give you pause or worry.

If text already exists in a text box but you still want to take advantage of Publisher's autoflow feature, click in one of the text boxes and press Ctrl+A, and then cut and paste the story to your target text box. Publisher treats pasted text just like it does inserted text, and initiates the autoflow process described in this section.

Rearranging chains

When you rearrange a chain, you have to tackle two tasks: Temporarily break the chain (disconnecting two text boxes in the chain) at the point at which you want to begin rearranging, and then reconnect the text boxes in the order you want.

Suppose that you have a chain, A-B-C-D, and you plan to add the text box X between text boxes B and C, to make the chain A-B-X-C-D. Follow these steps to rearrange the chain:

1. **Click text box B to select it.**

2. **Click the Break Forward Link button (the second button from the left; refer to Figure 6-6) on the Connect Text Boxes toolbar.**

   If the Connect Text Boxes toolbar doesn't appear when you click text box B, choose View⇨Toolbars⇨Connect Text Boxes from the main menu. You now have two chains: A-B and C-D.

3. **Click the Create Text Box Link button (the first button on the left; refer to Figure 6-6) on the Connect Text Boxes toolbar.**

   Text box B is still selected, and the mouse pointer turns into that cool pitcher again.

4. **Click text box X.**

   Now you have chains A-B-X and C-D.

5. **Click the Create Text Box Link button on the Connect Text Boxes toolbar.**

   Text box X is still selected.

6. **Click text box C.**

   Now you have one chain: A-B-X-C-D.

Voilà — you're ready to go into the chain-repair business!

If you don't reconnect C-D to your chain but continue to add new text boxes, eventually your story flows into your new additional text boxes. Text boxes C and D are still connected to each other; they just aren't connected to your linked chain.

Text box X in this example can be an empty, unconnected text box or an empty, connected text box that's the first text box in another chain — no surprise there. Because you're rearranging a chain, however, text box X also can be any empty text box that was, but is no longer, an original part of the current chain. For example, if you disconnect text boxes B and C in the chain A-B-C-D, you can then click text box D to make it the third frame in the chain A-B-D-C.

If you try to type in an empty, connected text box that isn't the first text box in a chain, Publisher informs you that this text box is part of another chain and asks whether you want to begin a new story at this point in the chain. Click OK to have the program disconnect that text box from the preceding text box in the chain. Any text boxes farther down the chain are now part of the new story.

You can use this technique only when typing; it doesn't work when you're importing or inserting a text file. To insert a text file into an empty, connected text box that's not the first text box in a chain, you must first manually disconnect that text box from the preceding text box in the chain.

After you know how to break a chain temporarily to rearrange it, permanently breaking a chain is easy. Just select the text box that you want to be the last in the chain and click the Break Forward Link button on the Connect Text Boxes toolbar. All text that follows in the next text boxes disappears from those text boxes and becomes overflow text for the last text box in the sequence. You can place the text where you want it at a later time when you connect this last text box to another text box.

Deleting stories

Connecting text boxes makes accidental text deletions a little less likely. Unfortunately, it also makes intentional deletions a little more difficult. Life is full of trade-offs!

When you delete a story's only text box, the story text has nowhere else to go, so it gets wiped out along with the text box. When you delete a text box from a multiple-text-box story, however, the story text has somewhere it can go: into the other text boxes in the chain. Publisher is also nice enough to mend the chain for you. If you have the chain A-B-C and you delete text box B, for example, the program leaves you with the chain A-C.

If you really want to delete multiple-text-box story text, follow these steps:

1. **Click any text box in the story and choose Edit⇨Select All or press Ctrl+A.**

2. **Press the Delete or Backspace key.**

   The entire story is deleted without deleting the text boxes.

Editing story text

Cutting and copying connected text boxes and the story text within them work similarly to deleting connected text boxes. If you cut or copy a connected text box, the pasting action results in only an empty text box; the story text in the original text box remains a part of the original story. To cut or copy multiple-text-box story text, you must highlight the text itself.

Although editing and formatting multiple-text-box story text is much the same as editing and formatting single-text-box story text, you can work yourself into a lather trying to highlight text in multiple text boxes by dragging over it with the mouse. Save yourself a whole lot of grief: Use the Shift key together with the keyboard-based movement techniques listed in Table 7-1 (over in Chapter 7). For example, press Shift+Ctrl+End to extend your selection to the end of the current text box, and then press Shift+right arrow to extend your selection to the next text box in your publication. You also can select all text in a multiple-text-box story by choosing Edit⇨Select All from the menu bar, as mentioned in the preceding section or press Ctrl+A.

If your connected text boxes are full of text, you can capitalize on the Select All command to zip to the beginning or end of a chain. Just choose Edit⇨ Select All and then press either the left- or right-arrow key. This technique is handy when you want to insert or delete text at the beginning or end of a story.

Select All is helpful for other processes too — for example, for deleting the entire text in a story. (Maybe you want to place a new version of the story in your publication.) Or, perhaps you want to edit your story in a word processor: You can use Select All to select the story and then export the story to a text or word processor file, open your word processor, open the file, and make your edits.

If you use Word, you can choose Edit⇨Edit Story in Microsoft Word from the Publisher main menu. (The command also conveniently sits on the context-sensitive menu of the text box. Right-click a text box and choose Change Text to see it.) This command launches the Microsoft Word OLE server and opens the program with your story displayed in a document window, as shown in Figure 6-9. When you finish making edits and close the Word window, you automatically return to Publisher. Except for the title bar in Word, you would never know that Publisher was the OLE client running the session. You just can't beat this kind of integration between these two programs.

Adding Continued notices

Publisher offers a feature to help readers locate the next and previous frames in a story in your publication: Continued notices. Publishing professionals sometimes refer to these handy guidance devices as *jump lines*. They come in two types: a Continued from Page notice tells readers where the story left off; a Continued on Page notice tells readers where the story continues.

Publisher manages Continued notices for you as an automated feature. You must manually insert and delete Continued notices to get things rolling, but after you set them up, Publisher keeps them up to date as your story grows (or shrinks) to new pages. Publisher even keeps the Continued notices up to date even when a text box is manually moved to a different page. To create a Continued notice, just right-click a linked text frame, choose Format Text Box from the context-sensitive menu, and select the Text Box tab in the Format Text Box dialog box. Select or deselect the Include Continued on Page and

Include Continued from Page check boxes to turn the notices on or off, respectively, for the selected text box. When you click OK, the program places the notices in your text box. Figure 6-10 shows you an example.

Publisher displays Continued notices only when it makes sense to display them. A Continued on Page notice is displayed only if the current story jumps to another text box on another page. A Continued from Page notice is displayed only if the current story jumps from a previous text box on another page. If you modify a story in such a way that a Continued notice no longer makes sense, the program automatically hides that notice.

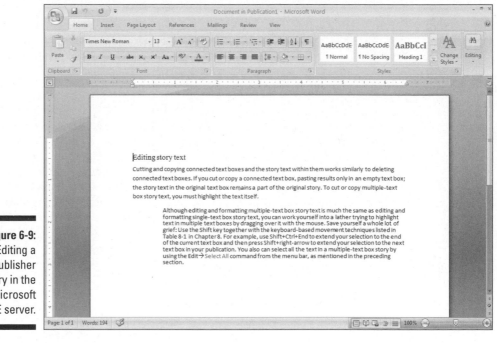

Figure 6-9:
Editing a
Publisher
story in the
Microsoft
OLE server.

Figure 6-10:
A text
box with
Continued
notices.

Story jumps can be distracting, and after readers jump to a new page, they don't often come back to the page from which they jumped. Use story jumps as little as possible to increase reader comprehension.

When a Continued notice is displayed, it always contains the proper page reference. If you move or delete the next text box in a chain or add or remove pages between connected text boxes, Publisher adjusts the page reference automatically; it certainly is smart in its handling of Continued notices!

If you don't like the wording of a Continued notice, you can edit it the same way you edit any other text. For example, you can change a Continued on Page notice to read "See page *x*" or "I ran out of room here, so I stuck the rest of the story on page *x.*" You can even add multiple lines to a Continued notice by pressing Enter while the insertion point is in the Continued notice, which is an improvement over earlier versions of the software. If you pressed Enter in a Continued notice in an earlier version, your computer just beeped at you. And, although you can add multiple lines to a Continued notice, you have to be careful not to type more than a full line of text on any of those lines. If you add so much text to a Continued notice that it no longer fits on one line, some of the text disappears.

If you accidentally delete a Continued notice's page-reference number, you can replace it by choosing Insert⇨Page Numbers from the main menu. Or, from the Format Text Box dialog box, turn off the Continued notice and then turn the notice back on. Your notice is reinserted in the text box as good as new. If you use this method, note that default text is used for the Continued On and Continued From notices after they're deleted and reinserted. If you want to use your own text, you'll have to retype it. (To open the Format Text Box dialog box, right-click a linked text frame and choose Format Text Box from the context-sensitive menu. You can also click inside the text box and choose Text Box from the Format menu.)

Aligning Your Text with Table Frames

As you discover in Chapter 7, you can use tab stops and tabs in paragraphs to create tables in text boxes. You can use a more elegant method, however — table frames — to create a predefined grid of columns and rows that automatically aligns your text perfectly, and keeps it perfectly aligned. Table frames are so easy to create and manage that it makes little sense not to use them throughout your publication whenever you need tabular displays.

Figure 6-11 shows you how a plain, unformatted table frame might look after you create it. You can tell by the selection handles that the table frame is selected.

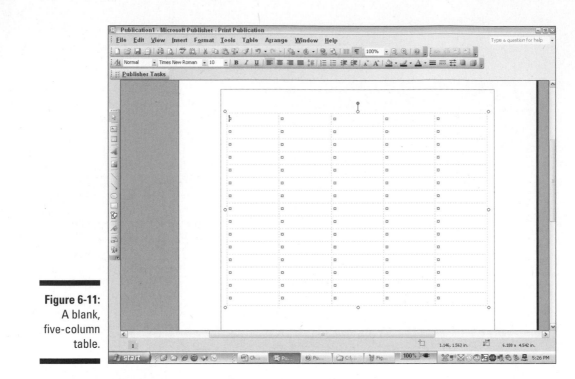

Figure 6-11:
A blank,
five-column
table.

Here are some important concepts to know about table frames:

✔ A table frame's selection handles are displayed only when the frame is selected — and they're never printed.

✔ If you can't see gridlines on-screen, choose View➪Boundaries and Guides or press Ctrl+Shift+O. You can hide gridlines by choosing View➪Boundaries and Guides again.

✔ If you choose a table format, elements that appear to be nonprinting gridlines in your table frame may instead be cell borders that *do* print.

✔ If you choose to show special characters in your publication (which I recommend), each cell also displays an end-of-story mark that looks like a small starburst. (You see these marks in text boxes too.) As with other special characters, end-of-story marks are displayed only on-screen; they aren't printed.

Moving around in tables

Publisher has only two navigation techniques specific to table frames:

✔ **Press Tab to move to the next cell (to the right).** If there's no cell to the right, the next cell is the first (leftmost) cell in the row immediately below. If you press Tab in a table frame's lower-right cell, however, you create an extra row of cells at the bottom of the table frame.

✔ **Press Shift+Tab to move to the previous cell (to the left).** If there's no cell to the left, the previous cell is the last (rightmost) cell in the row immediately above. If you press Shift+Tab in a table frame's upper-left cell, nothing happens.

If the cell you move to contains any text, these movement techniques also highlight that text.

Although pressing Tab and Shift+Tab can move the insertion point to any cell in a table frame, you may find it convenient at times to use other movement techniques. As with text boxes, you can move anywhere in a table frame by simply clicking at that position. You can also use many of the same keyboard shortcuts to move the insertion point around in tables. For information on moving around in text boxes, see Chapter 7.

Creating a table frame

Chapter 5 briefly explains how to create a table frame: Click the Insert Table tool in the toolbox and then click and drag the frame outline. Table frames are different from text boxes in this respect: After you create a frame outline, you have to make a selection from the Create Table dialog box that then appears. (See Figure 6-12.)

You make three selections in this dialog box:

✔ Number of rows

✔ Number of columns

✔ Table format

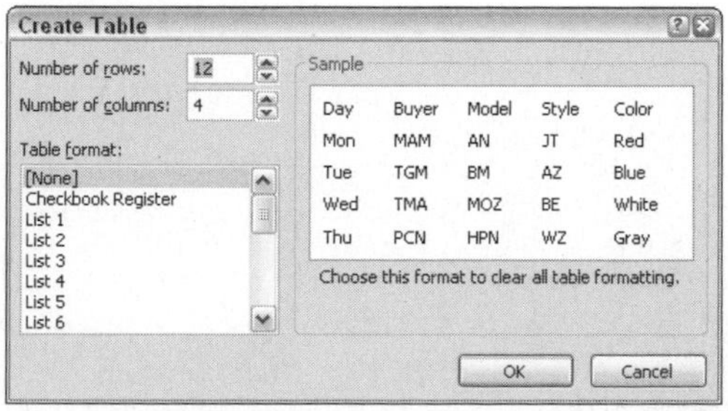

Figure 6-12:
The Create
Table
dialog box.

Create Table					
Number of rows: 12					
Number of columns: 4		Sample			
Table format:		Day	Buyer	Model	Style	Color
[None]		Mon	MAM	AN	JT	Red
Checkbook Register		Tue	TGM	BM	AZ	Blue
List 1		Wed	TMA	MOZ	BE	White
List 2		Thu	PCN	HPN	WZ	Gray
List 3					
List 4		Choose this format to clear all table formatting.			
List 5					
List 6					
			OK	Cancel	

Publisher lets you create tables as large as 128 x 128 cells and offers 21 different table styles, or *formats*. As you select a format, the program shows you a sample of the format in the Sample area of the dialog box. The [None] format displays a plain, unformatted table frame. When you click OK in the Create Table dialog box, Publisher creates your table in the frame you drew. If the size of the frame you draw is too small to contain the number of columns and rows you chose, Publisher displays a message box asking whether you want to resize the table to hold the selected rows. Click Yes to have Publisher resize the table so that it's larger; click No to reduce the number of rows and columns in your table.

Each table format has a minimum default cell size. If you select a larger number of cells than can be accommodated, Publisher displays a dialog box asking your permission to resize the frame. If you click No, you return to the Create Table dialog box, where you can then reduce the number of rows and columns in your table. If you click Yes, you create a table with the number of rows and columns you specified using the minimum cell dimensions.

Modifying tables

When a table is selected, the Table menu commands become active. This menu, shown in Figure 6-13, contains commands you can use to modify the appearance of the table. If you choose the Table AutoFormat command, the Auto Format dialog box appears. (See Figure 6-14.) This dialog box is almost identical to the Create Table dialog box, shown earlier, in Figure 6-12. The differences are that you can't change the number of rows or cells, but you can control some of the formatting options you apply to the table.

Although applying manual formatting is a good way to get your table frame to look just the way you want, it sometimes can mean plenty of work. Rather than manually format a table frame, use AutoFormat; it can do a lot of work for you. The AutoFormat feature not only applies character and paragraph formatting but also can merge cells and add cell borders and shading. Cell borders overlay table-frame gridlines and, unlike gridlines, are printed. Cell *shading,* a color or pattern that fills the interior of a cell, is also printed.

Click the Options button in the Auto Format dialog box to open a list of formatting options, such as Text Formatting, Text Alignment, Patterns and Shading, and Borders. You can select and deselect the options you want or don't want to apply.

Resizing tables, columns, and rows

The structure of a table frame truly differentiates it from a text frame. Whereas a text frame is one big rectangle into which you dump your text, a table frame is divided into a grid of separate text compartments (cells). After you create a table frame, you're not stuck with its original structure. You can resize the entire table frame; resize, insert, or delete selected columns and rows; merge multiple cells into one; and split a cell into separate cells. In short, you can restructure a table frame in just about any way you want.

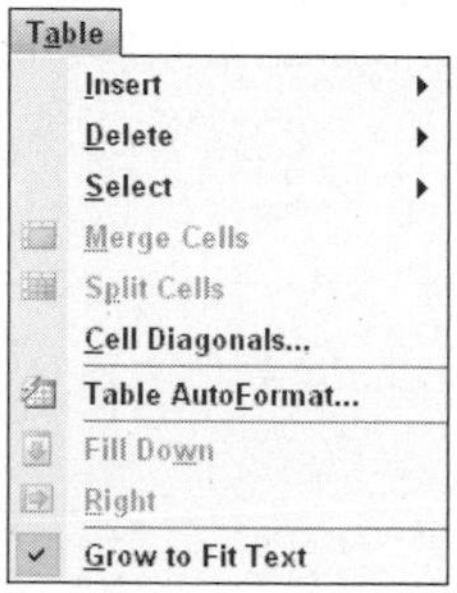

Figure 6-13:
The Table menu.

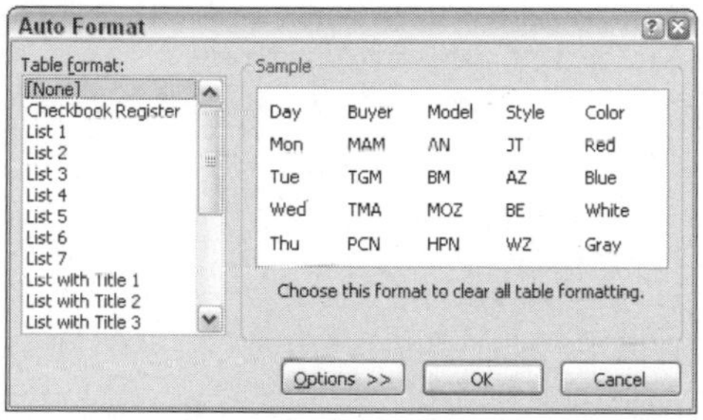

Figure 6-14:
The Auto Format dialog box.

Here are some guidelines for resizing a table frame:

- ✔ You can click and drag any of its selection handles. Publisher automatically adjusts the height of each row to fit each row's contents.

- ✔ When you narrow or widen a table frame, thus decreasing or increasing the available horizontal area in each cell, Publisher often compensates by heightening or shortening some rows, thus heightening or shortening the overall frame.

- ✔ When you shorten a table frame, Publisher reduces each row to only the minimum length required to display the text in each row.

- ✔ Regardless of whether your table frame contains text, you can't reduce any cell to less than ⅛-inch square. You can heighten a table frame as much as you want, however; and Publisher heightens each row by the same proportion.

- ✔ If you choose Table⇨Grow to Fit Text, the table's row height expands to accommodate the text you enter.

Here are some guidelines for resizing a column or row:

- ✔ Move the mouse pointer to the edge of a column until it becomes a double-headed arrow. Then click and drag until the column or row is the size you want.

- ✔ You can't shorten a row to a shorter length than is required to display its text, and you can't shrink any cell to less than ⅛ inch wide by ¼ inch tall.

- ✔ By default, when you resize a column or row, Publisher keeps all other columns and rows at their original size. Columns to the right are pushed to the right or pulled to the left, whereas rows below are pushed down or pulled up. The table frame increases or decreases in overall size to accommodate the change.

- ✔ To keep a table frame the same size when resizing a column or row, hold down the Shift key as you resize. You then move only the border between the current column or row and the next one. If you enlarge a column or row, the next column or row shrinks by that same amount. If you instead shrink a column or row, the next column or row enlarges by that amount. In either case, all other columns and rows remain the same size, as does the overall table frame.

- ✔ If you use the Shift key while resizing, you face even more limits. Unless you first lock the table frame (by selecting Table➪Grow to Fit Text from the main menu), you can't shorten the row below the row you're resizing to less space than that lower row requires in order to display its text. And, you can't shrink any adjacent column to less than ⅛ inch wide or a row to less than ¼ inch tall. In addition, even if you lock the table frame, you can increase a column or row only by the amount you can take from the next column or row.

- ✔ You can resize multiple columns or rows simultaneously. Just highlight those columns or rows, point to the right or bottom edge of the selection bar button that borders the right or bottom edge of your highlight, and then click and drag. Note that if you use the Shift key to resize, however, the program ignores your highlighting. You resize only the rightmost highlighted column or bottommost highlighted row.

- ✔ If you resize an entire table frame after resizing individual columns and rows, Publisher resizes the columns and rows proportionally. For example, if the first column is 2 inches wide and the second column is 1 inch wide, and you then double the width of the entire table frame, the first column increases to 4 inches wide, and the second column increases to 2 inches.

Inserting and deleting columns and rows

You can insert and delete as many as 128 columns and rows apiece. If you move to the last cell and press Tab, Publisher adds a new row at the bottom of the table frame and places the insertion point in the first cell of that row. You're now ready to type in that cell. How convenient!

To insert rows elsewhere, or to insert columns anywhere, you need to do only a little more work:

1. **Place the insertion point in the column or row adjacent to where you want to insert a new column or row.**

2. **Choose Table⇨Insert.**

   Publisher displays the Insert menu, as shown in Figure 6-15.

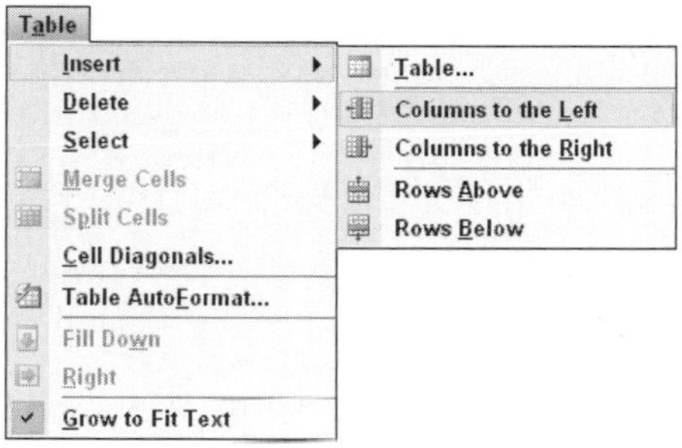

Table		
Insert ▶		Table...
Delete ▶		Columns to the Left
Select ▶		Columns to the Right
Merge Cells		Rows Above
Split Cells		Rows Below
Cell Diagonals...		
Table AutoFormat...		
Fill Down		
Right		
✓ Grow to Fit Text		

Figure 6-15: The Table Insert submenu.

3. **Select whether you want columns to the left, columns to the right, rows above, or rows below.**

   Even if a table frame is locked (refer to the section "Resizing tables, columns, and rows," earlier in this chapter), the program increases the table frame's size to accommodate the new columns or rows.

Deleting a column is easy. Follow these steps:

1. **Highlight the entire column you want to delete by placing the mouse pointer immediately above the column. When the pointer changes to a bold, downward-pointing arrow, click to select the column.**

   You can click and drag to select multiple columns.

2. **Choose Table⇨Delete⇨Columns.**

Deleting a row is just as easy:

1. **Highlight the entire row you want to delete by placing the mouse pointer immediately to the left of the row. When the pointer changes to a bold, right-pointing arrow, click to select the row.**

   You can click and drag to select multiple rows.

2. **Choose Table⇨Delete⇨Rows.**

The quickest way to delete a single row or column is to put an insertion point in the row or column you want to delete, and select the option from the menu. The row or column is now deleted, and you didn't have to highlight or drag over anything.

Before choosing the Table menu, decide how many rows or columns you want to add or delete, and select that number of rows or columns in the table. Then choose Insert or Delete from the Table menu. Choose Columns to the Left, Columns to the Right, Rows Above, or Rows Below[0].

Merging and splitting cells

You may occasionally want to merge multiple cells so that they become one cell. For example, you may want to merge cells so that you can center a heading over multiple columns, as shown in Figure 6-16.

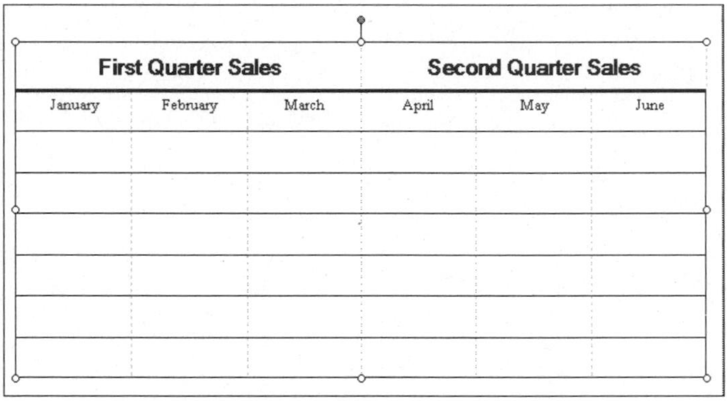

First Quarter Sales			Second Quarter Sales		
January	February	March	April	May	June

Figure 6-16: Cells merged to create column headings.

Keep these concepts in mind when you're merging cells:

- ✔ **To merge cells, highlight the cells you want to merge and then choose Table⇨Merge Cells.** Your highlighted cells become one. Any text in the individual cells moves into the single merged cell. You then can work with this merged cell as you would work with any other cell.

- ✔ **After you merge a cell, you can split it into individual cells again.** Click or highlight the merged cell and choose Table⇨Split Cells. The merged cell splits back into the original number of separate cells. The text, however, doesn't return to the original, individual cells. Instead, all the text moves intact to the leftmost and topmost cell.

The table's context-sensitive menu contains commands for inserting and deleting rows and columns and for merging and splitting cells. After you right-click the table, choose Change Table to see them.

In addition to being able to split cells horizontally, you can split cells diagonally in Publisher. Select the cells you want to split diagonally and choose Table⇨Cell Diagonals. In the Cell Diagonals dialog box, pick the type of diagonal you want (Divide Down or Divide Up) and click OK.

Working with table text

As with text boxes, you can fill a table frame by either typing the text directly into the frame or importing existing text from somewhere else. Except for the differences that I point out in the next two sections, the techniques for typing and importing text into text boxes and table frames are pretty darn similar.

Each cell in a table frame works much like a miniature text box. For example, when you reach the right edge of a cell, Publisher automatically word-wraps your text to a new line within that cell. If the text you type disappears beyond the right edge of the cell, you have probably locked the table. Choose Table⇨Grow to Fit Text to unlock it. If you want to end a short line within a cell, press Enter. The easiest method is usually to fill in the table frame row by row; when you finish one cell, just press Tab to move on to the next one.

I don't know why you would ever need a tab mark in a table frame, but if you do, press Ctrl+Tab.

There's one important difference between typing in a cell and typing in a text box: When you run out of vertical room in a cell, Publisher automatically heightens that entire row of cells to accommodate additional lines of text. If you later remove or reduce the size of some of that text, Publisher automatically shortens that row. Compare this process to typing in a text box: When you run out of room, the text box remains the same size, and the program sticks the text into an overflow area or, if it's available, a connected text box.

Importing table frame text

Just as you can do with text boxes, you can paste or insert a text file into a table frame. Some important differences exist, however. If your text is arranged in a table-like manner, such as in a spreadsheet or a word processing table, Publisher senses the arrangement and imports that text across the necessary number of cells in your table frame. If the text isn't arranged in a table-like manner, Publisher imports all text into the current cell.

If no table-like feature is available in your other program, you can use tab marks or commas *(delimiters)* to indicate column separations and paragraph marks *(end-of-row markers)* to indicate row separations.

Although you may be able to use the Insert⇨Text File command to import text into a table frame (as described earlier in this chapter), the Windows Clipboard is much more reliable. Use it whenever possible.

Choose one of these two methods to paste or insert text into a table:

- ✔ Cut or copy the text to the Windows Clipboard; then click the cell that will become the upper-left cell of the range and choose Edit⇨Paste or press Ctrl+V.

- ✔ Select a table cell and choose Insert⇨Text File to import text into the table frame.

When you import text into a table frame, Publisher overwrites (replaces) any text that exists in the cells into which you import. To restore accidentally overwritten text, immediately click the Undo button or press Ctrl+Z.

Here are some other important concepts to remember about bringing text into your table:

- ✔ If the copied text is arranged in a table-like manner and the current table frame doesn't have enough cells to accommodate all the copied cells, Publisher opens a dialog box to ask whether it should insert columns and rows as necessary. Click Yes to make sure that you paste all your text.

- ✔ If you haven't selected a table frame and the copied text is arranged in a table-like manner, the program creates a new table frame and places the copied text into that frame.

- ✔ Although a table frame can look much like a spreadsheet, Publisher doesn't have the power to calculate numbers. If you want to calculate the numbers in a table, calculate them in a spreadsheet program before importing. If you don't have a spreadsheet program, pull out your calculator!

- ✔ You can also make objects *inline* to table cells or to the text in a cell. When the object is inline to the text in the cell, the inline object moves with the text. When the object is inline to the table cell, the object is embedded in the cell and moves with the table. To make an object inline to a table cell or to text, right-click and drag the object. Release the mouse button where you want the object to land and then select Move Here or Move into Text Flow Here.

Editing table-frame text is much the same as editing text-box text. You need to know just a few extra procedures to efficiently highlight, move, and copy table-frame text.

You can use all the same mouse techniques to highlight (select) table-frame text as you use to highlight text-box text: drag, double-click, and Shift+click. You can also highlight table-frame text by combining the Shift key with any table-frame-movement techniques that I mention earlier in this section.

You also can highlight the contents of an entire cell by pressing Tab or Shift+Tab to move to that cell.

When you highlight any amount of text in more than one cell, you automatically highlight the entire contents of all those cells.

Here are some additional ways to select table-frame text:

- ✔ **Select the entire contents of the current cell:** Choose Table⇨Select⇨ Cell or press Ctrl+A (for All).
- ✔ **Select every cell in a column:** Choose Table⇨Select⇨Column.
- ✔ **Select every cell in a row:** Choose Table⇨Select⇨Row.
- ✔ **Select multiple columns or rows:** Click in any cell and drag across the rows or columns you want to select. Then choose Table⇨Select⇨ Column or Table⇨Select⇨Row. Hold the Shift key and press the arrow keys to expand the selection.
- ✔ **Select every cell in a table frame:** Choose Table⇨Select⇨Table.

Moving and copying table text

As with text boxes, you can use the Clipboard or drag-and-drop text editing (see Chapter 7) to copy and move text within and between table frames. If you like, you can even copy text between text and table frames.

Working in a table frame involves a very important difference, however: Whenever you move or copy the contents of multiple cells into other cells, Publisher automatically overwrites any text in those destination cells. To retain the contents of a destination cell, be sure to move or copy the contents of only one cell at a time. If you accidentally overwrite text when moving or copying, immediately choose Edit⇨Undo from the menu (or press Ctrl+Z).

Because of the way in which Publisher overwrites destination cells, rearranging entire columns and rows of text requires some extra steps. First, insert an extra column or row where you want to move the contents of an existing column or row. Then move the contents. Finally, delete the column or row you just emptied. Repeat these steps for every column and row you want to move.

Two commands on the Table menu, Fill Down and Fill Right, enable you to copy the entire contents of one cell into any number of adjacent cells either below or to the right.

Follow these steps to fill a series of cells in a row or column:

1. **Select the cell containing the text you want to copy and the cells to which you want to copy the text.**

   To use the Fill commands, you must select cells adjacent to the cell containing the text to be copied.

2a. **Choose Table⇨Fill Down to copy the value in the topmost cell to the selected cells in the column below it.**

or

2b. **Choose Table⇨Fill Right to copy the value in the leftmost cell to selected cells in the row to the right.**

Formatting table text manually

You can format table-frame text manually to make that information easier to read and understand. You can use all the character- and paragraph-formatting options detailed in Chapter 7: fonts, text size, text effects, line spacing, alignment, tab stops, indents, and bulleted and numbered lists, for example. You can even hyphenate table-frame text.

The key difference when applying paragraph formatting in table frames is that Publisher treats each cell as a miniature text box. Thus, when you align text, the text aligns within just that cell rather than across the entire table frame. And, when you indent text, the text is indented according to that cell's left and right edges.

To improve the look of cells, you can also change cell margins, thus changing the amount of space between a cell's contents and its edges. To change cell margins, choose Format⇨Table and click the Cell Properties tab. The resulting dialog box is shown in Figure 6-17.

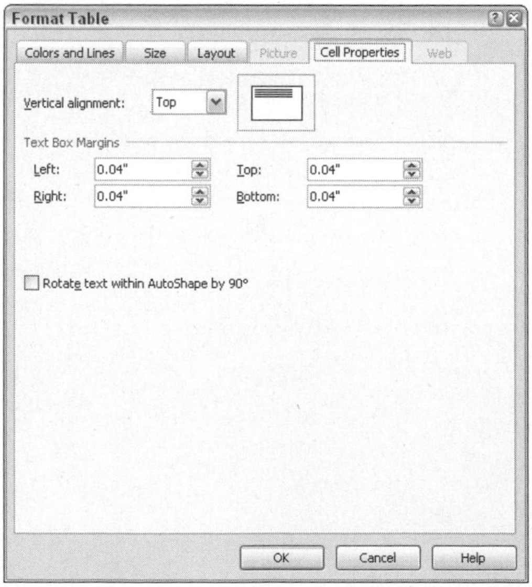

Figure 6-17:
The Cell
Properties
tab of the
Format
Table
dialog box.

Using Excel tables

Publisher lets you create and edit tables in your publication. It even has that cool Table AutoFormat command. However, if you're a Microsoft Excel user, you may find entering and formatting your tabular data in Microsoft Excel more convenient. Maybe you already have a Microsoft Excel worksheet that contains data you want to include in your publication. You don't have to waste time and risk data entry errors by retyping the information.

Importing an Excel worksheet

If you use Microsoft Excel and don't want to remember all the instructions for working with tables in Publisher, don't. Use Microsoft Excel to enter and format your tabular data and then import the worksheet into Publisher:

1. **In Microsoft Excel, enter and format some tabular data.**

2. **Save the Microsoft Excel worksheet.**

   If you're finished working in Microsoft Excel, you can close it.

3. **Switch to the Publisher window by clicking its button on the Windows taskbar.**

   If the Windows taskbar isn't visible, you can switch applications by pressing Alt+Tab. Hold down the Alt key and press Tab until the Microsoft Publisher 2007 icon is highlighted in the Cool Switch box that appears. Release both keys.

4. **Choose Insert⇨Object.**

   The Insert Object dialog box, shown in Figure 6-18, appears with the Create from File radio button selected.

5. **Click the Create from File radio button and then click Browse.**

   The Browse dialog box appears.

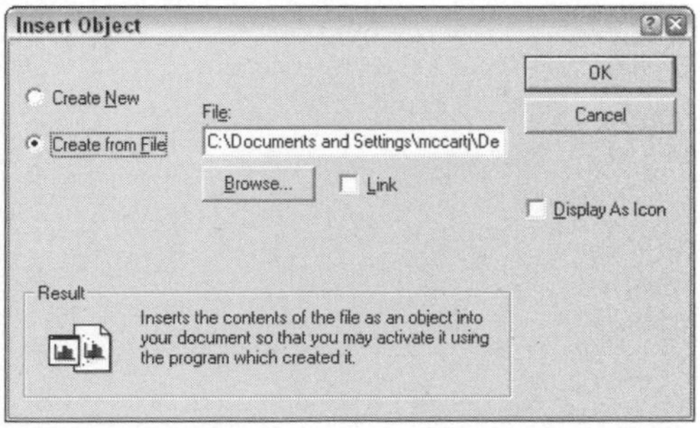

Figure 6-18:
The Insert Object dialog box.

6. **Navigate to (and select) the Microsoft Excel file you want to insert into your publication and then click Open.**

   You return to the Insert Object dialog box.

7. **Click OK to insert the Microsoft Excel worksheet into your publication.**

   Figure 6-19 shows an example of an Excel worksheet inserted into a publication.

The Excel worksheet you insert into your publication isn't really a table. I know: If it looks like a duck, waddles like a duck, and quacks like a duck, it must be a duck. Well, in Publisher, it isn't a duck, er, table. It's an object. If you select the newly inserted Excel worksheet and choose Table from the main menu, you notice that none of the Table commands is available.

Editing an Excel worksheet in Publisher

So you create a jazzy-looking worksheet in Microsoft Excel, save it to your hard drive, and import it into Publisher. That's great — until you realize that you spelled your company's name incorrectly. Do you have to launch Microsoft Excel, open the worksheet, correct the spelling of the company name, save the worksheet, and import it into Publisher again? Yes.

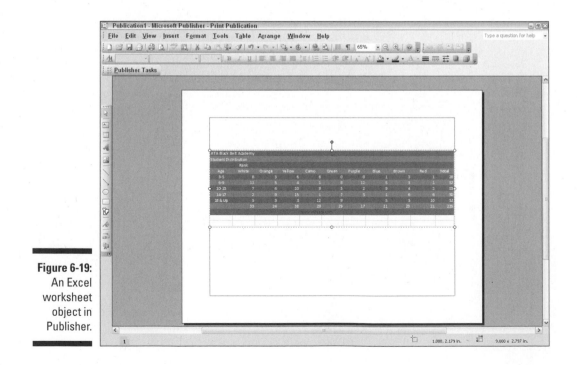

Figure 6-19:
An Excel worksheet object in Publisher.

Okay, just kidding. You don't have to do that. Just double-click the worksheet to launch Microsoft Excel inside Publisher. Although the title bar still proclaims that you're in Publisher, the menu bar and toolbars change to those belonging to Microsoft Excel. (See Figure 6-20.) In fact, because I created the sample worksheet in Microsoft Excel 2007, when I edit the worksheet, the Publisher menus and toolbars are replaced by the fancy new Excel 2007 Ribbon! Edit the worksheet as you would edit in it Excel. When you finish making changes, just click anywhere outside the worksheet. That's all there is to it!

Accessing tables in Access

If you're a database diehard who's wondering whether you can use your Microsoft Access tables in your publications, the answer is Yes. You can even use your Microsoft Access query results. Essentially, you have two options for getting data from your Access tables and query results into Publisher. You can import the entire table (or query results), or you can select part of the table (or query results) to bring into Publisher.

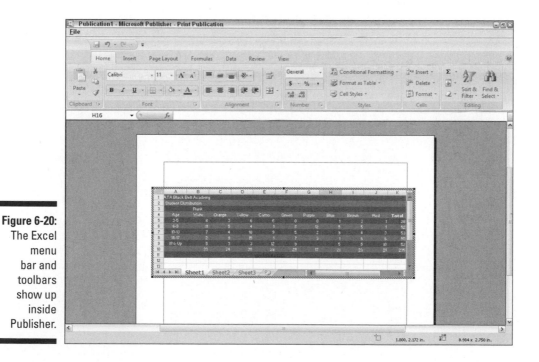

Figure 6-20: The Excel menu bar and toolbars show up inside Publisher.

Follow these steps to import an entire table or query results:

1. **In Microsoft Access, open the database that contains the table or query you want to use in your publication.**

2. **Click the Tables button in the Objects pane of the Database window.**

   To import the results from a query, click the Queries button in the Objects pane of the Database window.

3. **Select a table or query and then click the Copy button on the Standard toolbar. If you're using Access 2007, click the Copy button in the Clipboard section of the Home tab.**

4. **Switch to the Publisher window by clicking its button on the Windows taskbar.**

   If the Windows taskbar isn't visible, you can switch applications by pressing Alt+Tab. Hold down the Alt key and press Tab until the Microsoft Publisher 2007 icon is highlighted in the Cool Switch box that appears. Release both keys.

5. **In the Publisher window, choose Edit⇨Paste, press Ctrl+V, or click the Paste button on the Standard toolbar.**

   Publisher creates a new table containing the records from your Microsoft Access table or query.

Publisher creates an honest-to-goodness table from your Access table or query. Format the table just as you would format any other Publisher table. After pasting the table into Publisher, resize the table to your liking.

If you want to use only a portion of the records in your Microsoft Access table or query, select the records before clicking the Copy button in Step 3 in the preceding step list.

Chapter 7

Editors Are Bought, Not Born

In This Chapter

▶ Editing, navigating, and generally messing with text

▶ Searching, replacing, hyphenating, and checking the spelling of your text

▶ Formatting each and every character in your document

▶ Formatting paragraphs with style — and with styles

▶ Dressing your text — one text box at a time

*I*f you use a word processing or similar computer program, you know that editing (making changes to) text can be a breeze. Delete a word here, insert a couple words there, rewrite a sentence, add a comma, and the program takes care of the rest. The ease with which you can edit text in a computer program is one of the reasons that typewriters are choking landfills worldwide. My typewriter hasn't seen the light of day in years. I keep it just so I can say that I have one.

Editing text in Publisher is easy, too. Almost everything you know about editing text in a word processor applies to editing and formatting text in Publisher. Although, admittedly, Publisher doesn't have quite the editing muscle and sophistication of some full-blown, word processing programs, it still does a very respectable job.

Publisher is also more than a match for the formatting tools you find in any word processor. Its many text-formatting features enable you to take control of how your text looks, character by character, paragraph by paragraph, text box by text box. You control the horizontal; you control the vertical.

This chapter focuses on editing and formatting text in Publisher. It focuses specifically on working with text in text boxes, but you can use most of the techniques shown here to work with text in table frames as well.

Tricks of the Editing Meisters

You're probably an editing master already. If you've been banging away at a word processor for a while, chances are that this section is a review for you. In case it's not, I want to mention some tricks you can use to edit text in a text box.

To edit text, you first must position the insertion point in the text or highlight (select) the text. If you position the insertion point in the text, you can press Delete to remove any characters to the right of the insertion point or press Backspace to remove characters to the left. You can place the insertion point anywhere in a text box; when you do, Publisher also selects the text box for you.

If you select (highlight) text, any character you type replaces the highlighted text. This process works the same way in Publisher as it does in other Microsoft Office products. Be careful when selecting text: If you accidentally replace some text, press Ctrl+Z right away to undo your last action. (Have I mentioned backing up lately?)

If you haven't purchased Microsoft Publisher 2007 yet, save yourself some money and buy Microsoft Office Small Business 2007. In addition to buying Publisher, you get these Microsoft applications:

- Microsoft Office Word 2007
- Microsoft Office Excel 2007
- Microsoft Office PowerPoint 2007
- Microsoft Outlook 2007 with Business Contact Manager
- Microsoft Office Accounting Express 2007

Movin' and groovin'

If you're familiar with keys that move your insertion point in Microsoft Word, you find that they all work inside Publisher. You can also reposition the insertion point by using your keyboard's movement keys: Home, End, PgUp, PgDn, and the four arrow keys.

Some keyboards offer a separate bank of navigation keys, and some keyboards place them on the numeric keypad, at the right end of the keyboard. To use the keys on the numeric keypad as navigation keys, you must first turn off the Num Lock key on the keyboard. If the Num Lock key is turned on, the keys display numbers rather than move your insertion point. Figure 7-1 shows an ergonomic-style, 101-key computer keyboard.

Figure 7-1:
An
ergonomic-
style,
101-key
keyboard.

Table 7-1 lists some common movement keys and describes what they do. Notice that only the numbers on the numeric keypad (not on the main keyboard) move the insertion point. Turn off Num Lock on the keypad before using these keys to navigate.

Table 7-1	Navigation Keys
Key or Key Combination	*Where It Moves the Insertion Point*
Home or 7	Beginning of current text line
End or 1	End of current text line
Up arrow or 8	Up one text line
Down arrow or 2	Down one text line
Right arrow or 6	Right one character
Left arrow or 4	Left one character
Ctrl+Home or Ctrl+7	Beginning of current text box
Ctrl+End or Ctrl+1	End of current text box
Ctrl+up arrow or Ctrl+8	Beginning of current paragraph
Ctrl+down arrow or Ctrl+2	Beginning of next paragraph
Ctrl+right arrow or Ctrl+6	Right one word
Ctrl+left arrow or Ctrl+4	Left one word

If text is highlighted, pressing the left- or right-arrow key positions the insertion point at the beginning or end of the text and then removes the highlighting (*deselects* the text).

Selection tricks

As I mention earlier in this chapter, before you can edit or format a piece of text, you must highlight (select) it. The simplest way to highlight text is to select the Select Objects tool in the toolbox and then drag the cursor over the text you want to highlight. You also have a couple other choices for highlighting text:

- ✔ Double-click a word to select the word and any blank spaces following it.

- ✔ Click at one end of the text you want to highlight, press and hold down the Shift key, click at the other end of the text, and then release the Shift key.

- ✔ Combine the Shift key with any of the movement techniques listed in the preceding section. For example, to select an entire line of text, move the insertion point to the beginning of the line and then press Shift+End.

- ✔ Choose Edit➪Select All or press Ctrl+A (for *all*) to highlight all text in the current text box and in any connected text boxes.

You can also use the Shift key in combination with clicking or any movement technique to extend or reduce an existing highlight.

Drag and drop

Previous chapters in this book illustrate the use of the Cut, Copy, and Paste commands in several different applications. The cut/copy/paste technique is one of two ways to move text in text boxes. The other is drag and drop, which sounds like a training seminar for airport baggage handlers. By using *drag-and-drop* text editing, you can move and copy text within and between text boxes located on any single page or two-page spread without following all the steps of using the Windows Clipboard. I think of it as a direct form of cut and paste (or copy and paste, if you hold down the Ctrl key as you drag and drop).

To remove text from one spot and place it in another by using drag and drop, first highlight the text. After you complete that task, click the highlighted text and drag it to a new location. As soon as you release the mouse button, the text is dropped into its new location.

In previous versions of Publisher, the insertion pointer turned into a *T* with the word *Drag* next to it as soon as you moved it over your selected text — indicating that you were set to drag and drop. Publisher doesn't provide this little visual clue. The best that you get is a little box that appears under the arrow pointer when you click the selected text.

To copy text by using drag-and-drop, highlight the text you want to copy, press Ctrl, and then click and drag the selection to a new location. A small plus sign (+) shows up next to the arrow pointer, to indicate that you can now drag and drop and copy the selected text.

If the insertion point doesn't change to an arrow pointer when you place it over selected text, you may have turned off drag-and-drop text editing, although for the life of me I can't think of why you would want to do that. I love drag and drop. The Drag-and-Drop Text Editing check box on the Edit tab of the Options dialog box (it's on the Tools menu) disables this feature (which is turned on by default) in all your publications.

Drag-and-drop text editing isn't for everyone. My daughter, Becca (she prefers Warrior Princess), insists that the mouse pointer should turn into a dragon pointer when performing this mystical feat. Still, if you're mouse challenged, you might want to skip this feature.

Symbols

A big mistake that many new desktop publishers make is failing to use those special typographic characters that are known in Publisher as *symbols*. If you look carefully at this book, or any other well-produced publication, you can see symbols all over the place. These special symbols, which include fractions (such as ¼); special quotation marks (" "); special hyphens, such as en dashes (–) and em dashes (—); ligatures (Æ, œ, æ); and so on are a typographer's stock-in-trade.

Publisher provides two ways to put appropriate typographical symbols in your publications: automatically and manually. As you type, Publisher automatically replaces inch and foot marks (" and '), also known as *straight quotes,* with typographic quotation marks (" ", and ' '), and double hyphens (- -) with em dashes (—). (Typographic quotation marks are often called *smart quotes* or *curly quotes.*) If you import text, punctuation marks in that text remain as they were in your source document.

If Publisher doesn't replace these marks for you as you type, you probably turned off Publisher's autoformatting features. Choose Tools⇨AutoCorrect Options and click the AutoFormat as You Type tab of the AutoCorrect dialog box that appears. In the Replace as You Type area, select the Straight Quotes with Smart Quotes check box and the Hyphens (-, -) with dash (—) check box to turn on these settings. They apply to all your Publisher sessions.

If you like to import text into Publisher from another word processing program, try to set up that program so that it automatically replaces the text you type with the appropriate typographical symbols. Microsoft Word offers this feature, for example. Otherwise, you must search and replace the marks manually by either choosing the Edit⇨Replace command from the menu or pressing Ctrl+H.

What if you *want* to type an inch mark or a foot mark? You must turn off the Replace Straight Quotes with Smart Quotes option for a moment and then type the inch or foot mark. Don't forget to turn on the option again.

To insert a symbol manually into a publication, choose Insert⇨Symbol and make your selection from the Symbol dialog box, as shown in Figure 7-2.

The Symbol dialog box shows you all available symbols in your installed system fonts. The current font appears, but you can switch to other fonts — including Symbol. As you make your way through the various font sets, you find en dashes, fractions, copyright and registration marks, foreign letters and currency symbols, smiley faces, hearts, diamonds, clubs, spades, and even the *é* you need in order to type *résumé* correctly. Many of the most commonly used symbols are on the Special Characters tab of the Symbols dialog box. If you're looking for a special symbol, check out the Symbol font by selecting it from the Font list box. The Wingdings font is also a rich source of symbols, such as bullets, buttons, and bows.

Don't bother to insert symbols one at a time to create bulleted lists like the ones you see in this book. Instead, use the Bulleted or Numbered List feature in Publisher to create this special format. Bulleted and numbered lists are discussed later in this chapter, in the section "The Formatting toolbar."

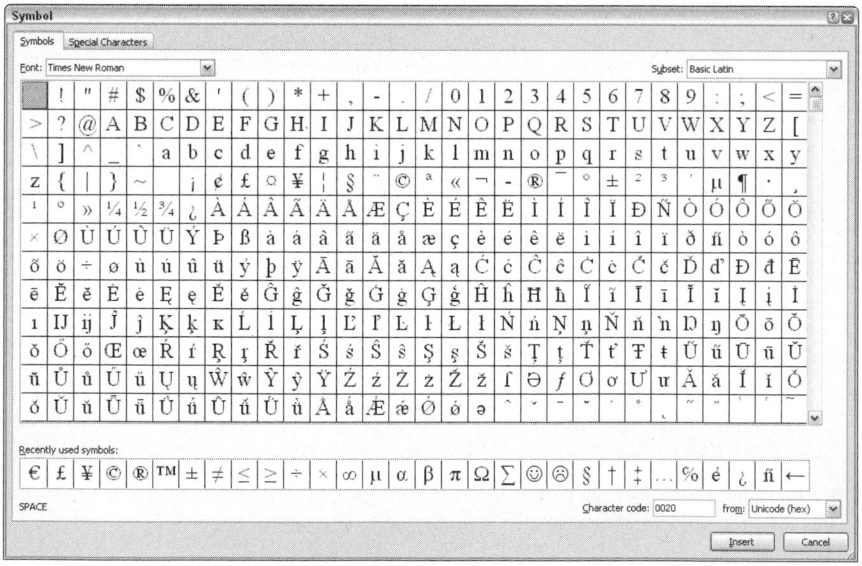

Figure 7-2:
The Symbol
dialog box.

Tools of the Editing Meisters

Any good page-layout program comes with a set of basic text management tools. Some of the heavyweight programs come with tools for formatting, text correction, seek and destroy, and other features that any word processor would envy. These tools are important; they increase accuracy and make your text more readable.

Publisher offers these tools:

- ✔ Search and replace
- ✔ A spell checker (including spell checking as you type)
- ✔ AutoCorrect
- ✔ Automatic hyphenation

Additionally, the Publisher Tools menu offers some other tools that aren't specific to text management. The Design Checker command looks at your document for common printing problems, and the Design Gallery contains such Publisher-designed objects as pull quotes, logos, calendars, and more that you can use in your publication. I discuss the Design Gallery and Design Checker in Chapters 9 and 12, respectively. The sections that follow examine the text tools.

Hide and seek: Find and Replace

Any good word processor has a *Find* feature, a command that enables you to hunt down a specific word or phrase in your document. Okay, even *poor* word processors have a Find feature. Publisher has a Find feature and even a Replace feature, which enables you to search and replace one word or phrase with another. If you need to correct text at story length, you just can't get by without these Search and Replace features.

Here's how to find text:

1. **Select a text box in the story you want Publisher to search.**

   Before finding and replacing text, press F9 to view your text at a readable size.

2. **Choose Edit➪Find or press Ctrl+F.**

   The initial Find and Replace task pane, shown in Figure 7-3, appears.

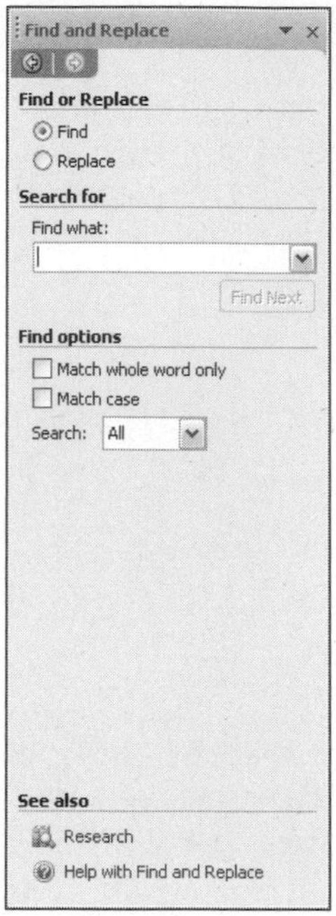

Find and Replace

Find or Replace
- Find
- Replace

Search for

Find what:

Find Next

Find options
- Match whole word only
- Match case

Search: All

See also
- Research
- Help with Find and Replace

Figure 7-3:
The Find
and Replace
task pane.

3. **In the Find What text box, type the text you want Publisher to find, using wildcard symbols, if you want.**

   If you ever worked in MS-DOS, you probably know about wildcards. One wildcard, the question mark (?), works in the Find and Replace task pane. If you use a question mark in your search criteria, any character can be a match for the character in the question mark position. For example, if you ask Publisher to search for the text *no?,* it finds the words *not, now, nod,* and others. If you need to search for an actual question mark, type a caret (^) before the mark, as in **^?**. To find a caret, ask a rabet. No, that's not right. To find a caret, type **^^**. Table 7-2 (appearing shortly) lists codes you can use to find other special characters.

4. **Select the Match Whole Word Only check box or the Match Case check box, or both, if you want those options.**

   The Match Whole Word Only option finds any occurrence of your search string that's surrounded by spaces or punctuation marks. This option ignores any matches that are part of larger words. With the option selected, a search for *publish,* for example, ignores the word *publisher.*

   The Match Case option searches your document for an exact match of your search string's characters, using upper- and lowercase characters as filtering criteria. With this option selected and the Match Whole Word Only option deselected, for example, a search for the word *publish* ignores any occurrence of *Publisher;* a search for the word *Publish,* however, finds *Publisher.*

5. **Select All, Up or Down in the Search drop-down list box to specify the direction of the search.**

   If you choose the Up option, Publisher searches from the location of the cursor upward to the beginning of the text box or story. If you choose the Down option, it searches from the cursor location to the end of the text box or story. If you choose the All option, Publisher searches the entire publication.

6. **Click the Find Next button.**

   Publisher scampers off to look for your text, and one of three things happens:

   - *The exact text you wanted is found and highlighted.*

   - *Publisher finds an occurrence of your text but not the one you were looking for.* Click the Find Next button to continue the search.

   - *Publisher reaches the beginning or end of the text without a match and opens a message box asking permission to continue looking through the rest of the publication (including master pages).* Click Yes if you want to continue looking. If Publisher then searches the entire story and comes up empty, it displays a message box saying that no matching text was found. Sorry!

7. **Click the Close button in the task pane to make the task pane run and hide when you finish searching.**

If you have used Microsoft Word, all this finding and replacing may look familiar to you. The Find and Replace procedures work essentially the same way in Publisher as they do in Word.

Publisher can't find text in a WordArt frame.

Publisher can't find the TV remote, your car keys, or your cellphone, either.

Sometimes, you may want to search for special characters, such as an end-of-paragraph mark or a tab space. You can do so by entering the codes listed in Table 7-2 into the Find What text box.

Table 7-2	**Find-and-Replace Codes for Special Characters**
To Find This	*Use This Code*
Two spaces	[two spaces]
Optional hyphen	^- (caret and hyphen)
Nonbreaking hyphen (a hyphen that doesn't break across a line ending)	^~ (caret and tilde)

(continued)

Table 7-2 (continued)

To Find This	Use This Code
Line break	^n
End of paragraph mark	^p
Nonbreaking space (a space that doesn't break across a line ending)	^s
Tab space	^t
White space (a tab character or space between words)	^w

Having Publisher help you find text is helpful, but getting the program to replace unwanted text is an even bigger labor-saving device. To find *and* replace text, choose the Edit⇨Replace command. Here's how:

1. **Select the story containing the text you want Publisher to replace.**

2. **Choose Edit⇨Replace or press Ctrl+H.**

   The Find and Replace task pane appears with the Replace radio button selected (see Figure 7-4). It's the same Find and Replace operation you see taking place in Figure 7-3; the program remembers the last text you typed in the Find What box during your current Publisher session.

3. **Type the text you want to find in the Find What text box, and the text you want to replace it with in the Replace With text box. Then specify the Search option.**

   Publisher searches in only two directions while running Find and Replace: Down and All. In this way, it's different from the Find feature.

   You can also set the same Match options described in the preceding set of steps.

4. **Click Find Next.**

   One of three things happens:

   - *A match is found.* To replace the found text, click the Replace button. Publisher then searches for the next occurrence of the text specified in the Find What text box.

   - *A match is found but not the one you want.* Click the Find Next button to continue the search.

   - *Publisher reaches the end of the text without finding a match, so it displays a message box asking whether to continue searching the rest of the publication (including master pages).* Click the Yes button to continue the search, or click No to end the search. If Publisher still can't find your text, it displays a message saying that it has finished searching.

5. **Click the Close button in the task pane to make the task pane disappear when you finish searching and replacing.**

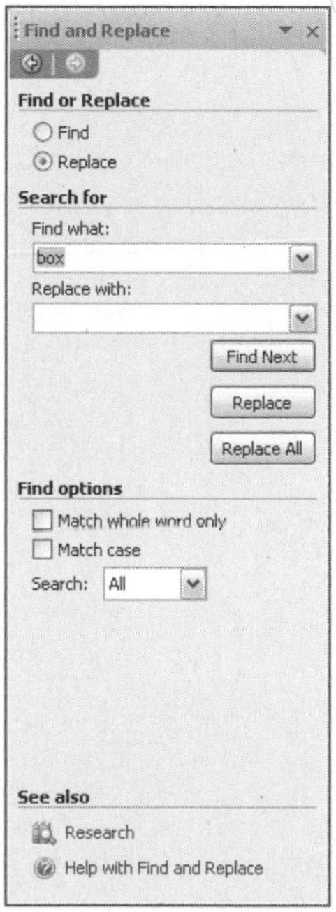

Figure 7-4:
The Find
and Replace
task pane
with the
Replace
radio button
selected.

If you click the Replace All button, Publisher replaces all occurrences of the matching text with your replacement text in one fell swoop. Take care when using the Replace All button: Unless you're careful, you may replace matches that you didn't intend to change. Mistakes are hard to catch in large stories.

The Replace command is an excellent way to repair text that wasn't prepared in the correct typographical way. For example, you can use the Replace command to replace all double spaces with single spaces. You can also replace other characters, such as double dashes and old-fashioned fractions, with their correct typographic counterparts. Use the Symbol dialog box (refer to Figure 7-2) to insert the correct symbol into your text. Cut or copy the symbol to the Clipboard, choose the Edit➪Replace command, and type the old-fashioned mark that you want to replace in the Find What text box. Then click the Replace With text box and press Ctrl+V to insert the symbol there. The symbol may appear as a bizarre shape totally unrelated to what you copied from the publication, but don't pay any attention to it. The symbol appears correctly again after it's back in the publication.

Now you're ready to replace at will. Just to be safe, however, always test your replacement text by replacing a single match before using the Replace All button to apply the replace universally.

Can you check my spelling?

There's no doubt about it: Spalling errors make you look bad. To begin checking your spelling, select a text box and then choose Tools⇨Spelling⇨Spelling or press F7. Publisher immediately searches for the first word that it doesn't recognize; if it finds one, the Check Spelling dialog box, shown in Figure 7-5, appears. Publisher places that word in the Not in Dictionary text box. You can correct the word in the Change To text box, and the spell checker even suggests close matches in the Suggestions list box.

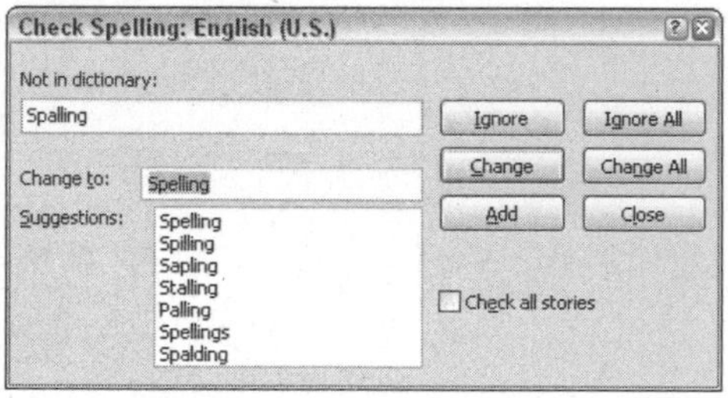

Figure 7-5: The Check Spelling dialog box.

Publisher can't check spelling in WordArt frames.

The spell checker is one of those "shared tools" in the Microsoft arsenal. (Know one, know them all.) Like other Microsoft programs with spell checking capabilities, Publisher doesn't find misspelled words per se: It compares every word it comes across against its own 100,000-word electronic dictionary. It considers any characters that appear between two spaces or similar delimiting characters to be a word. If a word doesn't match, Publisher points it out. That's why the dialog box has a Not in Dictionary text box rather than a Misspelled Word text box.

You have several choices for dealing with each word that Publisher flags:

✔ **If the word is incorrect and you can find the correct word in the Suggestions list box:** Double-click the correct word.

Alternatively, you can single-click the correct word and then click Change All to have Publisher automatically fix every occurrence of the incorrect word as it finds it.

✔ **If the word is incorrect and you can't find the correct word in the Suggestions list box:** Enter the correct word in the Change To text box and then click the Change or Change All button.

✔ **If the word is correct but it's not a word you use often:** Click the Ignore button to leave the word as is. Or, click Ignore All to leave every occurrence of the word that Publisher finds in this particular spelling check as is.

✔ **If the word is correct and it's a word you use often (such as your own name):** Click the Add button to add the word to the Publisher dictionary. Be careful with this button, though, because if you add an incorrect word to the dictionary, Publisher never points out the word again, in this or any other publication!

After you tell Publisher what to do with the first word, the spell checker continues until it reaches the end of your highlighted text or the end of the story. Publisher then asks whether you want to continue checking the rest of the current story. If you have more than one story in your publication, Publisher checks the current story first and then asks whether you want to check the next story (unless the Check All Stories check box is selected, in which case Publisher goes ahead and checks every story without asking).

Publisher checks spelling as relentlessly as my editor does. Eventually, though, it runs out of words to check and displays a dialog box telling you that it has finished checking your spelling. Click OK to close the Check Spelling dialog box.

If you typed a word but aren't sure whether you spelled it correctly, double-click the word and press F7. If Spell Check recognizes the word, a message box says that the spelling check is complete. If Spell Check doesn't recognize the word, the Check Spelling dialog box appears and offers alternative spellings. You can also right-click the word in question. Several alternative spellings appear at the top of the context menu.

What are those squiggly red lines in the text box? Publisher can check your spelling as you type. When you misspell a word, it's marked by a squiggly red underline to let you know that you made a boo-boo. Choose Tools➪Spelling➪Spelling Options and click to select the Check Spelling As You Type option. (This option is selected by default.)

A spell checker isn't a substitute for proofreading. Don't believe me? Ask my editor. Just because all the words are spelled correctly doesn't mean that they're the *correct* words. Did you know that *spalling* (which I misspelled for *spelling* a couple of pages ago) is a real word? In case this is news to you (it was to me), it means "to break up or reduce by chipping with a hammer" as in "I'll be out in the garage spalling the old computers, Honey. . . ."

Hyphenation

To fit more text in a given space or to make justified text easier to read, you can have Publisher hyphenate your text, by automatically breaking words in two at line endings. This process is automated, so Publisher continually removes and adds hyphens as needed as you type, edit, and rearrange text.

To have Publisher hyphenate your text automatically, follow these steps:

1. **Select the text frame or story that you want to hyphenate.**

2. **Choose Tools⇨Language⇨Hyphenation or press Ctrl+Shift+H.**

   The Hyphenation dialog box, shown in Figure 7-6, appears.

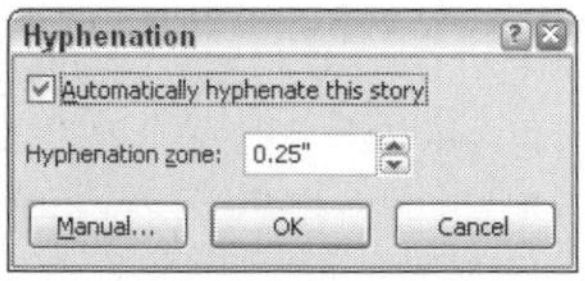

Figure 7-6:
The
Hyphenation
dialog box.

> **Hyphenation**
>
> ☑ Automatically hyphenate this story
>
> Hyphenation zone: 0.25"
>
> [Manual...] [OK] [Cancel]

3. **Verify that the Automatically Hyphenate This Story check box is selected and then click the OK button.**

Your text is now hyphenated. If you later change the text in any way, Publisher automatically re-hyphenates the text.

If you don't trust Publisher to hyphenate your text for you or if you want to manually control where a hyphen in a word occurs, you can click the Manual button in the Hyphenation dialog box. Then, when Publisher finds a word appropriate for hyphenating, it shows you that word and how it wants to hyphenate it. You can either approve, modify, or reject the hyphenation. If you use this option, though, Publisher doesn't re-hyphenate your text for you; you have to issue the Hyphenation command again.

Another control you have in adjusting hyphenation is the setting in the Hyphenation Zone text box. The smaller the hyphenation zone, the more hyphens Publisher uses and the more even the right edge of your text is.

To remove automatic hyphenation, choose the Tools⇨Language⇨Hyphenation command again. Click the Automatically Hyphenate This Story check box to deselect the option.

You can set up Publisher to hyphenate all text by default: Choose Tools⇨ Options and click the Edit tab. Select the Automatically Hyphenate in New Text Boxes check box if it's not already selected (it's selected by default), and then change the setting in the Hyphenation Zone text box, if you want. For any text box you now create in any publication, Publisher automatically hyphenates the frame's text. Publisher doesn't change the hyphenation in any existing text boxes, however.

Text Formatting

If you've worked in a word processor, you've formatted your share of text. Perhaps you're a text formatting meister. Even so, you may learn a trick or two in the sections that follow. If you don't, reward yourself with three gold asterisks and move on down the line.

Modern word processors and page layout programs divide the formatting that you can apply to text into three formatting levels:

- ✓ **Character:** You can apply this type of format to each character in your text: type styles, fonts, sizes, and cases, for example.
- ✓ **Paragraph:** This default format applies to paragraphs. Some formats, such as styles, you may be able to change. Others, such as line spacing, may not be changed, depending on the program you're using.
- ✓ **Document:** This type of format usually applies to the entire document. Page margins are an example of a document format. Because Publisher treats stories as though they're documents, document formats apply to text boxes and to connected text boxes with a story in them.

If you understand which formats belong to which category, you can quickly apply the format you want in order to get professional results — and often with dramatic time savings.

The Formatting toolbar

After you select a chunk of text, a Formatting toolbar appropriate to text formatting appears under the Standard toolbar. Figure 7-7 shows the Formatting toolbar for text. Most of the toolbar elements should be familiar to you if you have worked in a word processor.

Figure 7-7:
The Formatting toolbar.

This list describes the formatting options on the toolbar, from left to right:

- **Style list box:** Enables you to choose a style and apply it to your selection. A *style* is a set of formats that apply to a paragraph, as explained later in this chapter.

- **Font list box:** Shows the current font and enables you to select a different one.

- **Font Size list box:** Displays the current font size and enables you to enter a new one.

- **Bold, Italic, and Underline buttons:** Set the font style.

- **Align Left, Center, Align Right, and Justify buttons:** Apply text justification, which is a paragraph-level setting.

- **Line Spacing button:** Controls the spacing between lines.

- **Numbering button:** Accesses a paragraph-level setting that enables you to automatically number your paragraphs. (Great for creating numbered Steps lists!)

- **Bullets button:** Applies a paragraph-level setting that enables you to automatically place bullets at the beginning of paragraphs. (The Bullet List look.)

- **Decrease Indent button:** Moves the selected paragraph to the previous tab stop.

- **Increase Indent button:** Moves the selected paragraph to the next tab stop.

- **Decrease Font Size button:** Changes the selected text to the next smaller font size listed in the Font Size list box.

- **Increase Font Size button:** Changes the selected text to the next larger font size listed in the Font Size list box.

- **Fill Color button:** Applies color to the background of a text frame.

- **Line Color button:** Opens the Color Selector pop-up menu, which enables you to change the color of the selected line.

- **Font Color button:** Opens the Color Selector pop-up menu, which enables you to change the font color of selected text.

- **Line/Border Style button:** Enables you to place borders around text frames.

- **Dash Style:** Lets you choose the type of dashed line.

- **Arrow Style:** Allows you to choose the type of arrow.

- **Shadow Style:** Allows you to choose a shadow for the text box.

- **3-D Style:** Lets you choose a 3D style for the text box.

You must realize that the toolbar offers only highlights of what's possible format-wise. Many of the Format menu commands that the buttons duplicate open dialog boxes containing lots of additional options. Still, the buttons are a convenient, quick way to apply basic formatting.

Character formatting

Character formatting enables you to change the appearance of individual characters. Character formatting is most often used for emphasis, to set text apart from the text surrounding it. For example, words are often italicized to make them stand out in a block of plain text.

One confusing aspect of text formatting is that you can format the text in your paragraphs at the paragraph level and also format individual characters in that paragraph any way you want. You can think of paragraph formatting as a default format that you can override as needed.

Character formatting can make your text look great, but for even fancier text, try out WordArt, as described in Chapter 8.

Choosing a font

Perhaps the most noticeable character format is the font of your text. The *font* (or *typeface*) determines each character's basic shape. Microsoft Windows and Publisher together offer you lots of fonts. Text always uses one font or another; by default, it's Times New Roman. Some fonts, such as Vacation MT, Webdings, and Wingdings, are symbol fonts and aren't used for regular text.

As though the fonts that come with Publisher and Windows weren't enough, even more might be available to you: Other Windows programs might have installed additional fonts on your computer, and your printer might have its own set of built-in fonts. If you become a raving font addict, rest assured that you can buy and install even more fonts.

As Roger C. Parker says in *Desktop Publishing & Design For Dummies* (Wiley Publishing): "He who dies with the most fonts wins."

Choose one of these two methods to change the font for selected text:

  ✔ Select the font name from the Font list box on the toolbar.

  ✔ Choose Format➪Font to open the Font dialog box, shown in Figure 7-8. Click the font name in the Font list box.

    If no font name appears in the Font box, you probably highlighted text that's formatted with more than one font. You can still use the Font list box to apply the font you want.

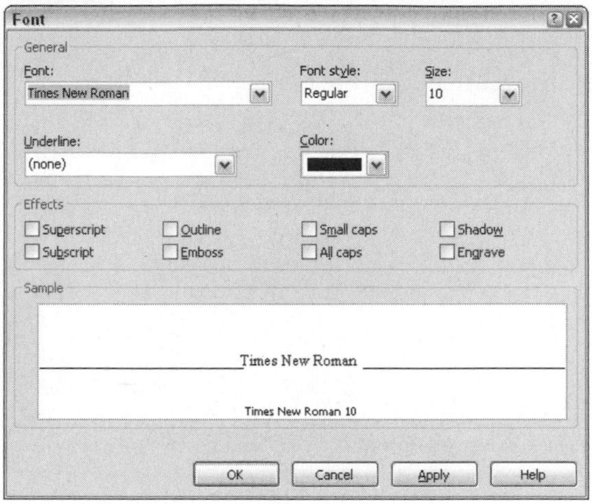

Figure 7-8:
The Font
dialog box.

Press Ctrl+Shift+F to highlight the font in the Font list box and activate the list box. Then press the up- or down-arrow keys to move to the font you want. Press Enter to select the highlighted font.

When you open the Font box's drop-down list, you see an icon next to each font name. The two *T*s icon indicates that the font is a *TrueType* font, an out-line font that any Windows program can use. The little printer icon indicates that the font is a *printer* font, built in to the current publication's target printer. No symbol means that the font is a *system* font, one that Windows itself uses to label windows, dialog boxes, and options, and other elements.

TrueType is generally the most hassle-free font type to use, but you may want to go with printer fonts if you're having a print service print your publication printed. Many print services use Postscript fonts that require printer descriptions.

Note that if you *do* use printer fonts, those fonts may look bad on-screen. Because Windows has only sketchy information about any given printer font, your on-screen characters may be misshapen, and lines of text may appear clipped off in certain views. Everything should look fine when you print your publication, though. Chapter 8 explains fonts and typography in detail.

Changing the font size

There must be something about publishing professionals that makes using standard English terms difficult for them. Even when they're simply measur-ing the size of text, they can't stick with inches, centimeters, or any other measurement that the rest of the world uses. Instead, they measure the height of text in points. A *point* is approximately ¹⁄₇₂ of an inch, and you can make text any size from 0.5 point to 999.9 points, in 0.1-point increments. In inches, those measurements translate from ¹⁄₁₄ inch to almost 14 inches high — that's quite a range! Unless you're making banners, though, you probably will keep your text somewhere between 6 and 72 points.

With typography, nothing is as simple as it seems. Even a standard point size changes depending on the font that's selected. These and other mysteries of typographic life are explained in Chapter 8.

Choose one of these methods to change the size of selected text:

✔ Select the size from the Font Size list box on the toolbar or enter your own size into the list box.

✔ Choose Format➪Font to open the Font dialog box (refer to Figure 7-8) and enter the font size there.

If no font size appears in the Font dialog box's Size list box, you probably highlighted text formatted with more than one size. You can still use the Size list box to apply the size you want.

Press Ctrl+Shift+P to highlight the font size in the Font Size list box and activate the list box. Press the up and down arrows to increase or decrease the font size, or type any size you want (between 0.5 and 999.9) and press Enter.

With TrueType fonts, you can enter any font size you want (in the allowed range), even decimal numbers. Some printer fonts support only a limited set of sizes, however. If you plan to use printer fonts, consult the printer's documentation to see whether this limitation applies.

Applying a type style

The last important character format is type style, which Publisher refers to as *effects.* If you want to make a word or two stand out, apply text effects such as **boldface,** *italics,* or <u>underlining.</u> You can apply these effects to selected text by using toolbar buttons or choosing options from the Font dialog box. You can specify whether you want to underline all selected text or just individual words and not the spaces between them. You can choose a double underline, a wavy underline, or a dotted or dashed underline. Go ahead — take a peek at the Underline list box in the Font dialog box. You can also create superscript or subscript effects, all caps or small caps, or outline, shadow, emboss, and engrave effects in the Font dialog box.

Here are some text-effect keyboard shortcuts — be sure that you know them cold:

Shortcut	*Applies*	*Shortcut*	*Applies*
Ctrl+B	Bold	Ctrl+I	Italic
Ctrl+U	Underline	Ctrl+Shift+K	Small caps
Ctrl+=	Superscript	Ctrl+Shift+=	Subscript
Ctrl+spacebar	Plain text (removes all style formats from selected text)		

With the exception of Ctrl+spacebar, all these keyboard shortcuts are *toggles:* Press the shortcut once to turn on the effect; press the shortcut a second time to remove the effect.

As with font and font size, you can use either the toolbar buttons or the Font dialog box (more generally) to make your type style selections. When you select text to which the bold, italic, or underline effect has been applied, the corresponding button on the toolbar has a pushed-in look. You can simultaneously select text that has one of these effects applied *and* text that does not. When you do this, you may notice that the corresponding toolbar button doesn't have the pushed-in look. If you click the button once, you remove the effect from all the highlighted text. Click again to apply the effect to all the selected text.

Some fonts (not common Windows ones, though) don't support boldface and italics. For these fonts, the B (bold) and I (italic) buttons are useless. You can click them all you want, but your text doesn't change.

Getting the yearn to kern

If you're really picky about how your text looks, you can even control the amount of horizontal space between characters, either squishing text together or spreading it apart. Publishing professionals call this effect *kerning.* (Don't confuse kerning with line spacing. Kerning controls the amount of *horizontal* spacing between characters, whereas line spacing controls the *vertical* spacing between lines of text.)

By default, Publisher automatically kerns between relatively large characters — any text that's 14 points or larger. To get Publisher to kern even smaller characters, choose the Format⇨Character Spacing command from the menu and change the setting in the Kern Text At scroll box. Publisher then adjusts the spacing between letters based on a list of letter pairs that are part of a font's definition.

Publisher does a good job of automatic kerning, but if you have some specific text that you want to kern manually, you have two choices, tracking or kerning. First, choose Format⇨Character Spacing from the menu. This command opens the Character Spacing dialog box, as shown in Figure 7-9, where you can adjust the spacing for large selections (Publisher calls it *tracking*) or fine-tune the spacing between two characters (Publisher calls it *kerning*). Perfect kerning is one of those power features that desktop publishers crave.

To quickly adjust the spacing of selected text, press Ctrl+Shift+[to move characters closer together or Ctrl+Shift+] to spread them apart.

Don't bother spending much time kerning text in a smaller font. Kerning is best done on large-font text, particularly headline text. Figure 7-10 shows you the difference between tight and loose kerning.

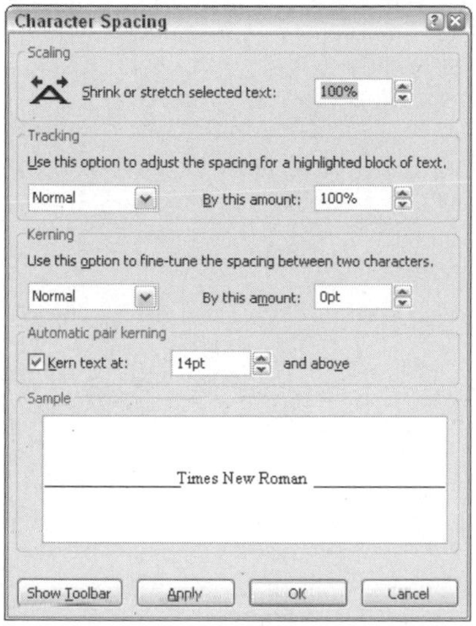

Figure 7-9:
The
Character
Spacing
dialog box.

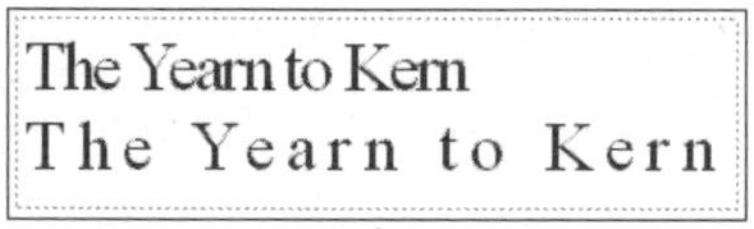

Figure 7-10:
Condensed
versus
expanded
kerning.

The Yearn to Kern
The Yearn to Kern

Paragraph formatting

Whereas character formatting enables you to control text one character at a time, *paragraph formatting* controls entire paragraphs. Paragraph formatting includes line spacing, alignment within a frame, tab stops, indents, and formatting text as bulleted or numbered lists.

You probably discovered in grade school that a paragraph is a group of sentences that forms a complete thought. Well, forget it! In Publisher, regardless of complete thoughts, a *paragraph* is anything that ends with a paragraph mark (one of those special characters that you create every time you press the Enter key). Thus, if you type a three-line address and press Enter to begin each new line, that address consists of three separate paragraphs. If you want, you can format each of those paragraphs differently.

With character formatting, you must select all the text that you want to format. But you don't need to bother highlighting entire paragraphs to apply paragraph formatting. To mark a single paragraph for paragraph formatting, just click to place the insertion point anywhere in the paragraph or highlight text anywhere in the paragraph. To mark multiple paragraphs for formatting, just highlight some text in each of those paragraphs. Keep this in mind during the next few sections whenever I tell you to mark a paragraph.

Here's a weird tidbit: Publisher and word processors store *in the paragraph mark itself* the paragraph format and any variation you apply to characters in that paragraph.

Adjusting line spacing

If you've done a decent amount of word processing, you know all about setting line spacing *within* a paragraph — the old single-space-versus-double-space dichotomy. You may not have known, however, that you can control the amount of space that appears *above* and *below* each paragraph. This option is important for making headings stand out and for many other purposes.

To change a paragraph's line spacing, follow these steps:

1. **Select the paragraphs you want to affect, and then choose Format⇨Paragraph from the menu.**

   The Paragraph dialog box appears, as shown in Figure 7-11.

2. **In the Line Spacing section of the dialog box, use the Before Paragraphs drop-down list to specify the amount of space to appear before the first line of each paragraph.**

3. **In the same section, use the After Paragraphs drop-down list to specify the amount of space to appear before the last line of each paragraph.**

   The Sample box shows you the result of your settings.

4. **(Optional) Specify the line spacing within a paragraph by using the Between Lines drop-down list in the Line Spacing section of the Paragraph dialog box.**

   Alternatively, you can press Ctrl+1 for single-spaced text; Ctrl+2 for double-spaced; Ctrl+5 for 1½ line space; and Ctrl+0 (zero) to remove the space before a paragraph.

It's considered good typographical practice to set line spacing rather than insert additional paragraph marks to create spacing. Then, if you decide to change the spacing between the paragraphs later, you need to work with the attributes of only the paragraphs that contain your content. You don't need to add or delete paragraphs you use as space holders.

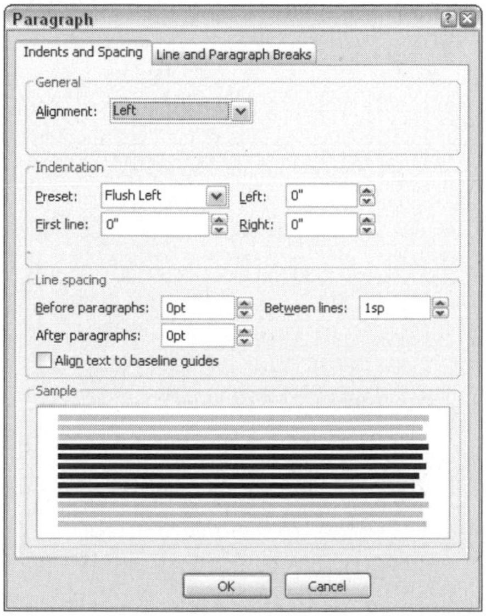

Figure 7-11:
Setting line
spacing
in the
Paragraph
dialog box.

You can specify any and all line spacing settings in terms of these measurements:

- ✔ **in:** Inches
- ✔ **cm:** Centimeters
- ✔ **pt:** Points
- ✔ **pi:** Picas
- ✔ **sp:** A special Publisher space measurement

One space in Publisher always equals 120 percent of the current text size — an ideal size-to-spacing ratio for single spacing. If you use the sp measurement (1 sp for single-spacing, 2 sp for double spacing, and so on), the line spacing changes as the text size changes. If you use any other measurement, the line spacing remains the same when you enlarge or reduce your text size, even if the result is wildly squished or spaced-out text lines.

You can enter any of the measurement units just listed into the Line Spacing text boxes in the Paragraph dialog box. Publisher automatically converts the units (except for the sp unit) to the default measurement units. You set the default measurement unit in the Options dialog on the Tools menu.

Setting paragraph alignment

By default, Publisher lines up paragraphs along the left edge of the text frame that holds them. Text aligned in this manner is said by typographers to be *ragged right,* or *left justified.* To push text instead to the right edge (*ragged left,* or *right justified*), to center it between the edges *(fully ragged),* or to stretch it from edge to edge *(fully justified),* you change its *alignment,* also called *justification* in publishing lingo.

Here are some ways to set paragraph alignment for selected paragraphs:

- ✔ The easiest way is to click one of the four alignment icons on the Formatting toolbar (from left to right across the toolbar): Align Text Left, Center, Align Text Right, or Justify.

- ✔ Use the following keystrokes: Ctrl+L for left justified; Ctrl+R for right justified; Ctrl+E for center (think *even!*); or Ctrl+J for fully justified. Press Ctrl+Q to return your paragraph to the default format.

- ✔ Use the Alignment drop-down list on the Indents and Spacing tab of the Paragraph dialog box.

Justified text can stretch your text out so far that it's difficult to read. To remedy this, try hyphenating the text, as described earlier in this chapter, in the "Hyphenation" section.

The justification, hyphenation, line spacing, and other paragraph-level formats you use are important determinants in how your publication looks. They "color" your text and make it either more or less readable. A full explanation of this topic would require more space than I have available in this book, but you should try to take the time to visit the style guides that I recommend at the end of Chapter 2. See Chapter 12 too, for more information on hyphenating and justifying text.

Setting tab stops

When you press the Tab key in a text box, Publisher inserts a *tab mark.* How this special character affects the text following it depends on the tab stops that are set for the paragraph.

By default, left-aligned *tab stops* are set every half-inch on the horizontal ruler. (When you're working in a text box, a special subsection of the horizontal ruler measures distances from the frame's left edge.) Thus, each tab mark you create usually causes the text following the mark to left-align with the next available half-inch mark. For example, if your text is 1¼ inch from the left edge of a frame and you insert a tab mark before that text, the text left-aligns with the 1½-inch ruler mark.

By setting your own, custom tab stops, however, you can align tab marks in a number of other ways. Publisher supports four different kinds of tab stops:

- ✔ **Left:** This setting is the default, and a tab moves text to the right of the tab mark so that it aligns flush left to the tab stop.

- ✔ **Center:** A tab moves text so that it aligns centered on the tab stop.

- ✔ **Right:** A tab moves text so that it aligns flush right to the tab stop.

- ✔ **Decimal:** A tab moves text so that any decimal point aligns to the tab stop. This tab is useful for aligning numeric data in tables.

You can quickly set a tab stop for selected paragraph (or paragraphs) by clicking the Move Both Rulers button at the intersection of the two rulers until the type of tab that you want appears. Then click the spot on the horizontal ruler where you want the tab to be placed. To remove a tab stop you set, simply drag it from the horizontal ruler.

Sometimes, you might want to use a *tab leader,* a set of characters that fill any gap created by a tab mark. Publisher offers dots, dashes, lines, and bullets as leaders. Dotted tab leaders are commonly used with right-aligned tab stops in tables of contents (such as at the beginning of this book). The dots connect the titles on the left with the page numbers on the right. In that case, you need to set tabs by using the Tabs dialog box, as explained in these steps:

1. **Select the paragraphs you want to affect.**

2. **Choose Format⇨Tabs.**

   The Tabs dialog box appears, as shown in Figure 7-12.

   If you know exactly where you want to place a tab, double-click the ruler at that location. A tab stop is inserted, and the Tabs dialog box opens.

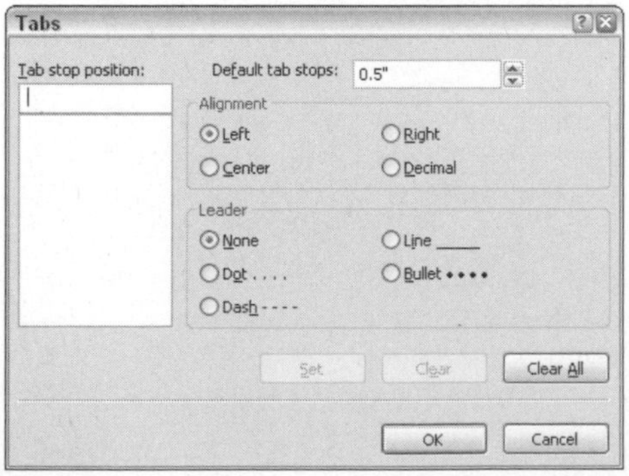

Figure 7-12:
The Tabs
dialog box.

3. **In the Tab Stop Position list box, specify a position for the tab stop in the upper text field.**

   You can type any of the units of measurement that Publisher accepts in the Tab Stop Position list box: inches, centimeters, picas, points, or pixels. Publisher automatically converts the units to the current default measurement units. (You set the default measurement unit on the Tools menu in the Options dialog box.)

   This position is the distance between the left edge of the text box and the tab stop.

4. **In the Alignment section, choose how you want text to align to your tab stop.**

5. **(Optional) Set a tab leader.**

6. **Click the Set button.**

   Your tab-stop position now appears in the lower section of the Tab Stop Position list box.

7. **(Optional) Set additional tabs by repeating Steps 3 through 6.**

8. **Click the OK button.**

After you set custom tab stops, the horizontal ruler displays those stops, using symbols for the four kinds of tab stops. If you're fairly adept with the mouse, you can fine-tune the position of a tab stop by dragging it back and forth on the ruler. Be careful to point directly to the tab stop you want to move, however, or you might accidentally create a new stop.

Here are some helpful shortcuts for working with tab stops:

- **To delete a tab stop:** Drag it down and off the horizontal ruler. Or, use the Clear and Clear All buttons in the Tabs dialog box.

  Notice that the Tabs dialog box provides an option for changing the Default tab stops from every half-inch to any other increment you like.

- **To modify the alignment or leader of an existing tab stop:** Open the Tabs dialog box and click to select the stop you want to change in the Tab Stop Position list box. Then set the alignment or leader (or both), click Set, and click OK.

Remember that tab stops are paragraph specific. If you click or highlight text in another paragraph, the horizontal ruler displays in that new paragraph any custom tab stops that are set. If the tab stops on the horizontal ruler are gray, you probably highlighted text in multiple paragraphs that use different tab stops.

Tab stops can be a pain. If you get frustrated from working with them, remember that just about anything you can accomplish with tab stops, you can often more easily accomplish with indents, table frames, and multiple text boxes.

Setting paragraph indents

Indents are like margins that affect only individual paragraphs. By default, all indents are set to 0, which makes paragraphs align with the text box margins. By increasing the indent setting, you can move paragraphs in from those margins.

If you want to move every line of text in a text box, you needn't bother with indents. Instead, just resize or move the text box.

To set indents, follow these steps:

1. **Mark the paragraphs you want to affect.**

2. **Choose Format⇨Paragraph from the menu.**

   The Paragraph dialog box opens. (Refer to Figure 7-11.)

3. **In the Indentation section of the dialog box, choose the type of indent you want from the Preset drop-down list.**

   - *Flush Left:* Aligns the entire paragraph with the left margin
   - *1st Line Indent:* Indents the first line of the paragraph by ¼ inch
   - *Hanging Indent:* Indents all lines except the first line of a paragraph by ¼ inch
   - *Quotation:* Justifies the text so that it's formatted into a block quote
   - *Custom Indent:* Allows you to create your own indent style

4. **(Optional) Use the Left, First Line, and Right options to fine-tune the preset indent.**

   The Left option indents the left edge of every paragraph line; First Line indents the left edge of just the first paragraph line; and Right indents the right edge of every paragraph line.

   The Sample box shows the effect of your choices.

5. **Click OK.**

After you set custom indents, *indent markers* — those little black triangles on the horizontal ruler — move to reflect the indenting. If you want, you can change the indents by dragging the indent markers back and forth:

- ✔ **The upper-left indent marker:** Controls the left edge of the first line in the paragraph

- ✔ **The lower-left marker:** Controls the left edge of every line in the paragraph except for the first line

> ✔ **The right indent marker:** Controls the right edge of every line in the
> paragraph
>
> ✔ **The rectangle under the lower-left marker:** Controls both the first line
> and left indents

Be careful to point the cursor directly at the indent marker you want to
move, however, or you might accidentally create a tab stop. If the indent
markers on the horizontal ruler are gray, you probably highlighted text in
multiple paragraphs that use different indents. You can still use the markers
to adjust your indents.

It's considered good typographical practice to use a first-line indent rather
than tab marks to indent the first lines of paragraphs.

As an example of how indents are used, consider the hanging indent, as
shown in Figure 7-13. You create a *hanging indent* by setting the left indent
larger than the first-line indent.

Unlike some word processors, Publisher doesn't allow you to set negative
indents. That is, your text can't extend beyond the text box margins. You
might, however, be able to get text to move closer to the edge of a text box by
reducing the internal margins of the text box. To do this, choose the
Format⇨Text Box command from the menu.

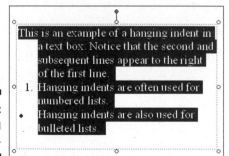

Figure 7-13:
A hanging
indent.

Using paragraph styles

You might not want to get into this subject, but many hard-core desktop publishers prefer to use text styles to apply text formatting. A *text style* is a named
set of attributes that you can apply to a paragraph. (If you've used a modern
word-processing program, you might already be familiar with text styles.)

I use text styles extensively because they are terrific labor-saving devices.
For example, if you want all your body text to be double-spaced, 12-point,
Arial italic text with a ¼-inch first-line indent, you can create a text style that
contains all those formatting instructions. When you then apply that style to
a paragraph, all the text in that paragraph instantly takes on each formatting

option specified by the style. If you later decide to edit a text style, all paragraphs that bear that style change instantly — it's quite the timesaver! So, most experienced authors, editors, layout artists, and publishers start the text-formatting process by creating a style sheet of all allowed paragraph types in their documents. Then they apply these styles to their work.

To create, change, rename, delete, and even import styles, choose Format⇨ Styles from the menu. The Styles task pane, shown in Figure 7-14, appears.

Start the style creation process by clicking the New Style button, at the bottom of the Styles task pane. Doing so leads to dialog boxes that direct you to the various character and paragraph formatting dialog boxes I cover earlier in this chapter. You can set the following properties as part of a text style:

- ✔ Character type and size
- ✔ Indents and lists
- ✔ Line spacing
- ✔ Character spacing
- ✔ Tabs

The Styles task pane lists the available styles — and shows you what the available styles look like.

Figure 7-14:
The Styles
task pane.

When you have your style looking exactly as you want it, give it its own name and then save it. The style is then listed in the Style list box, ready to do its thing for you at a moment's notice.

Has that moment arrived? Well, then, to apply your new text style to selected paragraphs, simply select the style from the Style list box at the left end of the Formatting toolbar, or change the selection in the Styles task pane.

Press Ctrl+Shift+S to activate the Style list box on the Formatting toolbar, and then press the up- or down-arrow keys to move to the style you want.

You might have noticed the Import Styles button at the bottom of the Styles task pane. Now, I write almost all my work in Word and import the text into Publisher. (Remember that you can also do editing-in-place with Word, as I explain in Chapter 6.) With the help of the Import Styles button, I can import any styles I might already have created in Word. Why duplicate work that you've already done?

Using the Format Painter

Publisher — like many other Microsoft Office products — offers the Format Painter feature. Format Painter enables you to copy the format of an object to another object. This feature is particularly useful when it's applied to text. It works generally with any object, however.

To copy and paste the formatting of selected characters or a paragraph:

1. **Highlight the text containing the formatting you want to copy.**

   You can select the characters or any part of a paragraph that contains the paragraph mark.

2. **Click the Format Painter button on the toolbar.**

   Your pointer turns into a paintbrush that looks like the Format Painter button.

3. **Click and drag the pointer over the characters or paragraph mark that you want to change.**

   The formatting is transferred to the selected text.

To apply the format to multiple selections, double-click the Format Painter button in Step 2. When you're done applying the format to your text, click the Format Painter button again.

Text box formatting

Two text formatting features affect entire text boxes:

✔ Hyphenating text

✔ Arranging text in snaking columns

Because these features affect entire text boxes, it doesn't matter whether you highlight text before you apply them.

The Hyphenation section, earlier in this chapter, discusses the Publisher Hyphenation feature. (Chapter 12 discusses this feature more fully.) In many programs, hyphenation is done at the paragraph level, but in Publisher, hyphenation is done an entire text box at a time.

In publications such as newsletters, text is often laid out in *snaking* columns, where text ends at the bottom of one column and continues at the top of the next. You can create snaking text columns by laying down text frames side by side and then connecting those frames, as described in Chapter 6. But that's the hard way of doing things. If you wanted to do things the hard way, you probably wouldn't be reading this book.

The easy way to do this, because the steps are so simple, is to set up multiple columns in a single text box (so that your text can snake through). To set multiple columns within a text box, follow these steps:

1. **Select the text box.**

2. **Choose Format⇨Text Box and select the Text Box tab.**

   The Format Text Box dialog box appears, as shown in Figure 7-15.

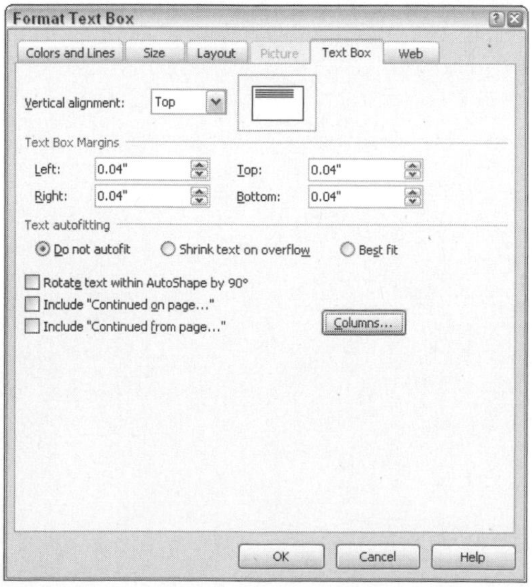

Figure 7-15:
The Format
Text Box
dialog box.

3. **Click the Columns button.**

   The Columns dialog box appears.

4. **In the Columns Number drop-down list, enter the number of columns you want.**

   You can have up to 63 columns in one text box.

5. **In the Columns Spacing drop-down list, specify how much space you want between columns.**

   Publishing professionals call this space a *column gutter.* The Sample area shows you an example of how your text box gets divided.

6. **Click the OK button to close the Columns dialog box, and click OK again to close the Format Text Box dialog box.**

   The text in your text box rearranges itself into multiple, snaking columns.

Publisher automatically ends one column of text and begins the next after it runs out of room at the bottom of a text box. To lengthen a column, try decreasing the top and bottom margins of the text box or resizing the text box.

To force Publisher to end a column before it reaches the bottom of a text box, place the insertion point where you want the column to end and then press Ctrl+Shift+Enter. This keyboard shortcut is the same one that Word uses to specify the end of a section, and this keystroke is imported from Word as a column end.

For nonsnaking columns, as in this book's tables, consider using table frames.

Chapter 8

Vintage Type: The Corkscrew, Please

*C*hoosing fonts for your publication is like decorating your house: It's great fun, and it's important in giving your publication a personality. Just as some people like Scandinavian and others like Southwest decor, different designers prefer different fonts. Although you *can* decorate your house with purple velvet wallpaper (don't look in my daughter's room, please!) or alternate orange and black paint on the bedroom walls, chances are that you want to choose more conventional design themes. The same is true in your publications.

In this chapter, I tell you how to buy (if necessary), install, and use fonts. Part of this chapter deals with the common practices that most desktop publishing experts recommend, and some sections give you the technical details, such as how to work with fonts, what font files are, and how best to use them.

About Type and Fonts

I was doing some consulting work at a client's office recently when I saw the most amazing sight: The client's secretary was busy typing a letter on an old IBM Selectric typewriter. Okay, I know — that isn't so amazing. The amazing part is that the typewriter was sitting next to his brand-new computer! Let's see . . . type a letter on this typewriter and choose any typeface as long as it's Courier, or type the letter on a computer and choose from hundreds of type-faces? Tough call! Of course, I smugly informed him of the superiority of the computer's technology over the typewriter. His response? "That old typewriter never locks up on me when the boss wants something typed in a hurry!"

Don't get me wrong: I like Courier. The widespread use of this extremely attractive font is a testament to its durability. I think that Courier's main problem is that it's overused. And, certainly, using the same typeface every day gets old fast, no matter how great the typewriter.

The point of this typewriter story is to introduce a basic typographic term: font. A *font* is one typeface, in one style. The print ball for that typewriter contained one font: Courier.

Of course, you can go out and buy other fonts for the typewriter I mentioned. When you need another font in your document, you simply replace the ball at that point and carry on. Compare that time-consuming process with creating text on your computer: On a computer, you can have as many fonts as you want, and switching to a different font is as simple as making a menu selec-tion. Until you print your document, you can go back and reformat your doc-ument to your heart's content — something that you would need gallons of correction fluid and unending patience to do on a typewriter. No wonder that those old IBM typewriters have been relegated to museums.

Font styles

The fonts used today come in four main styles:

- ✔ **Serif:** A *serif* is a small line that hangs off the upper and lower ends of the strokes that make up a text character. Serifs help guide the reader's eye, which is why serif fonts are typically used in body copy. (*Body copy,* or *body text,* makes up the majority of the paragraphs in a publication.) Examples of common serif fonts are Benguiat, Bodoni, Bookman, Courier New, Galliard, Garamond, Goudy, Jenson, Palatino, and Times New Roman. Many of these fonts are named after the designers who either created or inspired them.

- ✔ **Sans serif:** Sans serif fonts don't have serifs (*sans* is French for *without)* and are typically square and plainer than serif fonts. In earlier days, these fonts were described as either *gothic* or *grotesque* faces. They're more commonly used in headlines, in which a limited number of charac-ters need to be read. Examples of sans serif fonts in common use are Arial, Helvetica, Optima, Tekton, and Univers. (And, if you're wondering, it really *is* spelled Univers, without the *e* at the end.)

✔ **Decorative:** Decorative fonts are used to present letters in stylized form. Usually, they're thematic; a set of fonts may be created from pictures of jugglers and clowns or use cowboy motifs, for example. These fonts are appropriate for kids' birthday party invitations, and not so appropriate for your annual report to the Board of Directors.

✔ **Symbol:** This font style presents symbols as a character set. Chapter 6 shows examples of the Symbol and Wingdings fonts that are installed in Windows XP and Windows Vista. Vendors also sell symbol sets for maps (Adobe Carta) and for music (Adobe Sonata).

Fixed fonts

The first computer fonts emulated those found in older typesetting equipment or in typewriters. Each font was a single typeface designed for a specific size. Most of these fonts were designed as *bitmapped* descriptions (composed of a collection of dots), so they were called *bitmapped fonts*. You could install Courier 8, 10, and 12 on your computer in plain (roman), italic, bold, and bold italic styles, with one font file apiece for your screen and for your printer. You would therefore install 12 files altogether for these three sizes. What a mess!

As time went by, type vendors produced font descriptions that let you create a fixed font in any size from a single description. Now the use of fixed fonts is extremely limited.

Fixed fonts are usually sold in pairs that contain a *screen font* (used to display the font on your computer screen) and a *printer font* (used to print your text). In Windows XP and Windows Vista, an *A* icon in the Fonts folder indicates a fixed font. Choose Start➪Control Panel➪Fonts to see the fonts installed on your computer.

When you use a fixed screen font at the size it was designed to be used, the results look as good as with any font you can use. You get the added performance advantage of not having to have the font description *rasterized* (converted to a bitmap for display or output), which isn't much of an advantage in these days of very fast computers.

If you use a fixed font at a percentage that divides evenly into the size the font was designed for — for example, at one-half or one-fourth size — you also get perfect results. You can even get reasonable results when using a fixed font at two or four times its intended size. Your screen font looks distorted at other sizes, however, even though your printed material often looks perfect.

Some printers come with their own printer fonts. If Windows isn't familiar with your printer's printer font, it substitutes another font to display the document on-screen. Although you don't see a realistic display of how your document prints, it prints just fine by using the fonts contained in the printer. Most people have given up on fixed fonts at this point.

TrueType fonts

TrueType is one of two popular font formats. (The other is *PostScript,* discussed in the next section.) Unlike fixed fonts and PostScript fonts, TrueType fonts don't require separate screen and printer font-description files — Windows can use the same description file to display the font on-screen and to print your publication. Because the font information is contained in one file, you have half the file management chores as you do with fixed fonts and

TECHNICAL STUFF

Sizing up your font

You can make a font virtually any size you want. The size of a font is normally measured in points. A *point* is approximately ¹⁄₇₂ of an inch but varies somewhat from typeface to typeface. The normal font size used in correspondence is 12 points, but 8, 10, and 11 points are also common.

Remember that the size of a point depends on which font you're using. The size of 12-point type in one font can differ substantially from 12-point type in another font, for example. (The figure shows you samples in various faces at the same size.)

Not only do fonts have different vertical dimensions, but their widths are different as well. Font height is usually gauged by the height of the lowercase *x,* whereas the width is usually gauged by the width of the lowercase *m.* For this reason, a font's vertical dimension is referred to as its x-height, and its horizontal size is referred to as its m-width.

Serif fonts

Bookman
The quick brown fox jumps over the lazy dog. 0 1 2 3 4 5 6 7 8 9

Courier New
The quick brown fox jumps over the lazy dog. 0 1 2 3 4 5 6 7 8 9

Garamond
The quick brown fox jumps over the lazy dog. 0 1 2 3 4 5 6 7 8 9

Goudy
The quick brown fox jumps over the lazy dog. 0 1 2 3 4 5 6 7 8 9

Times
The quick brown fox jumps over the lazy dog. 0 1 2 3 4 5 6 7 8 9

Sans Serif fonts

Arial
The quick brown fox jumps over the lazy dog. 0 1 2 3 4 5 6 7 8 9

DESDEMONA
THE QUICK BROWN FOX JUMPS OVER THE LAZY DOG. 0123456789

Impact
The quick brown fox jumps over the lazy dog. 0 1 2 3 4 5 6 7 8 9

Univers
The quick brown fox jumps over the lazy dog. 0 1 2 3 4 5 6 7 8 9

Symbol fonts

Symbol
Τηε θυιχκ βροων φοξ φυμπσ οϖερ τηε λαζψ δογ. 0 1 2 3 4 5 6 7 8 9

Wingdings
✵〰♏❀ □◆✲♍&⚥ ♑□□•▪ ✗□⊠ ℯ♦○□• □✤♏□ ♦〰♏ ●⚽✆☒ ♤□Ⓨ◌🕮
◻ 🗀 ▤ ▤ 🗎 ⧄ ▤ ⑂ ▣ 🗋 🗷

PostScript fonts, which is a major benefit of using TrueType fonts. In Windows XP, an O icon in the Fonts folder indicates a TrueType font. In Windows Vista, an O icon in the Fonts folder indicates an OpenType font. OpenType fonts contain TrueType and PostScript font data.

PostScript fonts

Adobe PostScript fonts have been available since the mid-1980s. Most print services and professional designers favor PostScript fonts because of their high quality and large library of available font descriptions. An estimated 10,000 typefaces are available in PostScript form. (Sorry, but my editor won't let me list them for you.)

PostScript fonts come in two types: Type 1 and Type 3. The difference between the two types is that Type 3 doesn't contain special instructions *(hinting)* — that alter the appearance of fonts at small point sizes (11 point and smaller) to make them more readable both on-screen (if you have Adobe Type Manager installed) and in printed matter. Type 1 fonts (an TrueType fonts) come with hinting built in to their descriptions.

PostScript fonts require a special font rasterizer to convert them to bitmaps that can be displayed on the screen or printed by your printer. For a long time, PostScript fonts required a PostScript printer in order to print properly. PostScript printers contained a ROM chip which stored the PostScript interpreter that did the bitmap conversion for output. In 1989, under pressure from other vendors who finally cracked the technology of Adobe hinting, Adobe released Adobe Type Manager and published the specifications of PostScript type encryption and hinting.

Adobe Type Manager (ATM) displays PostScript fonts well and makes printing fonts to non-PostScript printers possible. Your computer's processor takes the place of the processor in a PostScript printer. Thanks to ATM, you can get great-looking output even from inkjet printers.

Choosing between TrueType and PostScript fonts

In regard to performance and quality, no one has yet been able to show me to my satisfaction that there's much difference — or, in fact, any difference — between TrueType and PostScript fonts. Of course, you get some TrueType fonts for free with the installation of Windows and other Microsoft products, such as Publisher. You can't beat that.

Here's the best advice I can give you regarding fonts: If you're an occasional desktop publisher, choose either TrueType or PostScript, but try not to use both. If you use both, pay particular attention to making sure that you don't use a font with the same name in both styles. In other words, if you set certain body text in TrueType Times Roman, don't set other body text in PostScript Times Roman. (It's easier said than done.)

If you're a professional desktop publisher, you might have no choice other than to use both typeface descriptions (TrueType and PostScript). The people who are my Gurus of Type favor PostScript type, largely because of the extremely large library of high-quality fonts available in PostScript, the fact that many print services prefer to work with PostScript, and the bias of many years of use. Desktop publishing professionals collect type like some people collect wine and toss around the same nonsense about flavor, bouquet, body, and other terms.

I remain unconvinced. I like the convenience of TrueType and think that PostScript is not worth the additional trouble of installing and using Adobe Type Manager or printing only to PostScript printers, except in those cases where a typeface exists in PostScript and doesn't exist in TrueType.

A primer on buying fonts

You buy fonts in sets. Fonts are sold, at minimum, as a single typeface, usually in different sizes and styles. Fixed fonts are sold as individual font files. TrueType and PostScript fonts are sold without regard to font size.

Initially, font vendors sold fonts in a general package meant to serve a variety of needs. The first Apple LaserWriter collection of 35 fonts in seven typefaces was this kind of package. A movement has been afoot for the past few years to sell fonts in related families for a related purpose. Now you can buy packages meant for newsletters, faxes, correspondence, or decorative purposes, to name just a few. Typically, these packages offer three or four typefaces in several styles. If you're font-minded (and who isn't, these days?), you can buy many vendors' entire font libraries on CD-ROM. The fonts on the CD-ROM are usually encrypted, and you need to obtain a serial number from the vendor to "unlock" the fonts so that you can install them. The vendor gives you the serial number for a particular font when you buy that font.

Buying fonts in families is an effective way to add to a collection. Most designers recommend that you be conservative in your use of fonts, so a collection of fonts in the same family makes sense. It's better to collect one typeface in many styles — even to collect special character sets such as Small Caps for a font such as Times — than it is to have an incomplete collection of several faces.

Without a doubt, font technology has undergone an explosion since the introduction of the personal computer. More and better fonts have been created in the past ten years than in all the previous five centuries of type design. I won't say that the best type designers are alive now, because that would be presumptuous, but I wouldn't be surprised if it were true. And, certainly, the most prolific designers are now out there working in their studios.

I want to mention some recent developments in font technology because they're important and valuable. First, several typefaces have been created that contain both sans serif and serif members. My favorite of this ilk is the Adobe Stone family, designed by noted type designer Sumner Stone.

Another development is the introduction of "intelligent font technology." Adobe has introduced the *Multiple Masters* typeface family. These fonts can be varied infinitely over a range through three or four axes so that you can have a single font description yielding plain, condensed, expanded, italic, bold, or different-size characters. These fonts require Version 2.6 or later of Adobe Type Manager.

Most computer stores and computer direct-marketing catalogs sell fonts in packages from one vendor or another. What you can find in these mass-market outlets are the most well-known and commercial font packages. These sources are adequate for the occasional desktop publisher.

For more complete collections of fonts, contact the font vendors themselves. Each vendor in the following list publishes attractive magazines with samples of all their fonts. Adobe's *Font and Function* appears quarterly, for example. The magazines also highlight new fonts that appear:

Adobe Systems, Inc.: www.adobe.com; 345 Park Ave., San Jose, CA 95110-2704 USA; phone 408-536-6000

Bitstream, Inc.; www.bitstream.com; 215 First St., Cambridge, MA 02142-1270; phone 617-497-6222, 800-522-3668

Esselte Letraset USA: www.letraset.com; 40 Eisenhower Dr., Paramus, NJ 07653; phone 201-845-6100, 800-343-8973

The Font Bureau, Inc.: www.fontbureau.com; 326 A St., Suite #6C, Boston, MA 02210; phone 617-423-8770

MiniFonts.com: www.minifonts.com

ParaType, Inc.: www.paratype.com; P.O. Box 3617, Saratoga, CA 95070-1617

PrimeType GmbH: www.primetype.com; Boxhagener Strasse 52, 10245 Berlin, Germany, +49 (0)30 53 09 71-10

Suitcase Type Foundry: www.suitcasetype.com; Tomas Brousil, Sobeslavska 27, 130 00 Praha 3, Czech Republic

If you still don't have enough fonts or haven't found just the right font for your publication, try searching the Internet. Use your favorite search engine (such as Google, Yahoo!, Dogpile, Excite, AltaVista, InfoSeek, or Lycos) to search on the word *fonts*. You will find more font resources than you can shake a stick at.

> # The Bézier versus the spline
>
> *TrueType* fonts are outline fonts based on the mathematical B-spline quadratic curve. These curves are similar to the Bézier curves on which Adobe PostScript fonts are based. Unlike PostScript fonts, TrueType fonts don't require separate screen and printer fonts. The rasterizing software in Windows contains the necessary interpreter to output the same file description to your printer as it does to your monitor — with excellent results to both. This is TrueType's major advantage; you have less file management to worry about with TrueType fonts.

Selecting fonts in your publication

In Chapter 7, I explain that you set the attributes for selected characters and paragraphs from either the Font drop-down list on the Format toolbar or the Font dialog box (choose Format⇨Font). Figure 8-1 shows you the Font dialog box again with the Font drop-down list open.

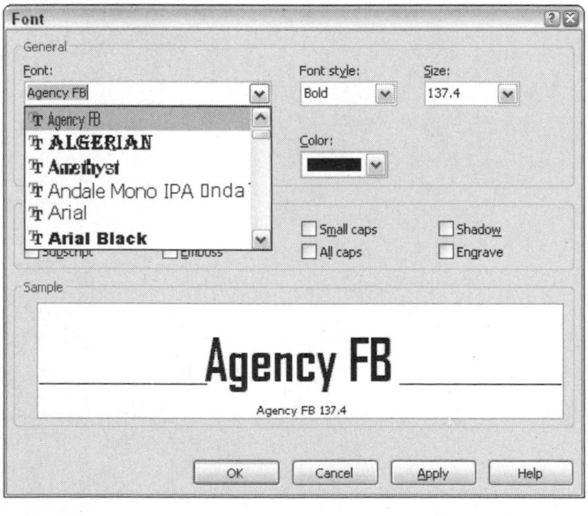

Figure 8-1:
The Font
dialog box.

Notice that when you select a TrueType font in the Font dialog box, it offers you four different font styles:

Regular	Bold
Italic	Bold Italic

You also have access to eight different effects:

Superscript	Emboss
Subscript	Engrave
Shadow	Small caps
Outline	All caps

And, you have 17 different underline options:

Single	Thick long dash
Words only	Dot dash
Double	Thick dot dash
Dotted	Dot dot dash
Thick dot	Thick dot dot dash
Thick	Wave
Dash	Double wave
Long dash	Thick wave
Thick dash	

You can mix and match styles, effects, and line placement options. As you might have figured out by now, the TrueType font rasterizer synthesizes these various options from the single TrueType font description.

Typography 101

I don't have room in this book to tell you everything about typography that you probably should know. Typography is a huge topic and one with a fascinating history. That history has generated more jargon than you can shake a stick at, so to speak — far too much jargon for me to explicate in any great detail. For now, though, a rundown of some basic terminology is in order. Figure 8-2 shows you a sample font with some of its features called out.

Most designers recommend that you choose a serif font for body copy. You can add some variety and visual interest to your pages by using sans serif fonts for headlines and subheads. A classic combination is to use the sans serif font Arial (also called Helvetica) for headings and the serif font Times Roman for body copy. This pairing, however, has been overused (as Courier has). For that reason, you might want to try other combinations.

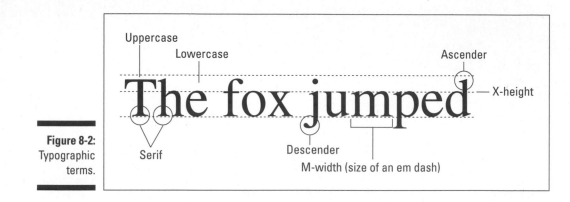

Figure 8-2: Typographic terms.

Consider using the 55 built-in Publisher font schemes for your publications. Each scheme uses two fonts that are designed to work well together and takes the guesswork out of it. Choose Format⇨Font Schemes to open the Font Schemes task pane.

The font you use for the body copy in a long story is of particular importance. That font colors your work and affects readability. Serif fonts have letters that are different sizes, which makes it easier for the human eye to recognize words. For this reason, italics, script fonts (elegant fonts with flourishes), and sans serif fonts are typically reserved for headlines or captions. Try taking a look at a page of body copy in several fonts to see which one works best with your piece.

The typographical size of a font varies according to its design. If you need to fit a lot of copy on a single page, select a compact font. Many leading fonts were designed for these special purposes. For example, the omnipresent Times New Roman font was created in the 1920s as part of a redesign of *The Times* of London. The intent was to make copy readable but very compact (the better to sell advertising space, my dear). Other fonts, such as Bookman, were created with a more open typestyle to make novels and other books easier to read. Most font catalogs offer suggestions for how to best use particular fonts and recommend fonts that go well with them as body fonts or display fonts, which are designed to grab readers' attention.

The one overriding piece of advice that most designers give is to avoid using too many fonts on your page. Too many fonts make publications seem cheap, poorly designed, confusing, and hard to read. We've all seen those "ransom note" designs, where each letter is in a different font. Most people's sensibilities are better than that — especially because we've been bombarded with well-designed printed material for our entire lifetimes.

The best way to impose good type practice in a publication is to create and manage your publication with styles, as described in Chapter 7. Or better yet, use one of the many templates that Publisher provides to give your publication a consistent and professional look.

You have a lot of control over the way the type on your page looks. You can use these strategies to adjust type characteristics that open up your text:

- ✔ Use bigger font sizes.
- ✔ Adjust letter spacing or kerning.
- ✔ Add line spacing.
- ✔ Add spacing between paragraphs.
- ✔ Use paragraph indents.
- ✔ Shorten the length of lines by adjusting the text box width.
- ✔ Change the justification of text boxes.

Left-justified text (refer to the last bullet in the list) is generally considered the most readable text and is the most frequently used. Right-justified and center-justified text are much less common and are generally used for special purposes, such as headlines, captions, and pull quotes. Fully justified text works reasonably well for line lengths of about 10 to 12 words and is commonly used in dense newspaper or newsletter pages. These methods are discussed in more detail in Chapter 7.

Display fonts are intended for limited use at larger sizes, to catch readers' attention. Using display text for headlines is a great way to pull a reader's eye to a section of a page. Often, headlines use larger and bolder fonts, display fonts, or some other special font treatment. Because the headline is the element that most people see first on a page, be particularly attentive to the selection of font and font size. Also, proper kerning of a headline is well worth the additional effort. (See Chapter 7 for details on kerning.) Be sure to adjust the line spacing of headlines so that the words clearly belong together. I like to use mixed casing in headlines unless the headline is very short. In that event, I sometimes use all caps or small caps. When I use script fonts (elegant fonts with flourishes) in headlines (infrequently), I tend to use them only in mixed case.

WordArt frames often give you an effective way of creating attractive headlines. (See the next section for more information.)

Another way to set off headlines and sections in your documents is to use rules. *Rules* are lines, either horizontal (for headlines) or vertical (for columns). The use of rules is very effective, and they don't even have to be thick. A single-point rule suffices in most cases except for separating the headline of your page. (Rules are also discussed in Chapter 5.)

No matter how much time you take in designing your publications, you can always learn something from other people's work. When you're working on a project, take a look at the best examples you can find of similar pieces and see which fonts were used, and how.

WordArt

Microsoft WordArt enables you to create especially fancy text objects, called — pause for effect — *WordArt* objects. Publisher provides WordArt frames for the very purpose of creating and holding WordArt objects.

To see how easy it is to create WordArt objects in Publisher, check out these steps:

1. **With your Publisher publication on-screen, click the Insert WordArt tool on the Objects toolbar.**

   This step opens the WordArt Gallery dialog box.

2. **In the WordArt Gallery dialog box, select a WordArt style and then click OK.**

   This step opens the Edit WordArt Text dialog box.

3. **In the Edit WordArt Text dialog box, type the text that you want to use as the WordArt object.**

   If you want multiple-line text, press Enter to create new lines.

   Notice that the Edit WordArt Text dialog box lets you select the font and font size and specify whether you want the WordArt text to appear in Bold or Italic format.

4. **Click OK to close the Edit WordArt dialog box.**

   The WordArt object on your publication page now displays the text you typed, as shown in Figure 8-3.

5. **Use any or all of the WordArt toolbar tools (see Figure 8-4) to "fancify" your WordArt object.**

   As you use each tool, the WordArt object automatically changes to show the effect you set.

   This step closes WordArt and returns you to Publisher. The WordArt toolbar disappears, Publisher takes back control of the menu bar and the top toolbar, and the WordArt selection handles go away.

6. **When your WordArt object looks the way you want, press Esc or dese-lect the WordArt object.**

Figure 8-3:
A sample
WordArt
object.

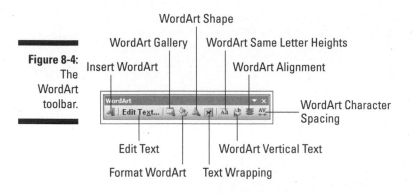

Figure 8-4:
The
WordArt
toolbar.

Take the time to explore all the tools on the WordArt toolbar. Table 8-1 gives you an overview of those tools and what they do. For more information about using WordArt, search for WordArt in the Publisher Help system.

Table 8-1	WordArt Toolbar Tools
Tool	*What It Does*
Insert WordArt	Opens the WordArt Gallery dialog box so that you can choose a WordArt style
Edit Text	Opens the Edit WordArt Text dialog box so that you can edit the WordArt text
WordArt Gallery	Opens the WordArt Gallery so that you can choose a different style for your WordArt text
Format WordArt	Opens the Format WordArt dialog box, in which you control how your WordArt text looks
WordArt Shape	Displays a menu of shapes that enables you to fit your text to a specific path or shape
Text Wrapping	Opens a menu that lets you specify the way the text in a text box flows around a WordArt object
WordArt Same Letter Heights	Changes your WordArt text so that all letters are exactly the same height
WordArt Vertical Text	Converts WordArt text to a vertical orientation
WordArt Alignment	Displays a menu that lets you specify the alignment of your WordArt text
WordArt Character Spacing	Displays a menu with character spacing (kerning) options

If you inadvertently click in the publication (but not on the WordArt text or any menu button or tool), the WordArt toolbar and the selection handles around the WordArt object disappear. Just click anywhere on the WordArt text to bring them back.

Be careful of your typing in WordArt. WordArt doesn't have a spell checker, and because Publisher treats a WordArt object as a picture rather than as text, it doesn't check the object's spelling, either.

Other Special Text Effects

Many publications use special large letters to start a text block. When this letter extends below the top line of the text, it's a *drop cap*. A large letter that appears above a line of text is a *raised cap*. Figure 8-5 shows you an example of each letter: The top *W* is an example of a drop cap, whereas the bottom *A* is an example of a raised cap.

> W e offer what we believe is the best martial art in the world. Taekwondo is an exciting and powerful martial art known for its dynamic kicking and hand techniques. Although these martial art techniques are centuries old, our programs are always evolving to keep pace with the rapidly changing world.
>
> A t Indianapolis ATA Black Belt Academy, we are not interested in just teaching self-defense, we are interested in the complete personal development of each student. Individual attention is a feature of each and every class, allowing all students to progress quickly and confidently toward their personal goals. Our instructors take their responsibility seriously as role models for younger students, teaching them the importance of strong

Figure 8-5: A drop cap (top) and raised cap (bottom).

Many people use drop caps in place of smaller headlines. Spread out these effects on the page, and don't put them on the same line as the headline. Typically, I try to use only one of these caps on a page at a time.

To add a fancy first letter, follow these steps:

1. **Click the paragraph that will contain the fancy first letter.**

2. **Choose Format⇨Drop Cap.**

   The Drop Cap dialog box, shown in Figure 8-6, appears. Notice that the styles under Available Drop Caps include drop caps and raised caps.

3. **Select the Drop Cap style you want and click the Apply button.**

   You can see the effect immediately because the choice you made is applied to the selected text in your publication. Apply as many styles as you want before making a final selection.

4. **Click OK when you're happy with your choice.**

   To create a Custom Drop Cap, click the Custom Drop Cap tab in the Drop Cap dialog box to open that tab, as shown in Figure 8-7. Publisher offers many options for creating your own drop caps, including font, font style, and color; the size and number of letters you want to stylize; and drop cap or raised cap options.

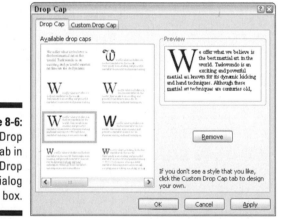

Figure 8-6:
The Drop Cap tab in the Drop Cap dialog box.

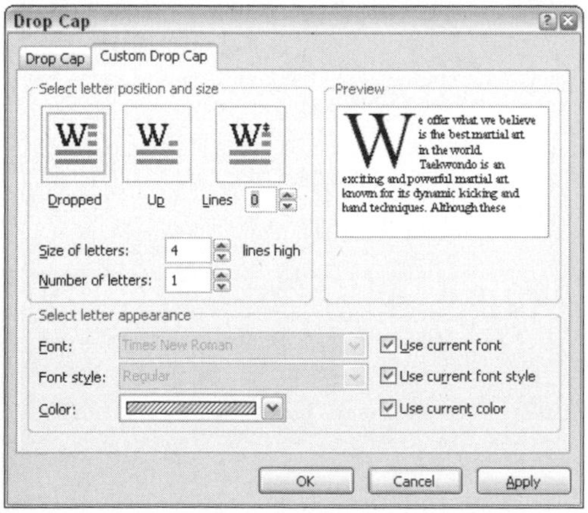

Figure 8-7:
The Custom Drop Cap tab in the Drop Cap dialog box.

Creating an electronic watermark

If you hold up to a light some expensive typing paper or foreign currency, you sometimes can see a *watermark,* an almost transparent image of a company logo, a dead king's portrait, or whatever. It's a very cool effect!

You can use Microsoft WordArt to create a similar effect electronically. Use WordArt to create an attention-getting message, such as Confidential or Important Notice, and then format the message the way you want. Then click the Format WordArt button on the WordArt toolbar. In the Format WordArt dialog box, select the Colors and Lines tab. Set the transparency to 70 percent or higher, depending on how dark you want the watermark to be. (You probably have to experiment with this setting. It varies, depending on the WordArt style you

select.) Click OK to close the Format WordArt dialog box. Lastly, right-click your WordArt text and choose Order⇨Send to Back. That's all there is to it! If you want the watermark to appear on every page of your publication, you can save yourself some time by creating the WordArt text on the master page. Choose View⇨Master Page from the menu or press Ctrl+M to view the master page. (If your publication has more than one master page, click the one you want to use.) Now create the watermark as just described. Click the Close Master View button on the Edit Master Pages toolbar when you're done.

If you do everything just right, you should be able to see the electronic watermark behind your other objects. Way cool!

Part IV
A Picture Is
Worth $6.95

In this part . . .

Okay, maybe a picture isn't worth thousands of dollars (unless you're Ansel Adams), but reading a publication without graphics or pictures is like listening to a basketball game on the radio. Sure, it can be interesting, but something seems to be missing. Microsoft Publisher 2007 lets you include graphical images in your pages to make them more visually appealing and to convey your message in a more compact form. In the three chapters that comprise this part, you can see the various ways of incorporating graphics as a design element in your publication. Publisher 2007 helps you import photographs, drawings, paintings, and even animated GIF files and video clips directly into your work with ease. You can also use a library of clip art or work with a library of design elements supplied by Publisher to create snappy, sophisticated layouts. Publisher 2007 makes it easy, and you'll find it a lot of fun to work with this aspect of the program.

Face it: Color sells. Color can highlight a section, set a mood, or perform any number of design functions. Microsoft Publisher 2007 lets you work with spot colors one at a time or create colors from the whole universe of colors on a full-color page. The second chapter in this part is a primer on working with color. You can see what colors are, how they're represented, how to match colors, and how to produce the best and most accurate output from the colors you want.

The third, and last, chapter in this part gives you a brief introduction to the Publisher 2007 Graphics Manager. You can use this feature to easily and efficiently manage all the photographs and illustrations you use in your publications. Although it doesn't let you create your own graphical images for use in your printed or online publications, it does a great job of helping you keep track of them and keep them current.

Chapter 9

You Ought to Be in Pictures

In This Chapter

▶ Creating and working with picture frames

▶ Getting pictures in and out of Publisher

▶ Finding and using artwork and images

▶ Using the Design Gallery and BorderArt to enhance your publications

▶ Working with scanned images inside Publisher

*A*t the risk of repeating an old cliché, singing an old song, or seeing an old saw, a picture really can be worth a thousand words. Why explain in dozens of paragraphs what an Aurora X-100 looks like when you can just show your readers a picture of one?

Although Publisher really isn't the place to draw complex pictures, it's mighty flexible when you're importing pictures created elsewhere. Some desktop publishers rely heavily on collections of electronic clip art and libraries of photographs, whereas others are daring enough to create their own pictures by using specialized graphics programs. Whether you're working from a clip art collection or creating your own pictures, this chapter shows you how to get pictures into and out of your publications and how to work with pictures after they're in Publisher.

This chapter also shows you how to use some tools that come with Publisher and Windows. You find out how to use Microsoft Paint to create your own drawings, use the Design Gallery to obtain publication elements, apply border art, and even use your own scanner from within Publisher to bring images directly into the program.

Understanding More about Picture Frames

Publisher uses picture frames to display graphics on a layout; a picture frame can contain either drawings or images. The differences between drawings and images are described later in this chapter.

You don't create graphics inside a picture frame; they must be created elsewhere. The graphic contained in a picture frame can be either a data file or an OLE object that's managed by another program.

You can create picture frames in two ways: Draw them yourself or have the program create them for you when you insert or import a graphic. Which method is best depends on your purpose:

- **When you need to place a picture frame of a specific size at a specific position in your layout:** Draw the frame with the Picture Frame tool (in the toolbox) and fill the frame with a picture manually.

- **When the content and size of the graphic determine the size of the frame:** Have Publisher create the frame for you as you import the picture. You can always adjust the frame's size and position later on.

Getting Yours

Publisher provides four ways to insert or import pictures:

- Copy a graphic from another Windows program to the Windows Clipboard and then paste the graphic into a picture frame.

- Choose Insert⇨Picture⇨Clip Art to open the Clip Art task pane, which provides easy access to these types of clip art:

  - Thousands of pieces included with Publisher

  - Clip art collections on the Internet

- Choose Insert⇨Picture⇨From File to import any picture that's saved in a format Publisher can recognize.

- Choose Insert⇨Picture⇨From Scanner or Camera to scan a hard copy of an image or to capture an image from a digital camera.

If you don't want to make a trip to the Insert menu to choose one of the commands in the preceding three bullets, you can just right-click a picture frame to display the context-sensitive menu shown in Figure 9-1. Point the mouse cursor to the Change Picture option to see your choices. The context-sensitive menu also offers the Windows Clipboard commands: Cut, Copy, and Paste.

I assume that you know how to use the Windows Clipboard (refer to the first bullet in the preceding list), although you may want to know more about which kinds of graphic formats the Clipboard supports. The other three methods of importing pictures into a picture frame are discussed in the sections that follow.

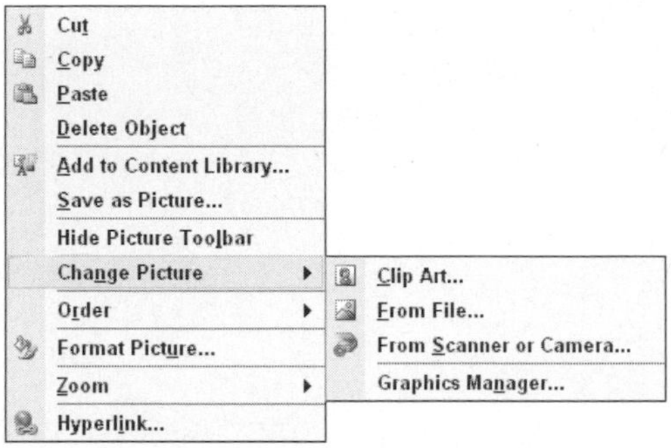

✂	C̲ut
▦	C̲opy
▦	P̲aste
	D̲elete Object
▦	A̲dd to Content Library...
	S̲ave as Picture...
	Hide Picture Tool̲bar
	Cha̲nge Picture ▶
	O̲rder ▶
✎	Format Pic̲ture...
	Z̲oom ▶
▦	Hyper̲link...

▦	Clip Art...
▦	F̲rom File...
▦	From S̲canner or Camera...
	Graphics Ma̲nager...

Figure 9-1:
A picture frame's context-sensitive menu.

No matter how you put a graphic into a picture frame, you can use any of the methods just described to replace that picture.

Using the Clip Art task pane

You can use the Clip Art task pane to search for clip art on your local hard drive, your local-area network, or on the Internet. Rather than choose the Insert⇨Picture⇨From File command to insert a clip art file, which requires you to remember the name and location of the picture file (files are stored in the Clip Art folder), you simply click a miniature version of the picture in the Clip Art task pane.

The clip art contained in the collection that Microsoft gives you are formatted as either .gif, .jpg, or .wmf (Windows metafile). A metafile format lets you save both drawn and painted images in the same file; .jpg and .gif are painted (or rasterized) formats. For more information about picture formats, see the section "Working with Different Picture Types," later in this chapter.

To insert a picture by using the Clip Art task pane:

1. **If you want to import the picture into a specific picture frame, select that frame.**

   Note: You can create a blank picture frame by choosing Insert⇨Picture⇨ Empty Picture Frame.

   Otherwise, make sure that no frame is selected. Publisher creates a frame for you in this case.

2. **Choose Insert⇨Picture⇨Clip Art or click the Insert Picture tool on the Objects toolbar and choose Clip Art from the pop-up menu that appears.**

   The Clip Art task pane, shown in Figure 9-2, leaps to the screen.

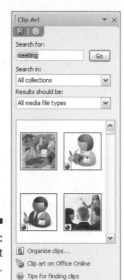

Figure 9-2:
The Clip Art
task pane.

3. **In the Search For text box, type a word or phrase that describes the clip art you're looking for.**

   If your search doesn't include searching online, the search returns fewer results.

4. **Choose a collection from the Search In drop-down list.**

   If you aren't sure which collection to choose, pick Everywhere. It results in the largest number of results.

5. **In the Results Should Be drop-down list, choose the media file type or types that you want to search.**

   Your choices are Clip Art, Photographs, Movies, and Sounds.

6. **Scroll as necessary through the thumbnails in the main pane of the Clip Art task pane and then click to select the picture you want.**

   This step inserts the Clip Art image into your publication.

7. **Click the down arrow next to the clip art image to see more options for working with clip art.**

   These options are covered later in this chapter, in the section "Using the Clip Organizer."

8. **If you want to recover some desktop real estate, click the Close button in the Clip Art task pane to close it.**

If you draw a picture frame before you import a picture from the Clip Art task pane, Publisher automatically resizes the frame to keep the inserted image in proper proportion. After the image has been inserted into the frame, you can resize it to your heart's content.

You can very easily replace the picture from the clip art collection with another picture: Just double-click the existing picture to reopen the Clip Art task pane. Click to select a different picture and then choose Insert from the clip's drop-down menu. You also can replace an existing picture by using the context-sensitive menu to open the Clip Art task pane: Right-click the picture you want to replace and then choose Change Picture⇨Clip Art from the menu that appears. (I find that double-clicking the picture is much faster.)

If you have other Microsoft programs on your computer, such as PowerPoint or other Office 2007 components, they share the Clip Art task pane that you use in Publisher. (In fact, you can access clip art from almost any modern Windows program, if you know how.) So, you might find more than just Publisher pictures there; you might also find pictures installed by Word or Excel or other programs.

Using the Clip Organizer

The Microsoft Clip Organizer tool is installed along with Publisher. The Clip Organizer helps you, er, classify (you thought I was going to say *organize!*) your clip art into collections. Two collections are created by default:

- ✔ **My Collections:** Stores any clip art collections you create
- ✔ **Office Collections:** Contains clip art and other media files included in Office 2007

In addition, you might encounter two other collections in Clip Organizer:

- ✔ **Shared Collections:** Created by a network administrator and can be shared by any user on the network. You see this category only if your network administrator has set it up for you.
- ✔ **Web Collections:** Contains, as its name implies, the collections located on the World Wide Web. Initially, the only collection in this category is the Microsoft Office Online collection, which contains about 150,000 clip art and other media files, free for you to use. Using the Web Collections category requires that you have a connection to the Internet.

You can do a couple of cool things in the Clip Art task pane and with the Microsoft Clip Organizer that many people never check out. One is to search for pictures by description, collection, or media type. Click the Collection List down arrow in the Clip Organizer and select Search. Now you can enter a keyword or description, tell Clip Organizer which collections to search, and specify the type of media you're looking for (Clip Art, Photographs, Movies, or Sounds, for example). You can even choose a file format for each of the media types to search.

Here's how to add pictures to the Microsoft Clip Organizer:

1. **Select the image you want to add and copy it to the Clipboard.**

   You can choose Edit⇨Copy from the menu, press Ctrl+C, or right-click the image and choose Copy from the context menu that appears.

2. **Click the Organize Clips link, at the bottom of the Clip Art task pane. (Refer to Figure 9-2.)**

   The Microsoft Clip Organizer, shown in Figure 9-3, appears.

3. **In the Collection List task pane, navigate to the collection that you want to add the image to and click to select the collection.**

   If you don't want the image to reside in any existing collection, create a new one. Right-click any collection in the collection list and choose New Collection from the context menu. Type a name for the new collection and click OK.

4. **Paste the image into the selected collection by using your favorite paste method.**

   You can choose Edit⇨Paste from the menu, press Ctrl+V, or right-click the collection and choose Paste Clip from the context menu that appears.

   Make sure that the collection is selected (highlighted) in the collection list of the Clip Organizer before pasting the image.

   Note: You aren't limited to specific image formats; you can select files in TIF, BMP, JPG, GIF, and other formats that Publisher understands.

   The Clip Organizer adds your picture to the selected collection.

5. **Using the Collection List task pane, navigate to the folder containing the newly added piece of clip art and locate the piece.**

6. **Click the down arrow next to the newly pasted clip art and select Preview/Properties to open the Preview/Properties dialog box, as shown in Figure 9-4.**

7. **If you don't like the caption and keywords you see in the Preview/Properties dialog box, click the Edit Keywords button and make any changes you want. Click OK when you're finished.**

8. **Click Close to close the Preview/Properties dialog box.**

   You return to the Microsoft Clip Organizer window with your newly imported image selected.

9. **Click the Close button to dismiss the Clip Organizer.**

It may seem like whimsy or technobabble to walk you through the process of adding pictures to the Microsoft Clip Organizer. If you manage large numbers of images, however, you'll find this process valuable.

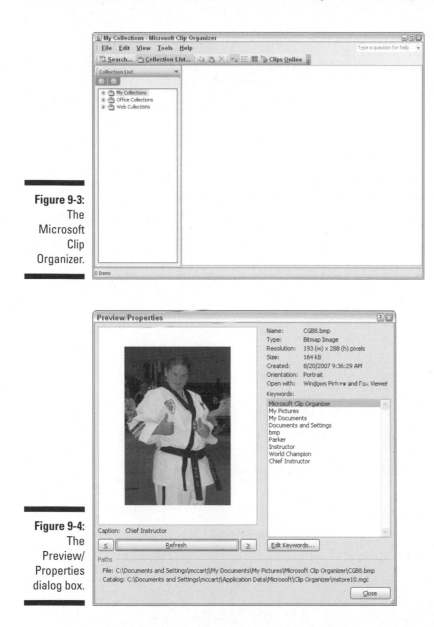

Figure 9-3:
The
Microsoft
Clip
Organizer.

Figure 9-4:
The
Preview/
Properties
dialog box.

One other aspect of using the Clip Art task pane deserves mention: If the clip art and images supplied on the Publisher 2007 CD aren't enough for you, check out the Microsoft Web site for even more. Click the Clip Art on Office Online link, at the bottom of the Publisher Clip Art task pane. There, you find additional clip art images, sounds, videos, and photos — more than 150,000 items! Any clips you select from this Web site can be added to the Microsoft Clip Organizer. (Need I mention that you must have an Internet connection to use this feature?)

By default, Clip Organizer and the Publisher Clip Art task pane offer only those pictures that are installed with Publisher and other Microsoft programs. Thus, if you create a picture yourself or obtain it from some non-Microsoft source, you don't find the picture in Clip Organizer (unless *you* place your picture in the Clip Organizer).

Inserting picture files

The Insert⇨Picture⇨From File command imports a picture stored on your hard drive into your publication. The Insert Picture dialog box, shown in Figure 9-5, shows the pictures in the selected folder. Use the Views button (in the upper-right corner of the window) to decide how the pictures should be displayed in the dialog box. Your options are Thumbnails, Tiles, Icons, List, Details, Properties, Preview, or WebView.

You might occasionally run across an image format that Publisher can't insert, but it's unlikely because Publisher supports many image formats.

To insert a picture by using the Insert⇨Picture⇨From File command, follow these steps:

1. **If you want to import the picture into a specific picture frame, select that frame.**

   Otherwise, make sure that no frame is selected — Publisher creates the frame as needed.

2. **Choose Insert⇨Picture⇨From File.**

   The Insert Picture dialog box appears. (Refer to Figure 9-5.)

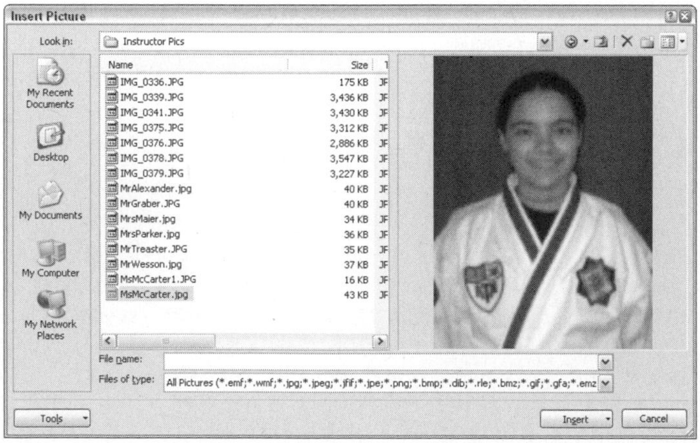

Figure 9-5: The Insert Picture dialog box in Preview mode.

3. **With the help of the Look In drop-down list, navigate to (and select) the file you want to insert, and then click Insert.**

   The picture is inserted into your publication. If you select a picture frame before importing a picture from a file, Publisher changes the frame to maintain the picture's correct proportions. You can always resize the frame later, either manually or by using the Scale controls in the Format Picture dialog box, described later in this chapter.

If you import a picture and later decide that you want a different one, just double-click the existing picture. The Insert Picture dialog box reopens. Select a different filename and then click Insert.

If Publisher doesn't understand the format of the picture you're trying to import, it whines: `Cannot convert this picture`. If you have access to the program that created that picture, try saving the picture in a different format. Or, if you can open the picture in any other Windows program, try copying the picture to the Windows Clipboard and pasting it into your picture frame.

If you import a picture by using the Clipboard and later want to change internal components of that picture, try double-clicking it in your publication. Depending on how your computer is set up, your double-click action may load the program that created the picture. Make your changes in that program and then close it. Your changes are displayed in Publisher.

Scanning pictures

Another way of importing a picture into Publisher is to scan the image into your computer or capture the image with a digital camera. Of course, you need a scanner or digital camera and some software to run it. Don't have one of these items? You can pick up a color flatbed scanner for around $50. Not that long ago, a scanner with those specs would have cost hundreds of dollars. (When I was a kid, I had to walk five miles through the snow, uphill both ways, to get to school. . . .)

Where was I? Oh, yes — scanning pictures into your computer. Choose Insert⇨ Picture⇨From Scanner. Select the device (scanner or digital camera) that you want to use in the Insert Picture from Scanner or Camera dialog box. If you selected a scanner, click Insert to scan the image into your publication. If you selected a digital camera, click Custom Insert. You can resize the scanned picture just as you would resize any other picture in your publication. (For more about scanning, see the appropriately named "More on Scanning" section, later in the chapter.)

Double-clicking an image that you scanned into your publication opens the Insert Picture dialog box. To replace the image with a new scanned image, click the picture frame and choose Insert⇔Picture⇔From Scanner or Camera. (I discuss scanned images in depth later in this chapter.)

Modifying pictures

After you import a picture, you can adjust it in Publisher in several ways: Resize it, crop it (chop off parts), and add some space between the picture and its frame to create a border.

If you want to edit the internal components of a picture (for example, to change a zebra's black-and-white stripes to purple and green or to add extra hair to a digital photograph of yourself — not that I have ever done this!), forget Publisher. You need to use a specialized graphics program instead. If you used the Clipboard to import the picture, you might be able to load the appropriate program just by double-clicking the picture. If that doesn't work, try using the Clipboard to export the picture to the graphics program, make your changes there, and then import the picture again.

Try using Microsoft Paint or, better yet, Adobe Photoshop Elements to edit your image. One of these two programs should enable you to open and modify most images. If you know the picture's file type, consult the section "Reviewing File Formats," the last one in this chapter, to find out which kind of image it is.

Resizing a picture

To resize a picture, you resize its frame. By default, both the picture and its frame are the same size and have the same proportions. You can resize a picture frame much as you would resize any other frame: by dragging any of its selection handles.

To maintain the proportions of a picture and its frame, hold down the Shift key as you drag a corner selection handle.

If Publisher distorted your picture when you imported it, holding down the Shift key as you drag a corner selection handle simply maintains that distortion. To "undistort" a picture, try using one of the Scale controls described next. (*Scaling* in Publisher is just another term for *resizing*. Scaling in snakes and pipes is another thing entirely.) The Format⇔Picture dialog box is also a way to resize a picture without using the mouse.

Here's how to resize a picture by using the Format Picture dialog box:

1. **Select the picture you want to resize or restore (or both).**

2. **Choose Format⇔Picture from the main menu.**

3. **Click the Size tab.**

   The Size tab of the Format Picture dialog box appears, as shown in Figure 9-6.

   You can use the same procedure to scale a WordArt object. Choose Format⇨WordArt from the menu and click the Size tab. The Format WordArt dialog box appears; it works the same as the Format Picture dialog box does.

4. **Enter Height and Width values in the Scale section to set the percentages to which you want to resize your picture.**

   These percentages vary according to the picture's original file size. Use the same percentages in the Height and Width boxes to retain the figure's proportions.

   If you want your picture to scale proportionately while resizing, select the Lock Aspect Ratio check box. Your pictures then scale proportionally while resizing diagonally. Holding down the Shift key while dragging a corner selection handle does the same thing as turning on this option. If you resize horizontally or vertically, though, the picture doesn't scale proportionately.

   To see the picture at its original file size, click the Reset button in the Original Size section of the Size tab.

5. **Click OK.**

   Both the picture and its frame are resized accordingly.

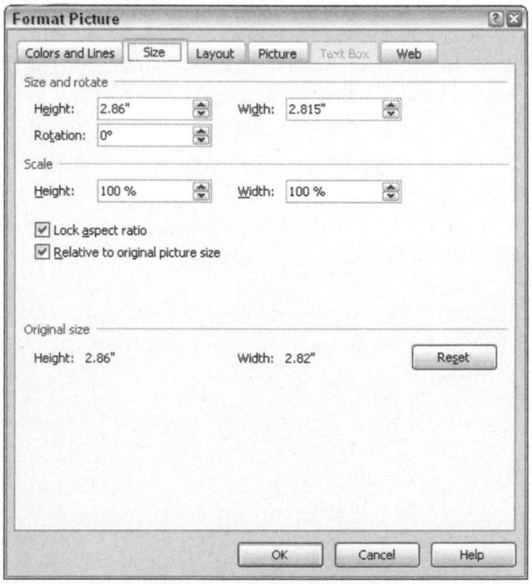

Format Picture

| Colors and Lines | Size | Layout | Picture | Text Box | Web |

Size and rotate

Height: 2.86"   Width: 2.815"

Rotation: 0°

Scale

Height: 100 %   Width: 100 %

☑ Lock aspect ratio
☑ Relative to original picture size

Original size

Height: 2.86"   Width: 2.82"   [Reset]

[OK] [Cancel] [Help]

Figure 9-6: Scaling a picture by using the Size tab of the Format Picture dialog box.

Don't forget that resizing a bitmap graphic lowers the quality of the image. You can, however, resize vector graphics (drawings) to your heart's content without doing any damage.

Cropping a picture

Publishing professionals who still assemble publications *without* using a computer often remove unwanted edges of a picture by lopping off those edges with a pair of scissors. In the publishing world, editing a picture in this way is called *cropping.* Why bother with scissors, though? You can use Publisher to crop a picture *electronically.*

To crop a selected picture, follow these steps:

1. **Click the Crop button on the Picture toolbar.**

   The Picture toolbar automatically pops up whenever you've inserted a picture into a publication, but if for some reason the Picture toolbar isn't displayed, choose View⇨Toolbars⇨Picture.

2. **Aim the mouse pointer at one of the picture frame's selection handles.**

   The mouse pointer changes to a *cropper* pointer, showing the same Crop icon as the Crop button on the Picture toolbar.

3. **Drag inward until you exclude the part of the picture that you don't want, and then release the mouse button.**

Cropping a picture doesn't permanently remove any picture parts; it only hides them from view. To restore a picture part that you cropped, repeat the preceding steps but drag outward. Regardless of whether you cropped, you can drag outward on any picture to *reverse crop,* thus adding space between the picture and its frame. You can also use the Picture tab of the Format Picture dialog box to crop images. Just specify the amount (in inches, by default) that you want to crop in the Left, Right, Top, and Bottom controls. If you want to add space between the picture frame and the picture, specify a negative number in the Crop From controls!

Here are a few more cropping tips to keep in mind:

- ✔ **To crop or reverse crop the same amount at each edge (thus keeping the picture in the center of its frame):** Hold down the Ctrl key as you drag a corner selection handle.

- ✔ **To crop in a more customizable, irregular manner:** Click the Text Wrapping button on the Picture toolbar and then choose the Edit Wrap Points menu option to create or modify the adjustment handles. (By default, Publisher enables you to crop in only a rectangular fashion.)

- ✔ **To resize a picture immediately after cropping:** Click the Cropping tool again to turn off the cropping option. You can also turn it off by deselecting and then reselecting the picture.

> ✔ **To remove all cropping and reverse cropping from a selected picture with the least amount of effort:** Click the Reset button on the Picture tab of the Format Picture dialog box and then click OK.

Working with captions

Sometimes, pictures aren't enough. They require an explanation. You can create captions for your pictures and have the captions move with their respective pictures across your layout. Unlike high-priced layout programs, Publisher doesn't automate the process of creating and renumbering captions for you. But you already possess the skills required to create a caption and attach it to a picture.

To create a caption, follow these steps:

1. **Draw a text box and enter the text of your caption into it.**

2. **Move the text box next to the picture and select both the picture and the text box.**

   You can select multiple objects by clicking and dragging the mouse pointer to draw a box around them. Or, hold down the Ctrl key while you click multiple objects to select them.

3. **Choose Arrange⇨Group or press Ctrl+Shift+G to lock together your picture and its caption to create a group.**

   Figure 9-7 shows you an example of a figure with a caption.

Figure 9-7: A picture with a caption.

Hey, that's it! What do you think this is — rocket science? You can apply another trick to make a caption even better. Select your text box and then choose Format⇨Text Box from the main menu. On the Text Box tab of the Format Text Box dialog box, set all margins to 0. Then your captions can get up close and personal with your graphics.

If you want a fancy caption, use a WordArt frame rather than a text box. (WordArt is described in Chapters 6 and 8.)

Applying borders and BorderArt

You can give your picture frame a border by using the Lines and Colors tab of the Format Picture dialog box or the More Lines option on the pop-up menu that appears when you click the Line/Border Style button on the Picture toolbar. If the picture frame is a regular rectangle, you can also apply BorderArt to it. (You can't apply this feature to irregular picture frames.) You can also apply BorderArt to text boxes, table frames, and even WordArt frames.

Follow these steps to apply BorderArt to a selected text box or frame (or frames):

1. **Choose Format⇨Picture.**

   The Format Picture dialog box appears.

2. **In the Format Picture dialog box, click the Colors and Lines tab.**

   The Colors and Lines tab appears, as shown in Figure 9-8.

3. **Click the BorderArt button, located in the Line section of the Colors and Lines tab.**

   The BorderArt dialog box appears, as shown in Figure 9-9.

   The BorderArt dialog box is one of those simple features that's so well implemented that using it is a breeze. Simply use the arrow keys to move through the list of available borders in the dialog box. The up- and left-arrow keys scroll up; the right- and down-arrow keys scroll down. As you scroll through the list, the Preview section displays the borders. This dialog box offers tons of fun borders for you to try, and you'll definitely enjoy playing with it.

4. **Make your selection from the Available Borders list box and then click OK.**

   You return to the Colors and Lines tab of the Format Picture dialog box.

5. **Adjust the thickness of the BorderArt border by changing the Weight setting on the Colors and Lines tab of the Format Picture dialog box, and then click OK to return to your publication.**

Working with Different Picture Types

Computers use two types of graphics: drawn graphics and painted graphics. The type of graphic you're using determines many of the characteristics of a graphical image displayed on your screen and the quality of its printed output. The two types use different file formats and require different types of programs for creating and editing graphics. But Publisher can work with both types of graphics, even in the same publication.

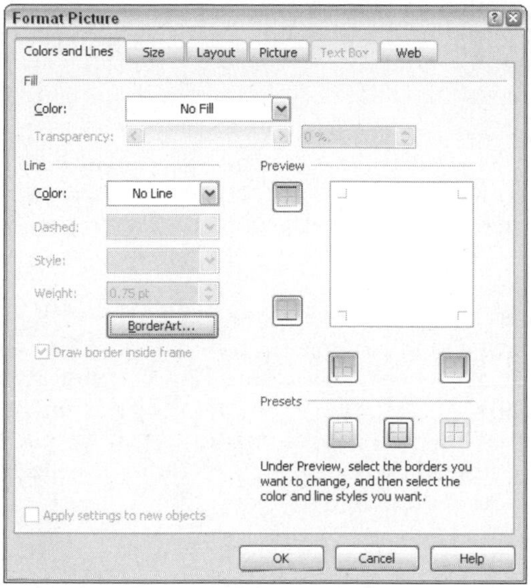

Figure 9-8:
The Colors and Lines tab of the Format Picture dialog box.

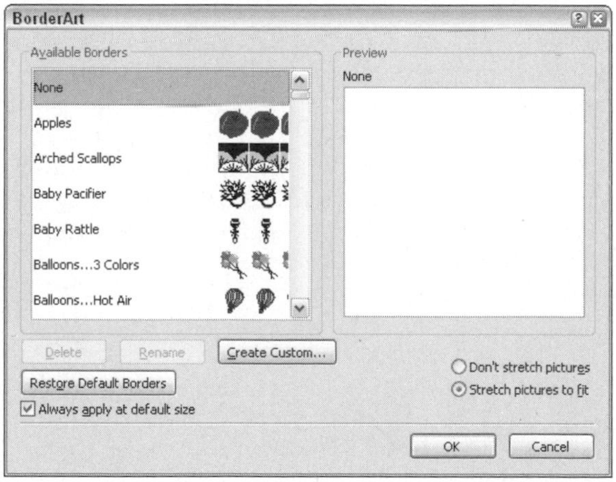

Figure 9-9:
The BorderArt dialog box.

Painted versus drawn graphics

Painted graphics are also referred to as *images* or as *bitmapped,* or *raster,* graphics. In painted graphics, the image is composed of a set of tiny dots (*pixels,* or *pels*) that forms a mosaic. The image is two-dimensional, although the manner in which the image is painted can give the effect of three dimensions.

A painted image is similar to a mosaic of tiles that you might see in a Roman temple. The smaller the tiles, the more realistic the image looks. The size of the tile — or in the case of a computer image, the size of the pixel — is the *resolution* of the image. This value is often given in *dots per inch,* or *dpi.* Because a bitmap is designed for a specific resolution, it looks good at that resolution. It can also look good at larger or coarser resolutions (smaller dpi) because you have more data than you need. Painted graphics don't scale up well, however. For example, a 72-dpi image that's displayed perfectly on-screen doesn't print well on your laser printer at 300 dpi.

Programs that create painted images are either paint programs, such as Microsoft Paint, or image-editing programs, such as Adobe Photoshop. I take a look at Paint in a moment — because it comes bundled with Windows, it's there for you to use, gratis. At the highest end of the spectrum, images can be photorealistic and can be rendered to show textures, reflections, and shadings. The file size of a bitmap image is directly related to the size of the image, its number of colors stored, and its resolution.

Drawn graphics are referred to as *vector* or *object-oriented* art. With a drawing, the lines, arcs, and other elements that make up a graphic are stored as mathematical equations. Because drawings are created in this way, they're resolution independent. They're calculated to display or print at the best capability of the output device — which is why they're referred to as *device independent.* This feature makes using drawings generally (but not always) preferable to using paintings in desktop publishing applications.

Here's an important point, though: Regardless of how a drawing is stored, it must be converted to a bitmap when it's printed or displayed on-screen. This process, referred to as *raster image processing (RIP),* displays graphics to any output device. When you "RIP" a bitmap image, the only conversion required is the resampling of the bitmap to either throw away or interpolate data from the bitmap.

When you RIP a drawing, the processing can be simple (for lines and simple drawing primitives) to very complex (for sophisticated descriptions of fill patterns). Thus, a complex PostScript drawing with many, many features and complex fills and strokes may take a while to calculate and process. These types of drawings may also require large file sizes — thus defeating their advantage over painted images. The crossover point is reached when you attempt to create a natural image as a drawing. This type of graphic is better stored as a bitmap.

Paint with Microsoft Paint

You can buy very expensive paint and image-editing programs as a supplement to Publisher. Still, if your needs are reasonable, you can create attractive bitmapped images (or edit the ones you have) in Microsoft Paint. Paint is one of the Accessories programs installed with Windows XP and Windows Vista.

To create a Paint OLE object in Publisher, follow these steps:

1. **Choose the Insert⇨Object command from the menu.**

   The Insert Object dialog box appears, as shown in Figure 9-10.

2. **Click the Create New radio button, select Bitmap Image or Paintbrush Picture from the Object Type list box, and then click OK.**

   The Paint OLE engine opens on your screen, as shown in Figure 9-11.

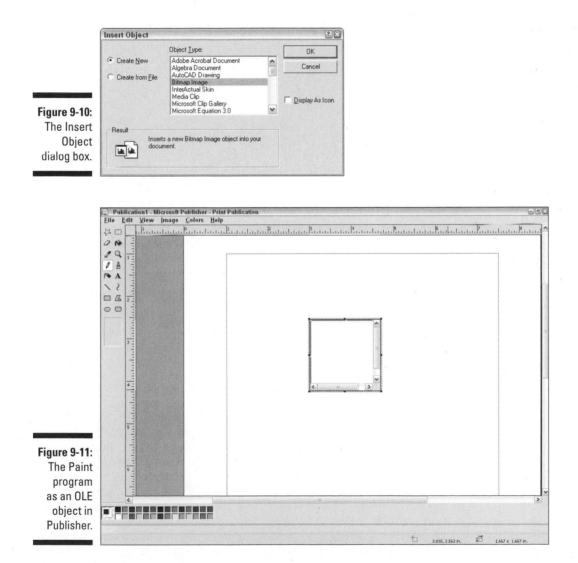

Figure 9-10:
The Insert Object dialog box.

Figure 9-11:
The Paint program as an OLE object in Publisher.

3. **Create your painting by using the paint tools in the toolbox on the left side of your screen and the color palette at the bottom.**

4. **When you're done, click outside the frame to return to Publisher.**

The connection of your painted object to Microsoft Paint is an intimate one. To edit the image in place again, simply double-click it. Because the image is part of the Publisher file, however, it doesn't have an outside, or independent, existence. That is, you can't open the image as a file from within Paint.

You often can use Paint to edit images from other sources. To do this, create a Paint frame on your layout, by following Steps 1 and 2 in the preceding step list. Then switch to the picture frame that contains your bitmapped image. Copy that image and paste it into the Paint frame. When you double-click the Paint frame now, it opens with your image in it.

Although Paint has many features and tools that I don't have room to tell you about in this book, you should know that it's useful for adjusting image colors. You might want to consult its online Help system for instructions.

Paint is based on an earlier version of ZSoft's Paintbrush, which was one of my favorite paint programs a number of years ago. If you open the Paint OLE engine inside Publisher, you need never worry about file formats. If you take the non-Publisher route to launch Paint, by choosing Start⇨Programs⇨ Accessories⇨Paint, you're limited to working with five (admittedly important and common) bitmapped file formats: BMP (the Windows native format), JPEG, GIF, TIFF, and PNG.

That makes Paint a good program to use to edit and print these kinds of images.

Draw with Publisher 2007

I have almost no drawing talent whatsoever, so I avoid drawing programs like the plague. I am, therefore, fond of clip art and choose collections such as the one that comes with Publisher. If you, however, can draw a horse that looks more like a horse than a cat, you might want to create your own pictures from scratch. Although you certainly can go out and buy a full-blown professional graphics program, Publisher has some helpful drawing features built in.

You use the Objects toolbar to create lines, arrows, ovals, and rectangles with ease, by first selecting the corresponding tool and then clicking and dragging in your publication. If that's not enough firepower for you, turn to *AutoShapes,* which are shapes that are ready for you to place in your publication. All you have to do is click the AutoShapes icon on the Objects toolbar, choose an AutoShape from the contextual menu that appears (see Figure 9-12), and then click and drag in your publication to create the selected shape. You can then resize it, color it, or fill it to your heart's content.

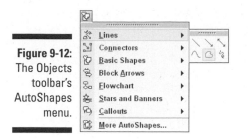

Figure 9-12:
The Objects
toolbar's
AutoShapes
menu.

The AutoShapes you can choose from are

- ✔ Lines
- ✔ Connectors
- ✔ Basic shapes
- ✔ Block arrows
- ✔ Flowcharts
- ✔ Stars and banners
- ✔ Callouts

If the list of predefined AutoShapes doesn't have what you're looking for, you can click choose the More AutoShapes option from the menu and browse the Microsoft collection of ClipArt AutoShapes. If you still can't find the exact shape you want, draw your own. Use the Freeform AutoShape tool in the Lines category to draw lines that have both curved and straight segments. Use the Scribble AutoShape tool to create a shape that looks like it was drawn with a pen.

Say OLE!

This book has presented three examples of using OLE servers in Publisher: WordArt (in Chapter 8), Clip Organizer (earlier in this chapter), and Paint. If you're reading the chapters in this book in order, you probably qualify as an OLE meister. But these examples just scratch the surface of the programs that are out there at your service. Many more OLE server programs get installed when you install Windows or other programs.

Before you know it, you have sound servers, video servers, coffee servers, and more. (*More* is the operative word here.) To see what you have installed in your system at the moment, choose the Insert⇨Object command from the menu to access the Insert Object dialog box. The servers are listed in the Object Type list box. You can then either create a new data object that will be part of your Publisher publication or you can insert an object contained in a data file. Typically, if you want other programs to access the data object, you should use the second option: the Create from File option. If you want to manage the object inside your Publisher publication, click the Create New radio button.

If you select the Display As Icon check box, as shown in Figure 9-13, you're telling Publisher to display the object as an icon instead of displaying the object itself. If you insert a Microsoft Office Excel Chart object and select the Display As Icon check box, for example, all you see in the publication is a small box with the word *Chart* in it. If you insert a an Office Excel Chart object and don't select the Display As Icon check box, the Office Excel Chart is displayed in your publication in all its glory.

Figure 9-13:
The Insert
Object
dialog box
with the
Display As
Icon option
selected.

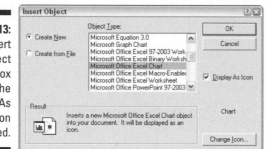

Microsoft Office Excel Chart is one of the OLE servers that you may find most useful. It can take Excel spreadsheet data and create charts and graphs from it.

If you insert a Clip Organizer object in your publication, then insert a Paintbrush Picture object, you notice that they behave differently. Whereas the Clip Organizer opens in its own, separate window, the Paintbrush Picture takes over the entire Microsoft Publisher window. The term *open editing* describes how clip art gallery loads: Each program displays in its own window. The term *editing-in-place* describes how Paintbrush loads: The object remains in place while the original program's window adjusts accordingly. In-place editing is one of OLE's newer features, so you see it more and more as you begin to use newer programs on your computer.

We are at the beginning of the era of compound documents or rich data type documents. Here, small programs manage your data within a file. Your publications will be all-singing, all-dancing wonders.

Using the Design Gallery

One feature you should definitely visit in your page layout work is the Design Gallery. The Design Gallery isn't a graphics creator per se, although it does rely on graphics in many instances. The *Design Gallery* is a browser that displays a collection of page layout parts you can use inside your document to create even more compelling publications. The original categories of parts you can use include Accent Box, Accessory Bar, Advertisements, Attention Getters, Barbells, Borders, Boxes, Calendars, Checkerboards, Coupons, Dots, Linear Accents, Logos, Marquee, Mastheads, Phone Tear-Off, Picture Captions, Pull Quotes, Punctuation, Reply Forms, Sidebars, and Tables of Contents. Then depending on the category you select, Design Gallery offers you many different styles, including Arcs, Kid Stuff, Marble, Nature, and Waves.

Follow these steps to insert a Design Gallery object into your layout:

1. **Click the Design Gallery Object button on the Objects toolbar.**

   The Design Gallery window appears, as shown in Figure 9-14.

2. **Click a category in the left-most pane of the window.**

   Design Gallery objects from that category are displayed in the center pane of the window.

3. **From the center pane, click to select an object that you want to insert.**

   Depending on the category you selected, you may have options available to you, as displayed in the far-right pane of the Design Gallery window.

4. **With your object selected, click the Insert Object button or double-click to have the object appear on your layout in a new frame.**

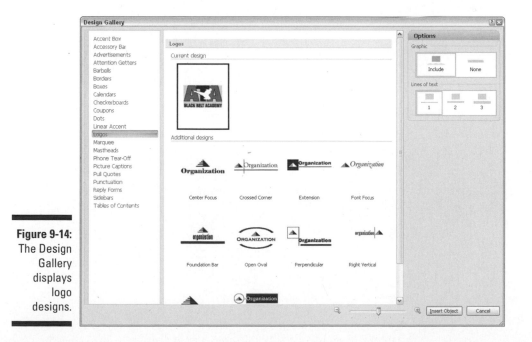

Figure 9-14:
The Design Gallery displays logo designs.

Figure 9-15 shows you a sample pull quote from the Design Gallery placed on a layout.

Using the Content Gallery

If you create something in your work or see something created by someone else that you want to save and reuse, that's easy to do. Just follow these steps to add the item to what Publisher calls your Content Library:

1. **Select the object or group of objects.**

2. **Choose Insert⇨Add to Content Library.**

   The Add Item to Content Library dialog box, shown in Figure 9-16, appears.

3. **Type a name for your new item in the Title box.**

4. **Select the relevant category check boxes (Business, Personal, or Favorites) and then click the OK button.**

   The object is added to the Content Library. Items stored in the Content Library are available to insert into any publication.

Figure 9-15: A pull quote from the Design Gallery.

"To catch the reader's attention, place an interesting sentence or quote from the story here."

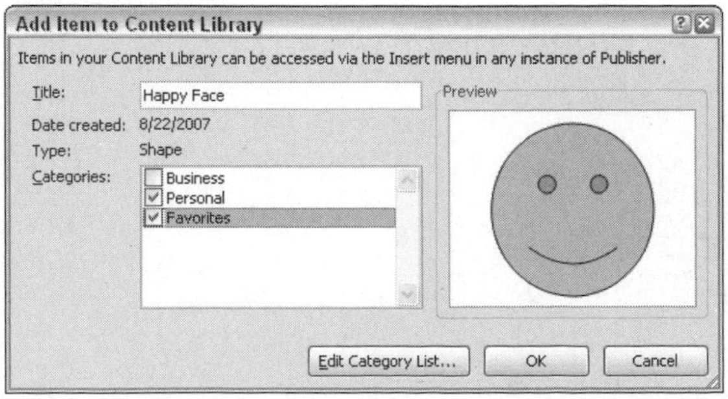

Figure 9-16: The Add Item to Content Library dialog box.

Add Item to Content Library

Items in your Content Library can be accessed via the Insert menu in any instance of Publisher.

Title: Happy Face
Date created: 8/22/2007
Type: Shape
Categories:
  ☐ Business
  ☑ Personal
  ☑ Favorites

Preview

Edit Category List...   OK   Cancel

After you have added objects to the Content Library, using them in the current (or any other) publication is simple:

1. **Click the Item from Content Library button on the Objects toolbar, choose Insert⇨Item from Content Library, or press Ctrl+Shift+E.**

   The Content Library task pane, shown in Figure 9-17 appears.

2. **Select the item you want to insert into your publication.**

   You may have to scroll to find it.

3. **Double-click the item, choose Insert from the item's drop-down list or click and drag the item onto your publication.**

   You can store as many items as you want in the Content Library (or as many as the storage space on your computer allows). If you have more than 20 or 30 items in the Content Library, you may want to use the Search features in the Content Library task pane to help you find the items you want.

   The Search options offered in the Content Library task pane are shown in this list:

   - *Category (the category the object is filed under):* You can edit the Category list by clicking the Edit Category List button in the Add Item to Content Library dialog box and then add, delete, and rename categories. The categories are None, Business, Personal, Favorites, and any category you created.

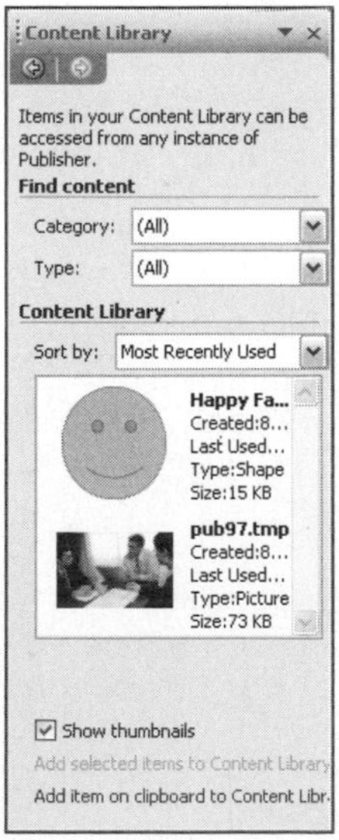

Figure 9-17: The Content Library task pane.

- *Type (the type of item that's stored):* Select a type — All, Group, Pictures, Shapes, Text, Text Boxes, Table, or Word Art.
- *Additional Sort By options (with cool search parameters):* Choose from Most Recently Used, Date Created, Title, Type, Size (Increasing), and Size (Decreasing).

4. Click the Close button to close the Content Library task pane.

Between the Clip Art task pane, the Design Gallery and the Content Library, Publisher gives you three very powerful methods for managing a collection of graphics and page layout parts to speed your work.

Tracking Down Other Picture Sources

With Publisher, you have just scratched the surface of available picture sources for your work. If you look on the Internet you discover an almost unlimited number of images you can use. Many of these images are freely distributed and of high quality. Most user group bulletin boards, for example, have graphics sections with images you can download. Many images that aren't free are very reasonably priced — or are free if you use them for non-commercial work.

Make sure that you check any downloaded files with virus detection software. Most services do a good job of checking files, but the Internet is wide open to viruses.

You can also find many commercial sources for images. I am inundated with e-mail from companies that want to sell me commercial clip art. Chances are that if a company is in the business of creating the images, the images that they sell are of high quality. If a company is in the business of harvesting images from other sources, as you often find in low-priced CD-ROMs, you can be less sure of quality.

Getty Images (www.gettyimages.com) has a tremendous collection of royalty free images. The Dover Publications image books (www.dover publications.com) are also excellent sources of images that you can scan into your publications.

Try to buy your drawn graphics in WMF formats, as they are the easiest to work with. If you need very high-quality drawn images, then use EPS graphics. (See the "Reviewing File Formats" section, later in this chapter, for more on these — and other — file formats.)

The New York Public Library Digital Gallery (http://digitalgallery. nypl.org) offers more than 500,000 images, many of which are in the public domain. For stock photographs, try FotoSearch (www.fotosearch.com) or ShutterStock Photos (www.shutterstock.com).

Inserting PowerPoint Slides into Publisher

You created a killer slide presentation in Microsoft PowerPoint and now you want to use some of the slides in Publisher. No sweat — follow these steps:

1. **In PowerPoint, open the presentation file that contains the slide you want to use in your publication.**

2. **Click the Slide Sorter button on the View Ribbon and then click the slide you want to use in your Publisher publication.**

3. **Choose Edit⇨Copy, press Ctrl+C, or click the Copy button on the Clipboard section of the Home Ribbon.**

4. **Switch to the Publisher window by clicking its button on the Windows taskbar.**

   If the Windows taskbar isn't visible, you can switch applications by pressing Alt+Tab. Hold down the Alt key and press Tab until the Microsoft Publisher 2007 icon is highlighted in the Cool Switch box that appears. Release both keys.

5. **In the Publisher window, choose Edit⇨Paste, press Ctrl+V, or click the Paste button on the Standard toolbar.**

   Your PowerPoint slide appears in your publication.

The slide you inserted can be moved and resized just like a picture frame. If you want to edit the contents of the slide, just double-click it. PowerPoint opens inside Publisher, complete with that new-fangled Ribbon interface! Make any changes you want; then click outside the slide to close PowerPoint.

More on Scanning

If you can see it on paper, you can get it into Publisher. The ultimate way to bring images into Publisher is by using a scanner. A *scanner* is a machine that digitizes images into bitmapped files. You can buy scanners that can read film or slides; you can also find related equipment for video digitization.

The most popular devices for desktop publishers probably are flatbed desktop scanners. You can get a medium-quality, full-color desktop scanner, such as a Canon CanoScan LiDE70 flatbed scanner, for about $80. This type of scanner creates files in 48-bit (full) color at 2400 x 4800 dpi. Images of this type are adequate for medium-quality magazine work.

You can also rent scanners at print services or have the service scan your images for you. In the latter case, the equipment that's used may be high quality, so expect the cost to be higher.

Scanners can create digital images in these four modes:

- **Black-and-white:** Creates images with only black or white pixels. This mode is suitable for images that are predominantly white or black and don't have much detail, but not for art with patterns or textures you want to preserve. This mode creates very small file sizes.

- **Line art:** Used for finely detailed artwork in black and white. Turn up the brightness level when you scan line art.

- **Grayscale:** Preserves any shades of gray in a black-and-white photograph or converts color values in a color image to shades of gray. This mode gives results of photographic quality and preserves patterns and textures. File sizes can be large but are still only a third of the size of color scan files.

- **Color:** Used to create images with pictures in full color. File sizes can be extremely large. Pay particular attention to minimizing the file size when creating these images and to making sure that the color fidelity is correct.

Many printed materials are printed as *halftone images,* in which black-and-white images are created with spots, dots, lines, or other repeating patterns. Because these images don't offer true black-and-white, they scan poorly. Scanner software often has special facilities to handle halftones in order to get adequate scans. Chances are that scanned halftones will result in images with *moiré* patterns (when two or more repeating patterns overlap each other and produce a distorted effect), which are quite unattractive. Often, you can avoid moiré patterns by reducing image size, positioning the picture in your scanner at an angle, and applying filtering to the image in an image-editing program. Then, if you're lucky, moiré patterns don't print. Your best bet is to avoid scanning halftone images, if you can.

Because large scanned images can take a long time to display on your layout and can make scrolling painful, Publisher has a feature that reduces the level of detail in your pictures or hides from view the pictures on a layout. You can also display pictures in a reduced form, which results in a slight improvement in performance.

To hide pictures on a layout, choose View➪Pictures. The Picture Display dialog box (shown in Figure 9-18) opens, where you can click the Hide Pictures radio button.

When you select the Hide Pictures option, your picture frames have an X through them, to indicate that they contain a picture. Frames without content appear without an X.

Scanners can be used to import not only pictures but also digitized images of any object: paper, marble, or cloth, for example. You can produce attractive and creative graphics by using scanned images in your work.

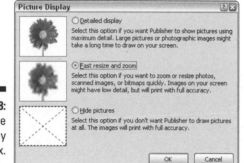

Figure 9-18:
The Picture
Display
dialog box.

Scanning is a complex topic that requires specialized knowledge to get professional-quality scans. I recommend one outstanding book on the topic of scanners and digital imaging technology: *Real World Scanning & Halftones*, 3rd Edition, by David Blatner, Conrad Chavez, Glenn Fleishman, and Steve Roth (Peachpit Press). This well-written book is technically excellent and was written with a sense of humor.

The most important concept you can remember about the scanning process is that you should scan images with the *purpose* of the image in mind. If you're scanning an image for screen display, a resolution of 72 dpi is sufficient. For a laser printer, you don't want to scan at more than 300 dpi; a higher resolution is wasted and can't be used. Similarly, although you can scan any image size to great color depth and your image can be reduced, doing so is a waste of resources. Use a color and an image size that are appropriate to your work. For example, an 8½-x-11-inch, 24-bit color image at 300 dpi (150 lines per inch, or medium-quality magazine printing at full color) consumes about 25MB of disk space! It pays to save.

For example, if you're printing only in black and white, scan in black and white. Or, better still, scan in shades of gray. You can create attractive results from 256 shades of gray, and create good results from 64 shades of gray, with enormous file size reductions. You just have to know the intended use of the graphics.

Publisher lets you directly incorporate scans by using software that supports the TWAIN standard. (TWAIN is scanner driver software that's installed on the Publisher Insert menu as a set of menu commands when the scanner is installed.) If your scanner doesn't support this standard, the From Scanner or Camera command on the Insert⇨Picture menu is grayed out. Even if the command is grayed out, all is not lost. Many scanner manufacturers upgrade their software, and you can check with your scanner manufacturer to see whether an upgrade is available. Also, third-party software that supports your scanner might be available. For example, the highly regarded VueScan software supports many common scanners and offers advanced features.

Reviewing File Formats

Graphical image file formats are a rat's nest of acronyms — a veritable alphabet soup. Unfortunately, you have to know something about each format in order to decide which one you want to import a file from. File formats come in three basic types: paint (or bitmapped image) files, drawing (or vector image) files, and metafiles, which let you store either type of picture. A file's extension tells you the format of the file. This section briefly describes the file formats that Publisher can import.

The following list describes some of the bitmapped or painted-image file formats supported by Publisher:

- **JPEG:** Files in the JPEG format take the JPG file extension. These high-quality color files offer advanced file compression techniques for reducing their image file sizes. Because JPEG is one of the best choices for full-color images, most image-editing programs save to JPEG format. You also find JPEG images in scientific work, and it's used as a standard file format on the Internet because the format is cross-platform.

- **Tagged Image File Format 5.0:** This format, also known as TIFF, is an industry standard file format that creates files that use the TIF extension. This format, created by Microsoft and Aldus, is openly published and supported. TIFF files are very high-quality images. All paint and image-editing programs open in and save to TIFF format. TIFF is probably the most commonly used bitmapped file format for printing from desktop publishing applications.

  Several variations of TIFF exist, so you can have problems opening TIFF files.

  Many programs, such as Photoshop, read one flavor of TIFF and save to another. If you're having trouble with a TIFF file, try converting it in a program such as Photoshop or a file-conversion program.

- **Windows Bitmaps:** These files, which are painted images in the Paint format, can be either black-and-white or color. You can open and edit these files, which take the `.bmp` file extension, in Paint. BMP files are simple files that don't use compression, so the file size on a high-quality image can be huge. They work well for lower-quality paint images but aren't commonly used for images.

TIFF, JPEG, and PNG files are the most commonly used high-quality image file formats.

You can import these two formats for drawn or vector images:

- ✔ **Encapsulated PostScript:** EPS files are written in the PostScript language, using plain text to indicate graphics and text with formatting. EPS files, which end with the EPS file extension, can be displayed but can be altered only by the creator application. You need a PostScript printer in order to print EPS files correctly.

  Although EPS files are sometimes saved without a preview file when they're created, and therefore appear as a black or gray box in a picture frame, they print correctly. EPS is a very high-quality format that many print services favor. You often find high-quality clip art stored in this file format. When you send an EPS file to a print service, it's complete — that is, it contains all the font information it needs and doesn't require the print service to set up its computer to print your EPS file.

- ✔ **WordPerfect Graphic:** This proprietary format is used for drawings inside the WordPerfect word processor and related products from WordPerfect (now owned by Corel). Otherwise, the WPG file format is infrequently used.

Publisher can import these three types of metafiles:

- ✔ **Computer Graphics:** This standard, which produces images with the CGM file extension, is widely used for drawn images and almost never contains bitmaps. CGM is used by many IBM PC clip art collections (and is never used on a Macintosh).

- ✔ **Windows:** This native file format for the Windows Clipboard creates files with the WMF file extension. Because WMF is specified by a single vendor (Microsoft), you encounter few difficulties with it. WMF files are nearly always drawings; rarely do you find a file of this type with a bitmap image in it. Many PC clip art collections now use the WMF format because it produces good results.

- ✔ **Macintosh PICT:** The PICT format is the native file format of the Macintosh Clipboard. In earlier days, the Macintosh was the source of many illustrations used on the PC. PICT files often contain either bitmaps or drawn images or both. Images are of moderate quality, and PICT isn't a commonly used high-quality format. The files take the PCT file extension.

Phew! I told you that the world of file formats was a rat's nest. Still, Publisher is blessed with a large and varied collection of file format import filters. All the popular ones are included, so you should have little trouble working with images from outside sources.

Image ethics

Pay particular attention to the source of any image you intend to use in your work. Someone created the image, and someone owns it, and the two "someones" aren't always the same person. Whoever the owner is controls the use of the image and can let you freely use it, let you use it for noncommercial use, or charge you a fee.

Don't be fooled into thinking that just because an image is a picture of something well known in the public domain (for example, a picture of the Statue of Liberty), it doesn't belong to the person who took the photograph. It does.

The Microsoft Publisher 2007 license allows you to freely use its clip art in your publications for your personal use. You cannot sell the clip art electronically as software, either individually or in a collection. Other companies let you freely use low-resolution images but charge you for the use of high-resolution images. You must check out the license that comes with the image. The problem, though, is that many images don't come with a license. In that case, err on the side of caution and use an image whose source and conditions of use are known.

Just to muddy the waters, an aspect of copyright law allows for the "fair use" of text and images in some instances. If you're using a piece of a document or an image for journalistic criticism, you're free to use the work of others. The restriction is that the piece you use must be a small part of the work and not something central to the use of the work. For example, you could use a still-frame image (but not hundreds of them) from a movie or a short video clip but not a long one. The fair use doctrine hasn't yet undergone long scrutiny of the law (something that could be said of much of current copyright laws). Each country also has its own copyright laws.

Chapter 10

Color by the Numbers

● ●

In This Chapter

▶ Figuring out what color is

▶ Using color in your publication to get your message across

▶ Printing spot colors or process colors

▶ Matching the colors on your monitor to colors on your printer

▶ Marking colors that cannot print on your printer

● ●

Color sells. What once appeared to be dull, listless text looks like super-text when you add color. Microsoft Publisher 2007 makes incorporating color into your publications easy. Some of its features can help you create effects close to those found in high-priced spreads you'll find in the glossy fashion mags.

In this chapter, I tell you how to use color in your publications. I also give you theories on color use and enough information about color modeling to get you started. I help you get more color in your publications for less money by explaining how to apply color in a cost-effective way.

Understanding How Color Improves Your Page

Which would you rather look at: a black-and-white photograph or a color photograph? A black-and-white movie or a color movie? Most people prefer color, even though black-and-white has its artistic merit.

Color creates highlights, blocks sections of your page, and draws the eye to important sections. Studies show that when color is used correctly, the average reader spends more time on a page and has a higher comprehension of its contents. When color is used badly — an easy thing to do — the average reader finds something better to look at. Studies show that, too.

Follow these keys to using color well:

✔ Don't go overboard when using color.

✔ Choose complementary colors. (More about this topic later in this chapter.)

✔ Be consistent in your use of color in a publication; use the same color for the same page elements.

✔ Create a *color scheme* — a set of colors producing the best impression — and then stick to it.

By following these suggestions, you help readers stay focused on the content of your page without being distracted by the color you put there. (If you think that these suggestions about not overdoing it with color sound a lot like the suggestions I made to not overdo it with type in Chapter 8, you're right.)

Defining Color

In technical terms, *color* is a reaction of the receptors in the eye, the optic nerve, and the human brain to different wavelengths of light. Color also has a certain strength, measured by the amplitude of its wavelength. If a color has no amplitude, it's black and you can't see it. Any color with a strong enough amplitude appears white.

If you mix a color with black, that color darkens and the resulting color is a *shade*. If you mix a color with white, the color lightens and the resulting color is a *tint* of your original color.

So far, so good. The color that an object appears to be is affected by whether the object is a source of light and transmits light (such as a colored piece of glass), or whether the light is reflected from its surface (such as printed paper). This feature affects not only the *range* of color but also its *intensity*. Transmitted light has a greater range and is usually more intense than reflected light. That's why you can get better scans from slide scanners than from desktop scanners that are scanning colored paper. It's also the major reason why output on your computer monitor looks great but printed output sometimes doesn't. Even great-looking printed output doesn't hold a candle to your computer monitor.

Color Models

I assume that your computer has a color monitor — a pretty safe assumption these days. Because a color monitor has to do a lot of the same work you do in trying to make your publication a smashing, colorful success (you know, combining all those shades and tints and ranges and intensities into a pleasing whole), it makes sense to take a look at how your monitor manages it all. To check out how color gets handled by your color monitor, follow these steps:

1. **Right-click your desktop and choose Properties from the pop-up menu that appears.**

   This step opens the Display Properties dialog box.

2. **In the Display Properties dialog box, select the Appearance tab and then click the Advanced button.**

   The Advanced Appearance dialog box appears, as shown in Figure 10-1.

Figure 10-1: The Advanced Appearance dialog box.

3. **Click the Color1 button to display the Color sample box.**

   The Color1 button is located in the center-right area of the dialog box.

4. **On the resulting pop-up palette, click the Other button.**

   The Windows Color dialog box appears, the holy grail of all color manipulation. (See Figure 10-2.)

Now I can talk a little about color theory and the various models of color.

Anytime you select color in a Windows program, the Color dialog box shown in the figure might open. Publisher tries hard to shield you from this monstrosity, but if you're working on a publication and you click "More Colors!" (as in "I must have *more* colors!"), eventually you open something that looks similar to the Windows Color dialog box, or selector. Oh, well.

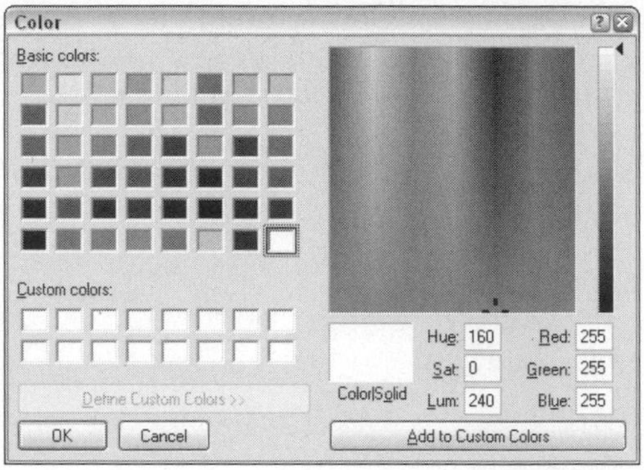

Figure 10-2:
The
Windows
Color dialog
box.

To select a color in the Color dialog box, click the color you want or drag the crosshair in the large pane on the right until you land on the perfect color. Whichever way you select a color, you see the values change for a color's hue (the Hue option) and saturation (the Sat option) in addition to all three values for red, green, and blue. *Hue* is the name of the color; *saturation* is the intensity of the color. The third value, which doesn't change, is the *luminosity,* or lightness. To change the luminosity value, you move the color on the vertical bar to the right of the Color selector box.

In one model, the HSL color model, these three values — *h*ue, *s*aturation, and *l*uminosity — uniquely identify a particular color. In the second model, the RGB model, any color is seen as a combination of three values of *r*ed, *g*reen, and *b*lue (the *primary* colors). Values in the RGB model can range from 0 to 255, thus describing 256 colors per primary color or 16.7 million possible colors in the spectrum. The number 16.7 million is one that computer programs and manufacturers often toss about.

Remember the color wheel? It's a representation of all the colors. (No, it doesn't *show* all 16.7 million of them.) Using the primary colors, the sequence around the wheel is red-orange-yellow-green-blue-violet.

You can describe four basic color schemes based on the position of the colors on the color wheel, as shown in Figure 10-3:

- ✔ **Monochromatic:** A single color on the color wheel. Monochromatic schemes appear uniform.

- ✔ **Analogous:** Colors that are close to each other on the color wheel. Analogous colors create color schemes that are soothing and harmonious.

- ✔ **Complementary:** Colors that are directly opposite each other on the color wheel. Complementary colors attract the most attention of all color schemes.

- ✔ **Contrasting:** Color combinations that consist of at least three colors that are an equal distance from each other on the color wheel. Contrasting colors are balanced.

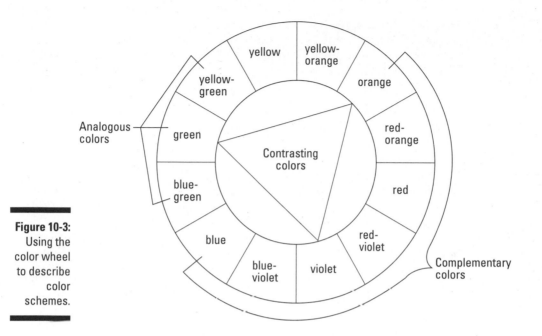

Figure 10-3:
Using the
color wheel
to describe
color
schemes.

I want to pass along some good recommendations for establishing color schemes. When using one color, create a monochromatic scheme by using that color's shades or tints. When using complementary colors, use one dominant color and shades or tints of its complement. When using contrasting colors, use the brightest color as a highlight and the palest color as the background.

Here's a piece of trivia about complementary colors. People who are color impaired are most often color impaired in pairs of complementary colors: Some people are red-green color impaired; others are orange-blue color impaired.

The RGB color model represented by the values in the Windows Color dialog box is a *computer color model.* That is, it represents color as though the human eye were a perfect measurement device — but it's not.

After having said all that about color, I suggest that you do yourself a favor and choose one of the more than 90 color schemes that Publisher offers, as spelled out in the next section. Microsoft spent a lot of money on talented designer types to come up with these color schemes, so there's no sense in reinventing the (color) wheel!

Perhaps the most widely accepted perceptual model of color was developed by the Commission Internationale de l'Eclairage (CIE) in the 1920s, based on populations of people matching a color to mixtures of three primary colors. The results of this model are probably the most accurate indication of true perceived color that we now have. In the *CIE space model,* similar colors appear near each other, and the CIE space looks like a set of hyperbolas with white at the center. Any paint or ink vendor worth its salt calibrates colors to one CIE space or another. Most advanced computer color-matching schemes are based on CIE space as well.

Changing the Color Scheme

A *color scheme* is a set of colors associated with a publication. Publisher comes with more than 90 color-coordinated color schemes. The easiest way to change the color scheme is from the Publisher Tasks pane. If the Publisher Tasks pane isn't showing, choose View⇨Task Pane from the main menu or press Ctrl+F1 to display it. Click the Format Publication down arrow and select Color Schemes from the list, as shown in Figure 10-4. As soon as you click on a color scheme, it's applied to your publication.

If you don't find any of the more than 90 color schemes to your liking, you're free to create one (or more) of your own. On the Color Schemes tab of the Format Publication task pane, click the Create New Color Scheme link. In the Create New Color Scheme dialog box, shown in Figure 10-5, select your favorite colors. The Preview and Sample areas give you an idea of the potential impact of your new color scheme. Type a name in the Color Scheme Name text box and click the Save button. Your new color scheme appears in the color scheme list in the task pane.

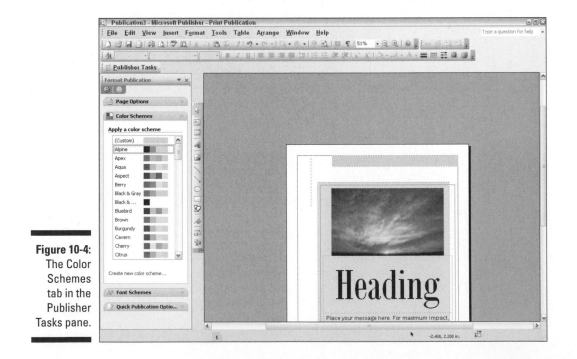

Figure 10-4: The Color Schemes tab in the Publisher Tasks pane.

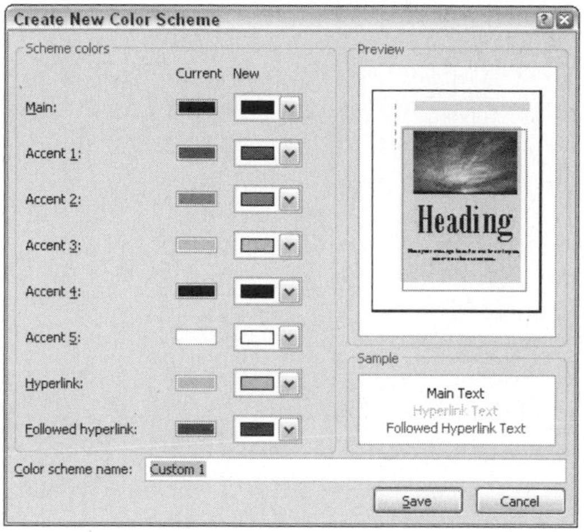

Create New Color Scheme

Scheme colors

	Current	New
Main:		
Accent 1:		
Accent 2:		
Accent 3:		
Accent 4:		
Accent 5:		
Hyperlink:		
Followed hyperlink:		

Color scheme name: Custom 1

Preview

Heading

Sample

Main Text
Hyperlink Text
Followed Hyperlink Text

Save   Cancel

Figure 10-5:
Find your true colors with the Create New Color Scheme dialog box.

Printing in Color

Printers can print color in one of two ways: by using a specific colored ink or by creating a color using a mixture of other colors. To assign color in a computer program, you specify a color as either a specific ink *(spot color)* or a process mixture *(process color).* You can use either, neither, or both in your work.

To print color correctly, you have to tell Publisher which print process you'll use — spot color or process color — and the printer you'll use. Publisher lets you print to a desktop color printer using a printer driver at any resolution offered by the printer (600 dpi, or *dots per inch*, is common, but 1200 dpi is probably more standard and even higher dpi (2400 dpi) is offered on some desktop laser printers.)

If you're creating a print-to-disk file for your local copy shop or commercial printer, you need to find out whether the shop has any special requirements. Ask your commercial printer to loan you a copy of its printer driver to work with, if you don't already have it. (Windows ships with many types of printer drivers.) Printer drivers affect not only color fidelity but also margins and other features. See Chapter 13 for more about printer drivers.

Publisher also has a Commercial Printing option. Using this option, you can specify process color or spot color. Spot color can print at high resolution, which can be 1,200 dpi or higher. (High-resolution image setters go as high as 2,800 dpi, and 2,400 dpi is common.) Process color, on the other hand, prints at medium resolution. I have more to say on this topic in Chapter 13.

Process color (full-color) printing

Publisher refers to process color printing as *full-color printing* and supports output to color printers to any resolution offered by the printer. With process color selected in the Color Printing dialog box (choosing Tools⇨Commercial Printing Tools ⇨Color Printing gets you there), you see eight colors in the Color palette of the Font Color, Fill Color, and Line Color toolbar buttons. If that isn't enough, you can click the More Colors button. The Colors dialog box then appears with the Standard colors tab selected. In that mode, you see 12 shades of seven colors (purple, blue, green, yellow, orange, red, and black).

Figure 10-6 shows the Standard color selections. If you use the Custom tab, you see all the colors that Windows makes possible in Publisher, as shown in Figure 10-7.

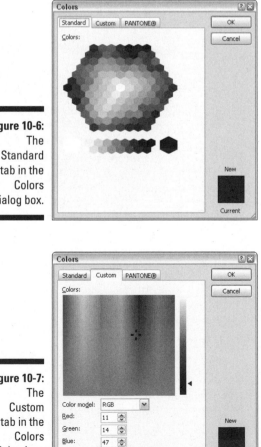

Figure 10-6:
The
Standard
tab in the
Colors
dialog box.

Figure 10-7:
The
Custom
tab in the
Colors
dialog box.

You can create colors with *gradient* patterns (colors that vary from light to dark or from one color to another in steps) by making selections from the Gradient tab of the Fill Effects dialog box. Doing so creates striking results.

Because of imperfections in the properties of CMY (*c*yan, *m*agenta, and *y*ellow) inks, they don't blend to form black. Instead, you get a dark brown. For this reason, and because this color, referred to as *process black* or *composite black*, requires more ink than most papers can absorb, black ink is used as a fourth color.

Process color can be applied in two ways:

- Inks are applied one on top of another and blended into a *contone,* or *con*tinuous *tone,* image.
- Color spots are placed side by side to create a halftone pattern. With well-crafted halftone patterns, the viewer's mind blends the colored spots to create the color.

Spot color printing

With the Spot Color option selected for an outside printer in the Color Printing dialog box (choosing Tools➪Commercial Printing Tools ➪Color Printing gets you there), you can see only black, shades of gray, and your selected spot colors in the Color palette. (See Figure 10-8 for a view of the Fill Color palette.) (Okay, you can't really see the colors in the figures, but the top two rows are blues, the next two are grays; the following are whites, and the bottom two rows are shades of black.) Note that the same palette appears under the Font Color and Line Color buttons on the toolbar. In either case, your selection of colors is always the same.

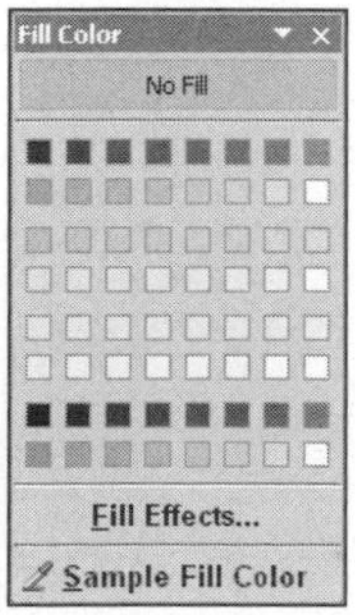

Figure 10-8:
The Fill
Color
dialog box.

A spot color adds an additional color to the black ink that's normally used in printing. Adding a single spot color to black is referred to as *two-color* printing because black ink is also a color. Some commercial print equipment can print two, three, or four colors, including black, in a print run. You can specify any number of spot colors, but because each color must be set up by your printer service, it may be more cost effective at some point to switch to full-color (or process color) printing. (Publisher recommends that you consider process color at the two-color stage, which is probably too conservative.) The number of copies being printed is also a factor in whether to use spot color or process color. Discuss color options with your commercial printer for the best deal.

When you use spot colors, you have the opportunity to mix your color with blacks (shades) or whites (tints) and thus extend the range of colors. You can also replace black ink with another color and use colored paper rather than white to further introduce color into your work. Be careful, though, because the color and quality of the paper affects the appearance of the color of the inks.

One Publisher option lets you print color separations as proof pages that you can hand to your printer when you use spot color. *Proof pages* serve as a check to see that color is being applied to your document in the right places for each colored ink; the term *separations* refers to the fact that each proof is a separate color. Each spot color is printed as a separate sheet in black, as is the color black itself. To enable this option, select Separations in the Print Colors As drop-down list in the Advanced Printer Setup dialog box before a print run.

To select Separations in the Print Color As drop-down list, you must have a color PostScript printer selected and use the Commercial Printing option with Spot Color selected.

Because of the high cost of full-color printing, I nearly always prefer spot color to process color. You can get good results by printing spot colors at high resolution and making good use of shades and tints. I often substitute another color for black ink and use colored paper for an additional color.

Color Matching

Every device that can display color also has a range of colors, or *color gamut,* it can create. Computer monitors have a color gamut, as do desktop scanners and printers. Because color monitors emit light, their color gamut is larger than the color gamut of printers. That's why the color that prints on your color printer often doesn't match the color you see on your color monitor. *Color matching* is a process that attempts to match the colors on one device to the nearest color available on another. The results are often less than satisfying.

Matching process color

Your computer monitor likely displays fewer than 16.7 million colors, and therefore, a number of colors are unavailable on your screen. Windows shows an unavailable color as a dithered pattern of two colors in the Color sample box in All Colors mode in the Color dialog box. The nearest pure color is displayed in the Solid color sample box. Dithered color happens quite a lot if your system (like mine) has 256 on-screen colors.

When the object can be displayed in the dithered, or *true,* color you have selected, Publisher does so. Colored text and objects with fill patterns cannot use dithered color (the text and fill patterns would *drop out* — be invisible to the eye); for those objects, Publisher uses the closest matching color.

In some printing processes, different-color inks are applied one on top of the other to produce a color of any kind. Three inks are used to create process colors: *c*yan, *m*agenta, and *y*ellow (CMY). These complementary colors should theoretically result in a process black (but don't, as I noted earlier).

Even when the color values on a monitor exactly match what a printer is capable of, printed color output often looks pale and washed out in comparison. Most times, special paper made for a particular printer dramatically improves print quality. Ask your printer service what paper options you might have.

Most print shops correct a publication for poor color, *if* you have made it clear that color matching is important. You should have reasonable expectations, though.

Matching spot color

If you print a spot color, you see a color that's uniform but perhaps not exactly the color you intended. If you need to match a particular spot color exactly, you must specify it by using a color matching system, available with many computer programs.

Several color paint matching systems are in use; the best known is Pantone. The Pantone company (www.pantone.com) produces about 1,100 standard color swatches that printers can match their printing to. Many ink manufacturing companies match their inks to Pantone colors. Publisher includes a Pantone tab in the Colors dialog box. The Pantone Color Matching system is recognized all over the world as *the* standard for describing color. Using colors from the Pantone tab of the Colors dialog box (see Figure 10-9) helps ensure that colors you want in your publication are the colors your commercial printer produces. I know that this concept seems simple, but keep in mind that your idea of 'blue' may not coincide exactly with someone else's.

You can buy a swatch book of Pantone inks at design retail stores and from most desktop publishing catalogs. With swatch book in hand, you can select the Pantone color you want and mark that color on each separation. Give those marked pages to your printer, and that should do the trick.

When you specify that a color in a publication should be a Pantone match, the printing service must match that color as part of its contract with you. The results vary, but not nearly as much as when you specify process color printing. Expect to pay more for Pantone inks because of the extra care that's necessary in their preparation.

I prefer Pantone colors to custom colors that your printer can blend. Custom colors are cheaper, however, and may be worthwhile if you don't mind some variance from print run to print run. Custom colors work best when you perform a single print run and don't have to do any matching.

Pantone has created a computer matching system that breaks apart standard colors into component inks so that they can be created with process inks. In the past, some programs (such as Adobe Illustrator) could specify Pantone inks in terms of their color values. Now Publisher offers the same functionality. Pantone uses a mixture of as many as seven ink color components to do its color matching. Pantone isn't the only matching system, just the most commonly used.

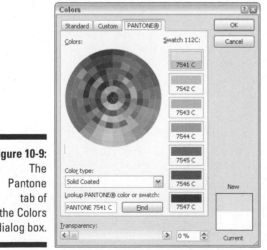

Figure 10-9:
The Pantone tab of the Colors dialog box.

Chapter 11

Grappling with Graphics Manager

In This Chapter

▶ Accessing Graphics Manager

▶ Finding pictures in your publication

▶ Working with embedded pictures

▶ Changing the way pictures are displayed

▶ Showing picture details

Microsoft Publisher 2007 provides a tool — the Graphics Manager task pane — for managing all the pictures in your publication. You can use the task pane to view a list of all publication pictures by name, page, file type, or even picture status. If that weren't neat enough, you can also use Graphics Manager to convert a linked image to an embedded image. You can even save an embedded image as a linked image and then save it as a new file.

Graphics Manager is pretty handy, but it can't do everything. First and foremost, it doesn't let you create pictures for your publication. If you used a previous version of Publisher, you might remember that the program used to have the Microsoft PhotoDraw program, which, unfortunately, is no longer available. Graphics Manager also doesn't help you manage OLE objects because OLE objects are now created and managed by other programs from within Publisher. And, going down the list of Publisher objects, Graphics Manager doesn't help you with AutoShapes, WordArt, BorderArt, or pattern fills, either.

Enough already with what Graphics Manager doesn't do. Let's take a look at the things it does.

Summoning the Graphics Manager Task Pane

Bringing the Graphics Manager task pane to life isn't difficult. Follow these steps:

1. **If the Publisher task pane isn't visible, choose View⟹Task Pane from the main menu or press Ctrl+F1.**

   The Task Pane opens to the Format Publication task pane or to the task pane most recently opened.

2. **Click the down arrow in the upper-right corner of the task pane to release the drop-down menu and then choose Graphics Manager.**

   The Graphics Manager task pane appears in Thumbnail view, as shown in Figure 11-1.

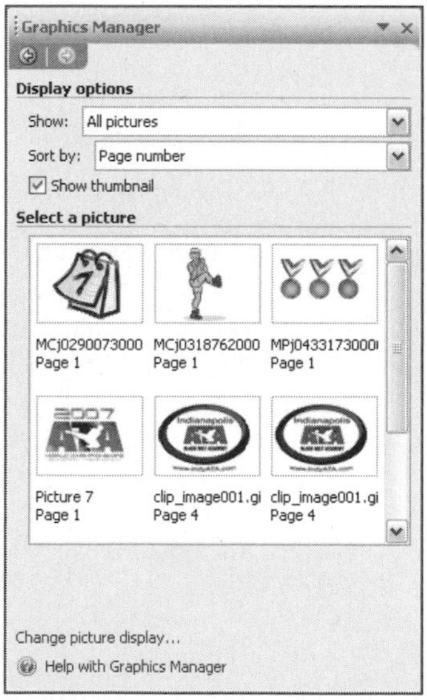

Figure 11-1: The Graphics Manager task pane in Thumbnail view.

After the Graphics Manager task pane appears, you can undock it from the side of the screen by pointing the mouse cursor to the left side of the task pane's title bar. When the cursor changes to a four-way arrow, you can drag the Graphics Manager task pane anywhere you want on the screen.

You can resize the Graphics Manager task pane when it's undocked by first pointing to any of the four sides and then dragging when the cursor turns into a double arrow. (You can also resize the Graphics Manager task pane when it's docked, but the only side you can move is the right side.)

When you're finished with the Graphics Manager task pane, you can dismiss it by clicking the Close button or pressing Ctrl+F1.

Pinpointing Your Pictures

Okay, finding pictures in your publication doesn't sound like such a big deal. Or is it? If your publication is only two pages long and has only a half-dozen pictures, you're correct. But what if your publication is a catalog that's more than a hundred pages long and has hundreds of pictures in it? And, what if you need to find an image named `widget137.tif`? Sure, you can page through the publication until you find it. (A better option is to have your intern do it. They love that stuff — trust me.) The best option is to use the Graphics Manager task pane to find it.

Here's how a search works:

1. **First, open the Graphics Manager task pane, as outlined in the preceding section.**

2. **Choose All Pictures from the Show drop-down menu.**

   Your files are listed in the Select a Picture pane of Graphics Manager.

   To view your pictures in Thumbnail view, select the Show Thumbnail check box, below the Sort By options on the task pane. If you're searching through a large number of pictures, turn off Thumbnail view to improve performance.

3. **On the Sort By drop-down menu, select the best choice for searching through your pictures.**

   The Sort By options are File Name, File Extension, File Size, Page Number, and Status. File Name is probably the most commonly used search options.

4. **Scroll through the Select a Picture pane until you locate the filename you want.**

5. **Click the down arrow next to the filename and choose Go to This Picture from the pop-up menu that appears. Or, just click the picture.**

   Publisher opens the page containing the selected picture and highlights the picture with selection handles.

   Note that the down arrow doesn't appear until you point the mouse cursor at the filename.

Figure 11-2 shows the Graphics Manager task pane with pictures listed alphabetically by filename.

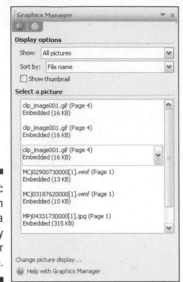

Figure 11-2:
You can easily find a picture by looking for its filename.

Embedding and Linking Pictures

You have essentially two ways to place a picture in your publication: Embed the picture, which means that the inserted picture is part and parcel of the Publisher publication, or link to the picture. When you link to a picture, your publication contains only a pointer to tell Publisher where the picture file is located and how to display it, which has the benefit of making your publication file smaller. The trade-off is that you have to keep track of that separate picture file.

If you're printing your publication with a professional printer, use linked pictures. The printer can then make edits to the pictures outside of Publisher, if necessary. You should insert pictures as linked pictures when you're creating this kind of publication. But, no worries! Publisher offers a way to change embedded pictures to linked pictures.

You might also decide to use linked pictures if your publication is very large because it contains numerous large images. If your publication is slow to load or if navigating in the publication is slow because of having numerous many large pictures, change embedded pictures to linked pictures.

To convert an embedded picture to a linked file, follow these steps:

1. **Using the Graphics Manager task pane, navigate to and select the file that you want to convert to a linked file.**

2. **Click the down arrow next to the filename and choose Save As Linked picture from the pop-up menu that appears.**

3. **Using the Save In drop-down list, navigate to the folder where you want to save your picture.**

4. **Type a name for the file in the File Name field or accept the name that Publisher suggests, as shown in Figure 11-3.**

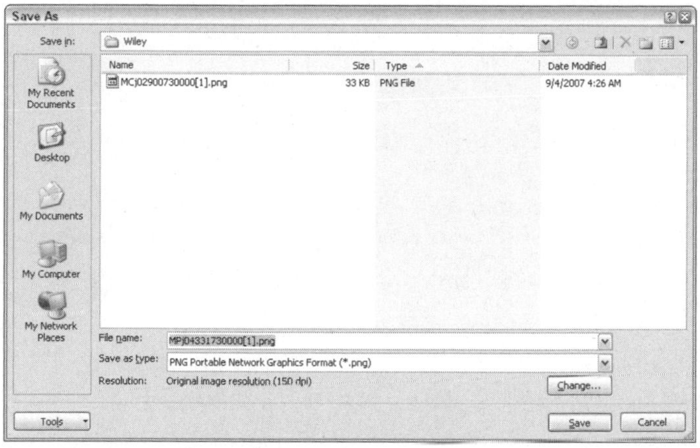

Figure 11-3:
The Save As
dialog box.

5. **From the Save As Type drop-down menu, select an appropriate file format for your picture.**

   When you convert an embedded file to a linked picture, Graphics Manager lets you choose the file type. Your options are `.gif`, `.jpeg`, `.tif`, `.png`, `.bmp`, `.wmf`, or `.emf`.

6. **Click Save.**

If you're tired of keeping track of all the linked picture files, you can change the linked pictures to embedded pictures. To convert a linked picture to an embedded picture, follow these steps:

1. **Use the Graphics Manager task pane to navigate to and select the file that you want to convert to an embedded file.**

2. **Click the down arrow next to the filename and choose Convert to Embedded Picture from the pop-up menu that appears.**

   Graphics Manager embeds a copy of your picture into your publication. It doesn't affect the picture file on your computer.

Changing the Way Pictures Appear in Your On-Screen Publication

You probably have lots of pictures in your Publisher documents. A picture is worth a thousand words, after all. But having many pictures in a document can really slow things down, especially if you're making a lot of changes to the size or other properties of the pictures. Publisher lets you decide how you want your pictures to be displayed on-screen by specifying settings in the Picture Display dialog box. Settings in this dialog box don't affect the way a publication prints.

To access the Picture Display dialog box, follow these steps:

1. **Call up Graphics Manager, as specified at the beginning of this chapter, in the section "Summoning the Graphics Manager Task Pane."**

2. **Click the Change Picture Display link, at the bottom of the Graphics Manager task pane.**

   The Picture Display dialog box appears, as shown in Figure 11-4.

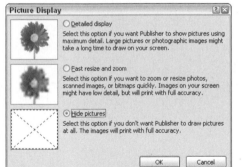

Figure 11-4: The Picture Display dialog box.

As you can see in this figure, you have these three display options:

- **Detailed Display:** Shows your pictures as they will print. Your pictures will look terrific on-screen but might be slow to draw.

- **Fast Resize and Zoom:** Causes your pictures to be displayed faster but possibly in a lower resolution. They will still print at full resolution.

- **Hide Pictures:** Does exactly what it says — hides your pictures, by displaying an empty picture frame with an X through it as a placeholder to show where your picture will appear. Your pictures print normally.

Getting the Details

Do you ever want to know how large a picture is in your publication is? Which graphic format it uses? Its effective resolution? Graphics Manager can tell you all that information and more.

To open the Graphics Manager task pane, follow these steps:

1. **Choose View➪Task Pane from the menu or press Ctrl+F1.**
2. **Click the Task Pane drop-down menu and choose Graphics Manager.**
3. **Click the down arrow next to the picture whose details you want to see and then choose Details.**

The Details dialog box, shown in Figure 11-5, appears.

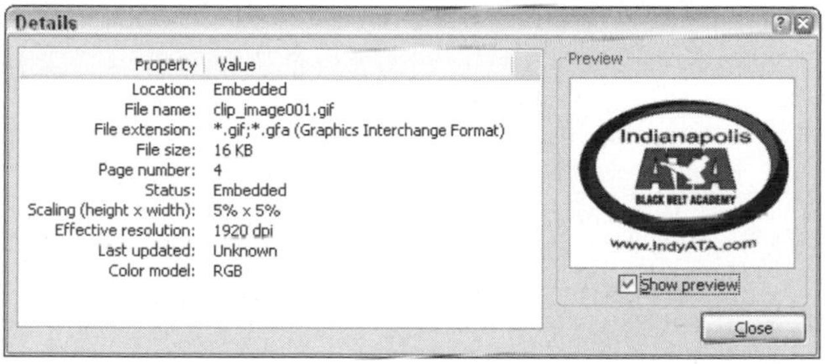
Details
Property Value
Location: Embedded
File name: clip_image001.gif
File extension: *.gif;*.gfa (Graphics Interchange Format)
File size: 16 KB
Page number: 4
Status: Embedded
Scaling (height x width): 5% x 5%
Effective resolution: 1920 dpi
Last updated: Unknown
Color model: RGB
Preview
Indianapolis
BLACK BELT ACADEMY
www.IndyATA.com
Show preview
Close

Figure 11-5: The Details dialog box with the Show Preview option selected.

Part V
Proof Positive

The 5th Wave   By Rich Tennant

In this part . . .

After your layout is complete, most of the hard work is done. Many "gotchas" can crop up when you begin to print your publication, however. Some are tiny errors that seem to bedevil everyone, and some errors are of the thorny, devilish type. In the chapters in this part, I discuss the most common problems that appear in a publication in its final stages of production and tell you how to get rid of them. If you're like most people, you spend some time tweaking your work to get it just right. It would be a shame not to take the next step and make sure that the printed work is as good as it can be. Printing can be expensive, and mistakes can be costly when you make them. The first chapter in this part can save you a lot of money and frustration.

Microsoft Publisher 2007 has a number of special features that help you guide a printing service to print your work. The second chapter in this part shows you how to set up your publication for a commercial printer and gives you a short treatise on paper and ink.

Chapter 12

Final Checks

. . . .

In This Chapter

▶ Giving your pages the once-over

▶ Using the Design Checker

▶ Discovering techniques for copyfitting text

▶ Adjusting text spacing and line endings

▶ Improving page design with special page elements

▶ Adding drawn objects, borders, shaded areas, and special symbols

. . . .

*P*roducing quality desktop publishing means sweating the details. I'm not talking about jumping up and down in your sweatsuit with the Richard Simmons *Sweatin' to the Oldies* video, but rather about getting absorbed in the details of your publication before you send it to the printer — where real money changes hands. In this chapter, I look at things you can do to make sure that your publication reflects the care you took in designing it.

The Eyes Have It

The single best piece of advice I can give you about checking your publication is this: Look it over in printed form. Publisher lets you create proof prints; avail yourself of this opportunity. You should also create a proof for an outside printer. The proof is your "contract" that tells the printer "This is what I want."

You can't (or at least you shouldn't) expect to catch all the errors in your publication the first time you look at it. The more people you have look at your work, the better chance you have of finding things that should be changed. Spotting your own errors can be difficult. When possible, try to live with the final design for a while before you commit to spending money for printing.

I highly recommend that you create a complete checklist of items you want to check in your publication after you complete its design.

The Design Checker

The Design Checker, an automated tool in Publisher, attempts to find things that are wrong with your publication. It catches many errors that you wouldn't be likely to catch until after the publication is printed, such as

- Empty frames
- Covered objects
- Text in the overflow area
- Objects in the nonprinting region
- Disproportional pictures
- Spacing between sentences

Follow these steps to check your design with the Design Checker:

1. **Choose Tools⇨Design Checker from the main menu or choose Design Checker from the Publisher Tasks drop-down menu.**

   The Design Checker task pane appears, as shown in Figure 12-1.

2. **Tell the Design Checker which type of design check you want to run by selecting the appropriate check box:**

   Run General Design Checks: Checks for problems that would apply to any type of publication, such as missing pictures or a story with text in the overflow area.

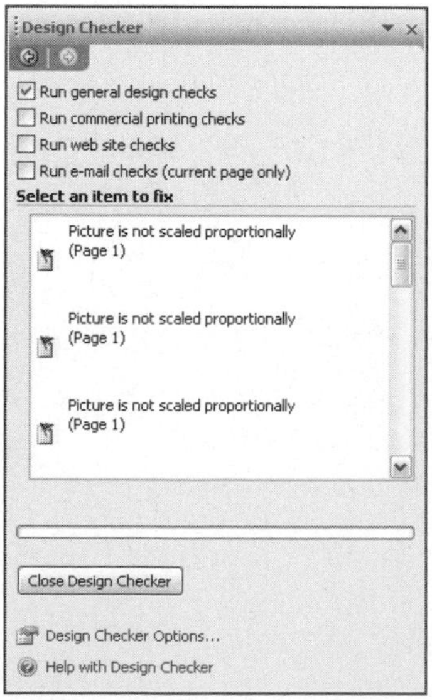

Figure 12-1:
The Design Checker runs a newsletter check.

Run Commercial Printing Checks: Checks for issues that can affect your commercial printer's ability to print the publication the way you intend. Too many or missing spot colors are common problems.

Run Web Site Checks: In publications that you plan to publish on a Web site, checks for missing (hyper)links and pictures that don't have alternate text.

Run E-Mail Checks: Checks primarily for problems that cause text to be sent as an image in an e-mail message, causing large messages (an object overlapping text or rotated text for example). It also checks for issues (hyphenated text) that cause gaps to appear in some e-mail viewers.

As soon as you select the type of check to run, the Design Checker starts looking for problems and displays potential problems in the Select an Item to Fix pane of the Design Checker.

3. **Click an item's down arrow in the Select an Item to Fix pane to see options for resolving the issue.**

   If you're not sure what the problem is with an item in the Select an Item to Fix pane, choose Explain from the drop-down menu. The Publisher Help screen opens with detailed information about the problem item.

4. **Click Close Design Checker when you finish.**

If you want more control over just what the Design Checker looks for, click the Design Checker Options link, at the bottom of the Design Checker task pane. Doing so opens the Design Checker Options dialog box, as shown in Figure 12-2.

Figure 12-2: The General tab of the Design Checker Options dialog box.

You can use the Sort By box to determine how to list items in the Select an Item to Fix box: Select Page Number, Description, or Status. If the Remove Fixed Items check box is selected, items disappear from the list as they're resolved. On the General tab, you can also choose which pages to check. You can select only the current page, all pages including master pages, or all pages not including master pages.

Figure 12-3 shows the Checks tab of the Design Checker Options dialog box with the Commercial Printing Checks option chosen in the Show drop-down list. This tab is handy if you want the Design Checker to ignore certain checks for a specified option. Just deselect the boxes in the Checks in This Category list.

As one of your final checks, you just can't beat running the Design Checker.

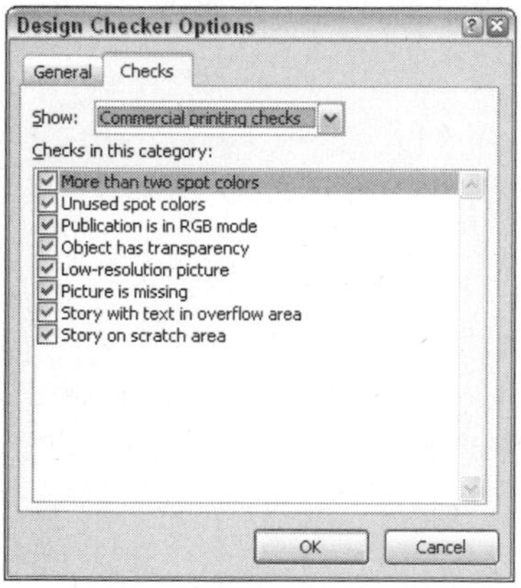

Figure 12-3:
The Design
Checker
Options
dialog
box with
commercial
printing
checks.

Word-Fitting Techniques

When you're working with a layout to make it look exactly the way you want, one of your hardest tasks is making the text fit into text boxes. If your layout *can't be changed,* the amount of text it can hold is set. Also, you might find that the formatted text simply looks ugly.

A common problem in fully justified text is that there can be a large amount of space between words throughout a text box — the text looks as though rivers are running through it. You probably can't change the justification of your text boxes, but you can work with the hyphenation feature (see Chapter 7) to break words and improve the look of your text. Even the automated hyphenation tool isn't perfect, so you might want to manually hyphenate justified text. In the following sections, I describe this technique and others for making your words fit into the text boxes in your layout.

Copyfitting

You can rephrase nearly every paragraph to reduce or add words without changing the meaning of the text. (My editor does this to me all the time!) People working with page layout generally don't have the luxury of being able to edit text — that job belongs to the author or the editor. If you're both layout artist and author, however, you can *copyfit* your text by adding and removing words.

Editing text written in short sentences or phrases is more difficult because you have fewer words to work with. In those cases, a thesaurus can be your best friend. To open the Publisher built-in thesaurus, follow these steps:

1. **Select the word you want to look up in the thesaurus.**

2. **Choose Tools⇨Language⇨Thesaurus.**

   The Research Task Pane opens, and the word you selected displays in the Search For text box. The Thesaurus is displayed as the reference material currently in use in the Research Task Pane. A list of choices from the Thesaurus is displayed in the Research Task Pane display pane.

The Publisher spell checker (see Chapter 7 for information on how to use it) contains more than 100,000 words. The spell checker's large dictionary doesn't help you if you use a valid word incorrectly — such as *two* rather than *to*.

Always proofread your text for errors caused by properly spelled but incorrectly used words.

If you're working with Microsoft Word, you can use its grammar checker to inspect your text. To open the grammar checker in Word 2007, click the Spelling and Grammar button on the Review tab in the Proofing group on the ribbon. (To check the grammar in your story in Publisher, choose Change Text⇨Edit Story in Microsoft Word from the context-sensitive menu of a text box.)

Incorrect word usage is particularly difficult for authors to spot. The best way to proofread is to have as many people as possible read your publication before you commit to printing it. If your publication is important, you may want to pay a professional proofreader to review it.

Adjusting spacing in headlines

Publisher gives you many ways to adjust the spacing in and between your text frames. Use the ideas in this section as a reminder and check list.

A common error in headlines is having too much spacing between letters and between lines. Headlines nearly always benefit from proper kerning and from reducing the default line spacing that Publisher applies to large letters. Kerning is particularly important in headlines with serif fonts.

Figure 12-4 shows an example of a headline that dominates the page. In Figure 12-5, the headline's spacing between characters *(tracking)* was changed from very loose to normal, and the line spacing was adjusted to 1.25 sp. In addition, the headline frame can now be reduced to make the headline less prominent.

Before you spend too much time formatting the tracking and line spacing of your headlines, try using the AutoFit feature. Right-click the text box that contains your headline and choose Change Text⇨AutoFit Text⇨Best Fit. You may find that substituting a WordArt frame for a text box in headlines works well.

If a headline belongs with a block of text, leave more space above the headline than below so that readers have a visual clue that the headline applies to the text that follows.

Another problem to watch for is a headline that breaks across lines in a way that makes the meaning unclear to the casual reader. If you can improve the readability of your headline by grouping phrases, do so. For example, in the headline Gas Prices Top $4 Per Gallon, break the line in front of the word *Top* rather than behind it. (Then go pull your bicycle out of the garage.)

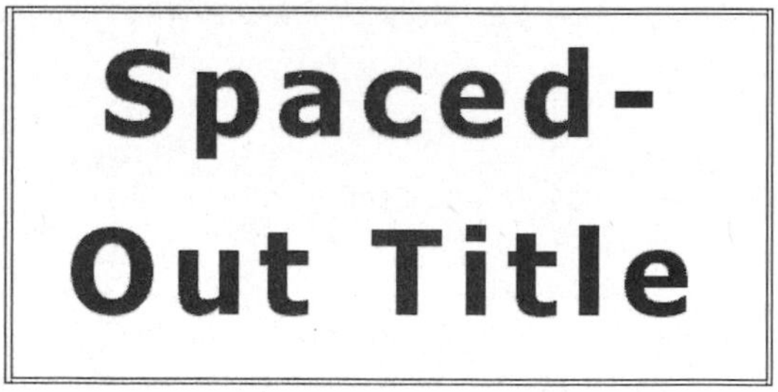

Figure 12-4:
A large
headline
before
adjustment.

Spaced-
Out Title

Figure 12-5:
The same
headline
after
tracking and
line spacing
adjustments
were made.

Make sure that your headline placement matches the page numbering in the table of contents (if your publication has one). Although many page layout programs automatically renumber the table of contents, Publisher does not. Also, if you use headlines as headers and footers and place these elements in the background, make sure that they're correct when you proofread the pages.

Getting words to fit in text boxes

One way to make text fit into a text box is to simply adjust the size of the text box. This task is straightforward if only a single text box is on the page. With several text boxes in a multicolumn page layout, however, resizing text boxes can affect all columns simultaneously. One subtle way to work around adjusted text boxes is to play with the lines and spacing in your headlines. If you made the text boxes smaller and now have extra space on the page, you can add a line to a headline or put in a secondary headline to occupy that space. If you made the text boxes larger, you can remove extra headlines to provide more room.

The amount of line spacing dramatically affects the amount of text you can fit into a text box. You can adjust line spacing in

- A single text box
- All text boxes on a page
- All text boxes on a two-page spread

You also can change the spacing before, after, and between paragraphs. If you adjust line spacing, you do so for the entire text box and, ideally, for all text boxes on a page or a two-page spread.

You don't have to make large changes in line spacing to get results. Check the results on a printed page to see whether the adjustments you make are acceptable; don't rely on the way your page looks on the screen.

I also like kerning and tracking as a way to slightly alter text to make it fit correctly in a text box. (When you use kerning and tracking in this way, the change isn't obvious to a casual observer.) Chapter 7 tells you about various techniques for adjusting the spacing between letters in your text.

Publisher refers to *kerning* as adjusting the spacing between two characters, and *tracking* as adjusting the spacing between characters for a large selection of text.

When you adjust text boxes, pay particular attention to preventing widows and orphans. A *widow* is a short line at the top of a page or column; an *orphan* is a word, or portion of a word, on a line by itself at the end of a paragraph.

One common mistake to watch for is two spaces between sentences. This practice is a holdover from the days when people used typewriters — the extra space made sentences more obvious.

To check for extra spaces, search for two space characters and replace them with one: Just type two spaces directly into the Find What text box in the Replace dialog box and replace with one space. Be sure to run this search-and-replace operation a second time, in case you typed *three* spaces between sentences.

Hyphenating and justifying text

Another method for altering the way text fits in a text box is to change the justification. Sometimes after a design is set, however, you don't have the flexibility to change the text justification. To fit the largest amount of text into a text box, apply full justification and automatic hyphenation to the text box. Remember, however, that you cannot use automatic hyphenation for only part of a text box.

Whenever you use automatic hyphenation, you can no longer control the location of line breaks. To regain control, turn off hyphenation; then turn it back on and request to confirm each hyphenation as it occurs.

When you use right- or left-justified text (also called *ragged* text) as opposed to full justification, you often make the text more readable even though you can't fit as much text in a column. To gain more space, hyphenate.

In ragged text, if you're tempted to force a line ending by using a soft carriage return (by pressing Shift+Enter), don't do it! When you force a line ending, however, you change the line endings of every line after that point. This situation isn't a problem if automatic hyphenation is turned on, but it can cause grief if you hyphenated the text manually. Therefore, forced line endings should be your last resort.

You can also force a line ending at the position where the automatic hyphenation tool places a hyphen. To do so, move the cursor to that position, click and press Ctrl+- (hyphen). An optional hyphen shows up only when the entire word doesn't fit on the line. Therefore, optional hyphens aren't affected by soft carriage returns. If you want to make sure that a word is never hyphenated (at the position where Publisher would hyphenate it), move the cursor to that position, click and press Ctrl+Alt+- (hyphen). I recommend this safeguard for a compound word that already contains a hyphen: for example, *double-barreled* rather than *double-barrel-ed*. The common practice is to never end a column or text box with a hyphen.

Always use optional hyphens rather than regular hyphens to hyphenate text.

When you hyphenate text in a paragraph, try to have no more than two consecutive hyphenated lines. Hyphenated text is harder to read and understand. For this reason, some page layout professionals avoid hyphenation, although it greatly increases the amount of work necessary to fine-tune the layout. Whatever you do, don't hyphenate headlines; they must be readable at a glance.

You can control the amount of hyphenation that Publisher uses by changing an option in the Hyphenation dialog box. Choose Tools⇨Language⇨Hyphenation from the main menu and enter a smaller number in the Hyphenation zone text box to smooth out your ragged edge and to reduce the amount of white space between words. To have fewer hyphens or to have fewer short syllables before and after the hyphen, make the Hyphenation zone larger.

You can also open the Hyphenation dialog box by pressing Ctrl+Shift+H.

Page Improvements

People tend to read a page from the upper-left corner to the lower-right corner. In a two-page spread, that principle applies to the upper-left corner of the left-hand page to the lower-right corner of the right-hand page. Putting your most important page elements along this diagonal path is good design practice.

One useful feature of page layout programs is that they impose a design structure on your pages. Readers should be able to instinctively find common elements, such as page numbers, on a page. I recommend setting common page elements on master pages, one master page for all left-hand pages and another master page for all right-hand pages. With these common elements in place, you can move on to break up the tedium of your pages by having some elements stand out. The longer the publication, the more important it is to have elements that draw the eye to specific sections.

Special page elements

Earlier in this chapter, I describe some techniques for breaking up a page and drawing attention to various sections. The following useful techniques help make your pages more interesting:

- **Pictures:** Pictures instantly attract attention. When you place a picture on a page, it becomes a focus of attention. Putting pictures off the reader's diagonal path — in the lower-left or upper-right corner of a page or two-page spread — creates an interesting effect. If you use too many pictures, however, you greatly reduce their effectiveness.

- ✔ **Drop caps or raised caps:** These design elements are an excellent way to start a chapter or section, and they draw the reader's attention regardless of where they appear on the page.

- ✔ **Rules and shaded boxes:** I like rules and shaded boxes because they're particularly valuable for making headlines stand out. If you think that a section of text is important, put it in a shaded box.

- ✔ **Pull quotes or sidebars:** A *pull quote* is a short section that highlights the important point you're making on a page. To make a pull quote stand out, place it outside the text box. *Sidebars* are longer sections that you want to make stand out. You can reserve sidebars for optional reading or make them central to your text treatment.

Don't forget that the Design Gallery comes with a selection of specially for-matted headlines, coupons, pull quotes, sidebars, tables of contents, and titles. If you create any design elements that you want to use elsewhere, create your own category in the Design Gallery and save those elements under it. I talk about the Design Gallery in Chapter 9, and I like it so much that I wish it were greatly expanded. Figure 12-6 shows you the Design Gallery with the Pull Quotes category selected.

Inserting an object from the Design Gallery is just the beginning. You're free to resize an object and to ungroup it so that you can work with its compo-nents. You can also change the text in a Design Gallery object, and adjust colors and shading.

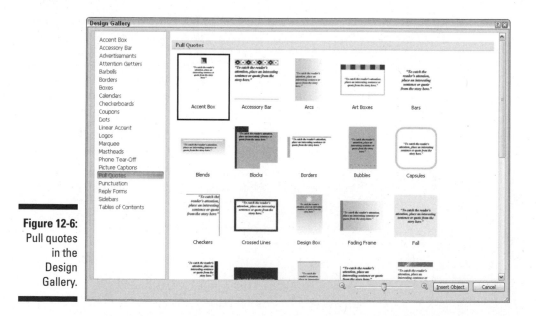

Figure 12-6:
Pull quotes
in the
Design
Gallery.

One interesting effect that you can make with shaded areas is a *bleed,* which is a section of color that extends past normal margins all the way to the edge of your page. You can use bleeds with single pages and to span the inside margins of a two-page spread. If you use bleeds in your work, consult with your printer shop to make sure that its presses are capable of printing bleeds. Bleeds often require special treatment and cost more money, but their effects can be worth the cost.

Drawn objects

Although most tools in the toolbox can't draw objects for you, you can use them to create interesting effects. You can also find special shapes on the AutoShapes tool on the Object toolbar. Drawn objects don't have to be small; they can be major page elements as well. For example, if you're creating a publication that includes a topic for discussion or the dialogue of a play, you can use a cartoon balloon shape — which is ordinarily used to hold captions — as your entire page frame. Be creative and have fun!

Also, you needn't be constrained by the shapes that appear in the toolbox. You can combine shapes to create other shapes, such as combining triangles, circles, and lines to create a mountain landscape with the moon rising in the background. When you combine shapes with colors, patterns, gradients, and shadings, you have a wealth of tools at your disposal.

Borders and shading

Borders and shading are helpful ways of separating a section of your page. You can place borders around pictures by using rectangles and circles or create a matted-photograph look by putting colored frames in back of pictures. If you try this technique, consider using bold colors to emphasize the picture.

When you use borders and shading with text, try to understate their presence. If a shaded block is colored gray, keep the gray level at 10 to 15 percent. You can overuse color on a page very easily. Similarly, if you use shading in back of text, make sure that the shading makes your text more readable, not less. As the shading gets darker, it's more difficult to see black text but easier to see white text. Note that white text, or *reversed text,* is generally less readable than black text. It works well only in front of black backgrounds and in short phrases, such as headlines.

Borders and shading are valuable when you create tables. The Publisher table frame automatically creates shades and borders for you. If you create an array of information without a table frame, consider adding these features to your work.

Do you want to know the most readable color combination for text? Take a look at the cover of this book. Surprise! It's black type on a yellow background. To change the color of text, use the Font Color tool, which appears on the Formatting toolbar when you have text selected.

Special symbols

If you use capitalization in a paragraph, you might find that using SMALL CAPS looks better, particularly for a whole sentence of capitals. Also, changing a line of capitals to small caps can shorten your paragraph measurably and help you with copyfitting. If you have a paragraph that must be lengthened to fit the text box, consider making the first sentence all caps — especially if the first sentence makes the point for the paragraph or section.

Keyboards have feet (') and inch (") marks for single and double quotation marks. Typographers prefer the use of stylized *smart quotes* instead: 'and' for single quotation marks and "and" for double quotation marks. To automatically insert these symbols into your text when you type single and double quotation marks, choose Tools⇨AutoCorrect Options to open the AutoCorrect dialog box. Click the AutoFormat As You Type tab and select the "Straight Quotes" with "Smart Quotes" check box, as shown in Figure 12-7. (This option is set by default.) If you have text that needs straight single or double quotation marks, you have to turn off the option temporarily. Don't forget to turn it back on when you finish. You can also use the Insert Symbol dialog box to insert any of these characters.

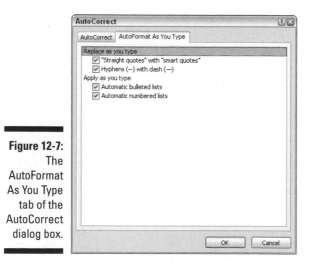

Figure 12-7:
The AutoFormat As You Type tab of the AutoCorrect dialog box.

Suppose that you want to align the first character of a headline or a pull quote with the text frame that appears below or above it. A regular quotation mark can disrupt that visual alignment and be distracting. Therefore, you might want to use the *hanging* quotation mark typographical technique to put an opening quotation mark to the left of the headline or pull quote.

Some page layout programs let you format a paragraph so that it has a hanging quotation mark. In Publisher, follow these steps to create this effect manually:

1. **Type a paragraph or pull quote with smart quotes at the beginning and end of the text.**

2. **Create a small text box that's large enough to hold the quotation mark.**

3. **Position the small text box to the left of the paragraph or pull quote for an opening quotation mark or to the right for a closing quotation mark.**

   Zooming in to see your text is helpful when placing the small text box.

4. **Select (highlight) the quotation mark in the paragraph or pull quote and then choose Edit⇨Cut to cut it to the Clipboard.**

5. **Click an insertion point in the small hanging text box; then choose Edit⇨Paste to paste the cut quotation mark into the frame.**

Unfortunately, because you have separate text boxes, the hanging quotation doesn't automatically follow the headline as it moves around on your page. Therefore, group the hanging quotation mark text box with the headline or pull quote text box. Other symbols that typographers use (which might be new to you) are the en dash (–) and em dash (—) in place of two hyphens (- -) and three hyphens (- - -), respectively. They're named en dash and em dash because they're the width of a capital *N* and *M*, respectively, in the font that's being used. Many desktop publishing programs automatically substitute these symbols whenever you type two or three hyphens. Publisher, for example, automatically substitutes the en dash when you type a space followed by a hyphen, and an em dash when you type two hyphens together.

Good typographical practice recommends using en dashes to indicate a range of numbers (where you would normally put the word *to*) or when you have a compound word, as in Barrington Smythe–Jones. Use an em dash to set off a parenthetical remark — as I do in this sentence — before you end your thought and use up your brain cells.

If your en and em dashes don't show up automatically, ensure that the Hyphens (-,- -) with en/em dashes (—) option is enabled on the AutoReplace Format As You Type tab of the AutoCorrect dialog box.

If you look closely at the symbols in different fonts, you find that most fonts contain typographer's fractions. The ½ and ¼ symbols appear to the right in the Insert Symbols dialog box, one line down from where the en and em dashes appear. Also, most fonts have characters for copyright (©), trademark (™), and registration (®) symbols. These special characters are best used as superscripts in the same font size. You also find various currency symbols ($, £, ¢), accented characters (Á, ç, é, ô), and ligatures (Æ, æ), for example.

It pays to study the Insert Symbols dialog box to see which special characters your current font offers.

You may require a special fraction beyond the ones offered in a standard character set. Here's how you create one:

1. **In standard text, type the fraction you want, such as** 3/8.

2. **Format the numbers to the left and right of the division sign at about 60 to 70 percent of the text size.**

   For example, if you have 12-point text, use 8-point numbers.

3. **Format the left number as a superscript and the right number as a subscript by choosing Format⇨Font from the main menu and clicking the corresponding radio buttons in the Font dialog box.**

Don't forget that you can use non-integer point sizes (such as 11.5) if you're using TrueType fonts or Postscript fonts and Adobe Type Manager.

What if you need a superscript number, such as 2^8, or a subscript number, such as H_2O? You can apply these formats to selected text from the Character dialog box or by pressing the Ctrl++ (plus) or Ctrl+Shift++ (plus) key combinations. Press these combinations again to toggle the superscript or subscript back to normal text.

Chapter 13

Printing, Print Shops, and Paper

● ●

In This Chapter

▶ Specifying which printer you want to use

▶ Printing page proofs on your own printer

▶ Setting up an outside printer

▶ Investigating the quality offerings of common printing devices

▶ Selecting and working with an outside printing service

▶ Deciding how and when to use your various paper options

● ●

Mom is a desktop publisher's best friend. A desktop publisher's next best friend is the person responsible for printing his or her publication. You should call your mother at least once every week and send her flowers on Mother's Day. And you should talk to your printing professional before and during the development of any desktop publishing project that you aren't printing yourself.

In this chapter, I consider how to work with professional print shops and other outside printing resources. Specifically, I show you how to set up your publication for whatever printer you're using, select paper, and take advantage of the special paper (from PaperDirect) that Publisher lets you use. I also describe common problems and concerns about using an outside printer. People sometimes find working with a professional printer for the first time to be something of a mystery.

Printers and Output Quality

Print quality is determined by the printer *engine* (the mechanism that makes the printer print). Typically, print quality is measured in the number of dots per inch (dpi) that a printer can deliver to a printed page. That measurement isn't the whole story, however. The shape of the dots, their placement in relationship to a letterform, and the density of the dots can dramatically change the perceived quality of a printed page.

For example, many printers, such as the Hewlett-Packard LaserJet series, use *resolution enhancement technology* to improve print quality. (HP named its technology *REt;* other vendors name theirs something else — Intellispot, Varidot, Omnishade, PrintGear, or whatever their lawyers can trademark.) When placing dots at the edge of a printed character, some laser printers vary the size and intensity of the spot to better conform to the character's border. The net effect is that the printed text appears to be at a higher resolution and that *halftones,* which print with shades of gray — created by black spots — appear to have more grays in them.

The following list briefly describes printer types and their common uses:

- **Impact:** Dot matrix and print wheel printers are included in the impact printer category. This type of printer prints by striking a ribbon (like a typewriter) and transferring the ink from the ribbon to the page. Some of these printers can print graphics, but as a group they aren't used in desktop publishing applications. The only reason I can think of for keeping an impact printer around is for printing multipart forms. Although impact printers aren't suitable for desktop publishing, if you need one, you can pick one up starting at about $150.

- **Inkjet:** An inkjet printer prints by spraying ink droplets under pressure. The output quality of this printer type varies widely. Desktop inkjet printers at the low end print up to 600 dpi in either color or black and white. Print quality is moderate, but print speeds are relatively slow. Special paper improves inkjet output. You can now buy very inexpensive — less than $25 — inkjet printers that deliver impressive color output at medium to high resolutions. What's the catch? A color ink cartridge for that low-cost printer costs nearly $40. There's no such thing as a free lunch, er, printer.

- **Laser:** Laser printers produce black-and-white grayscale (shades of gray) and color output. You can find black-and-white laser printers for less than $100. Color laser printers are now available starting at about $200. When looking for a new laser printer, whether it's black and white or color, keep in mind that your major expense over the life of the printer is the toner cartridges. It's definitely worth your time and effort to find out how much toner cartridges will cost for the printer you're considering buying. Common desktop laser printers print in the 600 dpi range, although laser printers that print to 1200 dpi are becoming the new standard.

- **Xerographic:** Many copy shops and printer services have printers that are essentially fancy copy machines. These xerographic printers offer fast speed and moderate resolution (1200 dpi). In this category, the Xerox DocuTech 6180 is a 180-page-per-minute *(ppm)* production scanner/printer.

- ✔ **Dye sublimation:** This type of printer works like an inkjet printer but uses heads to *sublime* (vaporize and deposit) special dyes on paper. Some printers in this category use crayons and waxes; others use low-melting dyes or liquids. They're used almost exclusively for color work. In most cases, inkjet printers produce a halftone image, but dye sublimation printers can produce contone (continuous tone) images.

- ✔ **Imagesetter:** This high-resolution laser printer prints at 2000–3000 dpi. The output it creates is printed paper or, more often, film that's used in turn to create printing plates. You can find imagesetters at print services. They're used in very low-volume printing to create original print masters.

You might find any or all of these printers, except for impact printers, at a copy shop or printer service.

Selecting the Target Printer

Each printer you use (whether in-house or in a professional print shop) offers different capabilities: page sizes, minimum margin widths, and color options, for example. When you print to your desktop printer, you set those options in the Page Setup dialog box. If you're using a printer that's at a professional print shop, you can install and use the *printer driver* (the interpreter that lets your computer talk to the printer) for the print shop's printer as the target printer on your desktop computer. (*Target printer* is just a spiffy term for the machine on which you intend to print a given publication.) Your target-printer selection and setup are *publication-level settings:* They're a part of your current publication but do not affect any other publications.

Note that the target printer doesn't have to be *your* printer. That is, although you probably have your own printer attached to your computer, you might not want to use that old banger. You might have access to an even better printer that offers color, faster speed, the capability to print on bigger sheets of paper, a slot that dispenses hot beverages while you wait, or whatever. If this other printer is the one you intend to use to print the final version of your publication, you should select it as the target printer.

Windows contains many printer drivers; some belong to expensive color printers or imagesetters. If you can't find the target printer that you intend to print to on this list, you can always ask your printer service to supply you with the driver. Most will "loan" you their printer drivers for free. Printer drivers are easily copied to CD or downloaded from a Web site and are installed on your machine using the Windows Add Printer Wizard.

Follow these steps to select and set up a target printer:

1. **Choose File⇨Print Setup.**

   A Print Setup dialog box, like the one shown in Figure 13-1, opens with your default printer listed. (Your printer might offer different options from the ones shown in the figure.)

2. **If you don't want to use the default printer, choose a different one from the Printer Name drop-down list box.**

   The default printer is determined by Windows. To change the default printer, choose Start⇨Printers and Faxes, right-click the printer of choice from the listing that appears, and select the Set As Default Printer command from the resulting pop-up menu.

3. **In the Orientation section, click to select a paper orientation, if it isn't already selected.**

   Your choices are Portrait (lengthwise) and Landscape (sideways).

4. **In the Paper section, use the Size drop-down list box to choose the size of paper on which you plan to print, if it isn't already selected.**

   The selected printer determines the available sizes.

5. **Also in the Paper section, use the Source drop-down list box to choose the appropriate paper source for your publication, if it isn't already selected.**

   I'm not talking about the Hamilton Paper Box Company or Staples here. The *source* refers to the part of the printer that has the paper you want to print on. The selected printer determines its available sources. Some printers have different trays, feeders, tractors, and other methods for loading paper into themselves.

6. **Click OK.**

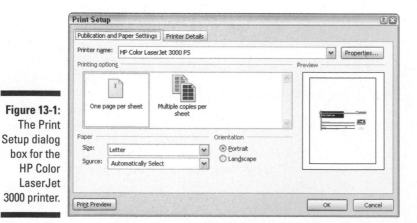

Figure 13-1:
The Print Setup dialog box for the HP Color LaserJet 3000 printer.

If you can't find the target printer in the Printer Name drop-down list box, use the Windows Control Panel to install a driver for that printer.

Printing Your Pages

The operations described in these sections are controlled by Windows; Publisher uses the services of the operating system to print. You can print to a local or network printer, or you can set up to print to an outside printer service. Often, you do both, by printing draft or sample copies on your local printer for proofing and then receiving final output from a printer service.

Printing problems are legion with computers — if you're having difficulties printing, try getting help by selecting the Troubleshooting topic in the Windows Help system. Use the Help command on the Start menu to access the Windows Help system.

If your publication prints but doesn't look the way you expected, search for the word **printer** in Microsoft Publisher Help. Press F1 or choose Help⇨Microsoft Office Publisher Help and type `printer` in the Search box. This command opens the Help system and shows you topics of interest in solving printer problems.

To print to a local or network printer, called *inside printing,* you can use various methods:

- ✔ Click the Print button on the Standard toolbar. Publisher immediately begins printing your entire publication by using the current print settings.

- ✔ Choose File⇨Print or press Ctrl+P. The Print dialog box, shown in Figure 13-2, appears with the default printer selected. Make your selections from that dialog box and then click OK.

- ✔ Drag and drop a publication file to a printer icon or shortcut on the Windows desktop or in Windows Explorer.

The Print dialog box

The Print dialog box contains these important features:

- ✔ **The Printer Name drop-down list box:** Select the printer you want to use from the list of installed printers. The default printer appears first in the dialog box. To send a print job to another printer, select that printer by name from the Printer Name drop-down list box.

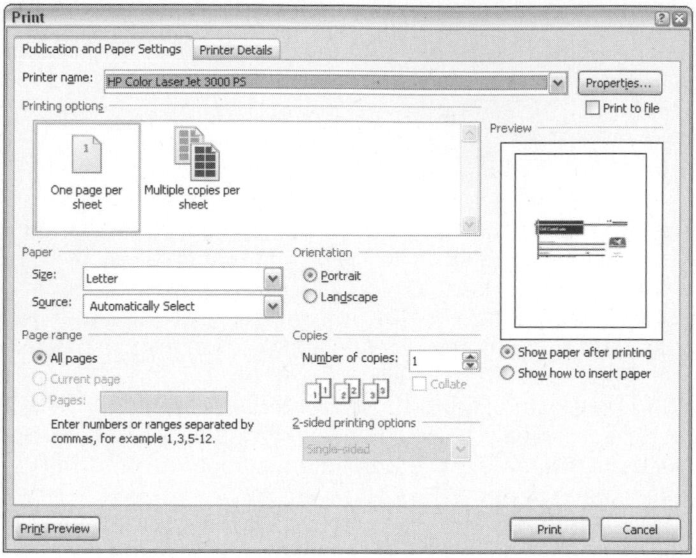

Print

Publication and Paper Settings | Printer Details

Printer name: HP Color LaserJet 3000 PS   ▼   Properties...

☐ Print to file

Printing options

[One page per sheet] [Multiple copies per sheet]

Preview

Paper
Size: Letter   ▼
Source: Automatically Select   ▼

Orientation
◉ Portrait
○ Landscape

Page range
◉ All pages
○ Current page
○ Pages:
Enter numbers or ranges separated by commas, for example 1,3,5-12.

Copies
Number of copies: 1
☐ Collate
2-sided printing options
Single-sided   ▼

◉ Show paper after printing
○ Show how to insert paper

Print Preview   Print   Cancel

Figure 13-2:
The Publication and Paper Settings tab of the Print dialog box for the HP Color LaserJet 3000 printer.

✔ **The Properties button:** Change settings for your printer: page size, type, orientation, and handling; graphics; fonts; and other properties specific to your printer.

✔ **The Page Range section:** You have three suboptions in this section:

• *All Pages:* Select this radio button to print all pages.

• *Current Page:* Select this option to print just the page in which you're working.

• *Pages:* To print a range of pages, select this radio button and enter the number of the first and last pages you want to print in the From and To text boxes.

✔ **The Copies section:** Specify the number of copies you want to print and whether you want them to be collated.

✔ **The Advanced Printer Setup button:** This button, located on the Printer Details tab, opens the Advanced Printer Setup dialog box, where you can choose to print linked graphics in full or low resolution. You can also decide not to print linked graphics. The specific printer model you're using determines whether you can specify the print quality, what to print, the printing order (for labels), and other options.

The Print to File option prints to a file as a `.prn` or `.ps` file, rather than printing to a printer. One main advantage of this is that you can "print to file" from Publisher even if no printer is connected and later, when connected to a printer, print the publication using just the captured file.

The capabilities you see in the Print dialog box and the Advanced Printer Setup dialog box are determined to some extent by which printer you select. Nearly all printers, however, allow you to select a range of pages to print and to print multiple copies or copy a file to disk and have the file printed on another printer. Many other capabilities — collating, color capabilities, two-sided printing, and other options — are specific to each printer. Check out the Properties dialog box by clicking the Properties button in the Print dialog box to find out more about your printer's capabilities. Also, your printer manual is a good place to learn more about your specific printer.

When you accept the Print dialog box settings, Publisher creates a print job and *spools* (sends) it to your printer. To see the *print queue* (the set of documents) sent to the printer, double-click that printer's icon in the Printer folder. A window opens, showing you the current print jobs and offering you the commands necessary to modify your print jobs. You can delete print jobs, suspend them, and move them around in the queue.

The Print Setup dialog box

If you're printing to a desktop printer, you owe it to yourself to choose File⇨ Print Setup and explore your printer's Print Setup dialog box. It's somewhat deceptive because it hides the most interesting settings in the Properties sheet. To access these settings, click the Properties button. You can then control such characteristics as paper size, graphical resolution (the number of dots per inch), and font quality.

Tips for printing

The Publisher Help feature includes some handy tips for printing your publication. To access this feature, open the Help window by choosing Help⇨ Microsoft Office Publisher Help or pressing F1. If the table of contents isn't visible, click the Show Table of Contents button on the toolbar. In the table of contents, click Saving and Printing, click Printing, and then click Tips for Printing Your Publication. One of the most valuable tips presented is a table that can help you decide whether you should print the publication yourself on your desktop printer, take the publication to a copy shop, or hire a commercial printer to create the final output.

Using Outside Printing Services

Publisher lets you print to any common desktop printer that you can attach to a PC. For low-volume output, a desktop printer is usually sufficient. You may sometimes need to print in large quantities, however, or with capabilities beyond those of most desktop printers (such as printing large jobs, printing in high resolution, printing spot color jobs, or printing on a paper size that your desktop printer doesn't support). In these cases, visit a printer service, copy shop, or commercial printer. Each of these establishments offers different capabilities, and each one offers different degrees of hand-holding.

The following ideas can help you in your quest to select an outside printing service:

- **If you know people who use printing services, get their recommendations.** If you don't, let your fingers, er, mouse do the walking through the Internet and try out a few services. Try searching for **printing services** or **commercial printing** at your favorite Internet search engine. Ask to see samples of a service's work and get the names of other clients they worked with. Good printers deliver quality work on time and on budget. You're paying good money for the work, and you should get good results.

- **Know what you expect from your service.** Use the Pack and Go Wizard, (described in the next section) to ready your publication for the commercial printer. By default, the wizard prints a composite and separations. The composite combines all the colors in your publication and should well represent the final product. The separations show your printing service how the colors are separated. Publisher prints one page for each color. Take the composite and separations with you to the printing service.

- **Evaluate the printing quotes.** If you need to print several thousand copies of a publication, a commercial printer is the best choice — and will likely save you money. Copy shops and printer services offer lower pricing at volume levels, but commercial printers can lower the cost per page even more.

- **Ask about their policy on** *overage.* Most printers, to be on the safe side, print a specific number of additional copies of your print order. Some charge for the overage — make sure that you know when they do. An overage charge of more than 15 percent of the print price is excessive.

- **Don't pick a printer that offers the cheapest price.** You usually pay anyway for the money you save with longer print turnaround times and less attention to your work. Printing is an extremely competitive industry. After you calculate the cost of paper and ink, labor is the only remaining variable.

Working with an outside service

Be sure that you understand what your outside printer service requires in order to print your publication. An outside service is likely to ask that you provide, at minimum, the following materials before it can complete your print job:

✔ Page proofs of each page, with each spot color or process color separation printed as a proof

✔ A listing of your fonts, files, and printing directions

✔ The files themselves in Publisher 2007, Adobe PDF, or Postscript format, with any needed font files and graphics files included

✔ Any original drawings or photographs that need to be scanned

Use the Publisher Pack and Go Wizard to ensure that you have everything you need to take to the printing service. Follow these steps:

1. **Choose File⇨Pack and Go⇨Take to a Commercial Printing Service.**

   The Take to a Commercial Printing Service task pane appears — almost as if by magic — as shown in Figure 13-3.

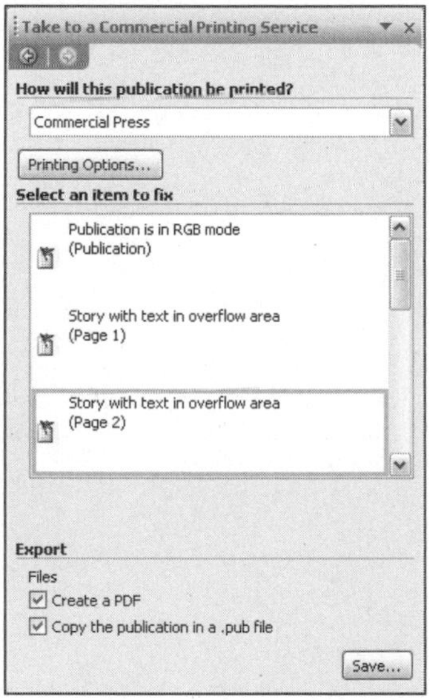

Figure 13-3:
The
Take to a
Commercial
Printing
Service
task pane.

2. **Choose Commercial Press from the How Will This Publication Be Printed? drop-down list, if it isn't already selected.**

3. **Click the Printing Options button.**

   Doing so displays the Print Options dialog box, shown in Figure 13-4.

   The Print Options dialog box is the place to change the orientation of the publication or choose which pages to include.

4. **Confirm your print options and then click OK.**

   The Take to a Commercial Printing Service task pane returns to your screen.

5. **If any items remain to be resolved in the Select an Item to Fix section of the task pane, click the down arrow next to each item and choose how you want to address the issue.**

   Items you might see here include Publication in RGB mode (best for desktop printing, although you're likely to choose spot or process colors) and Story with Text in Overflow Area.

6. **When all flagged issues have been resolved to your satisfaction, click Save.**

   The first screen of the Pack and Go Wizard appears, as shown in Figure 13-5, prompting you to enter a location to save your files.

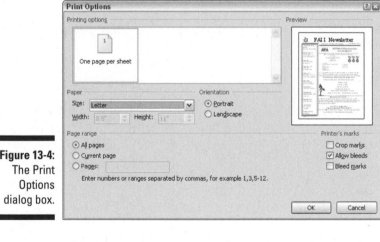

Figure 13-4:
The Print
Options
dialog box.

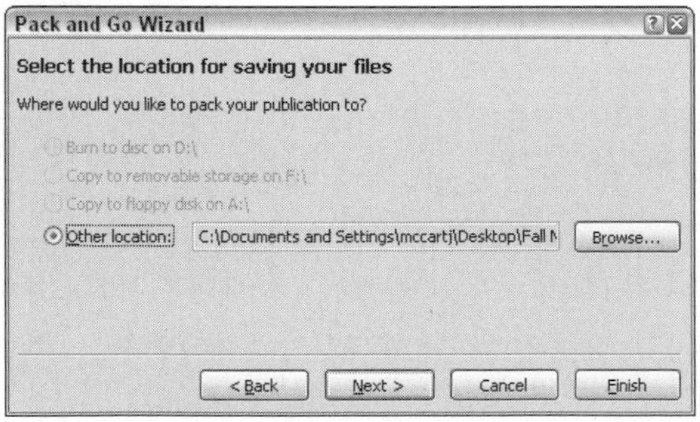

Figure 13-5:
The first
panel of the
Pack and
Go Wizard.

7. **Click Browse to choose a folder in which to store your publication, and then click Next.**

   The final screen of the Pack and Go Wizard appears, as shown in Figure 13-6, letting you know that your publication has been successfully packed.

Figure 13-6:
You're
packed and
ready to go!

> **Pack and Go Wizard**
>
> **Your publication is successfully packed**
>
> The wizard copied your packed file into the directory you selected.
>
> If you make changes to your publication, use the Pack and Go Wizard again.
>
> ☑ Print a composite proof
>
> OK

8. **Click OK to print a composite proof.**

   I recommend printing the composite proof but if you already have a copy (or just don't want to print it), clear the check box before clicking OK.

   The Pack and Go Wizard creates a zip file containing all the files you need to take to your commercial printer in the folder you chose. If the file isn't too large, you can e-mail it to the commercial printer. Otherwise, you can copy it to a USB drive or create a CD.

Avoiding problems

Using special fonts can be the most troublesome aspect of working with an outside printer service. The following list describes some of the troubles you can encounter:

✔ Many shops keep only a limited collection of fonts. In some cases, a busy shop might simply hand you the output of your file with whichever font it substituted for the fonts it doesn't have.

✔ If you overload a document with fonts, you can overload an imagesetter's memory and create Postscript overflow errors that add to your costs.

✔ Using gradient fills can quickly overload an imagesetter's memory, as can special WordArt effects.

Another troublesome aspect of working with outside printers is forgetting to include all the graphics files that your publication needs. Keep these concepts in mind:

- ✔ If you submit scanned graphics, make sure that the resolution of the scan is appropriate to the kind of printing you're doing.

- ✔ Try to use scanned graphics that are simply placed in your publication. If you crop, rotate, or otherwise modify your scanned images, you create large, complicated files.

Ensure that your printer service has the fonts you used in your publication. Also, if you submit EPS (Encapsulated Postscript) files, make sure that the printer service has the same creator application for your publication and its components.

If you're printing a costly print job, you might want to request a *press check,* where you ask your printer to set up the printing press and run off sample copies of the publication for you to check. The printer service is more likely to be willing to do this if you're on hand at the time that the shop runs your job.

Sit down and evaluate any print job that a printer returns to you. If you find a problem, let the printer service know about it. And, don't forget to let them know when you're especially happy with their work. My favorite way of letting my service providers know that their work was good is to recommend them to other people.

Setting Up for Outside Printing

The Tools⇨Commercial Printing Tools⇨Color Printing command lets Publisher select a printer driver that's best for the outside printing you're likely to do: black-and-white, full color, or spot-color printing. Figure 13-7 shows the Color Printing dialog box.

To set up your publication for black-and-white printing, select Single Color. Then click the down arrow of the Inks in Use color and click the Change button to display the Change Ink dialog box. Click Black and click OK.

Avoid using two spot colors in *gradient* fills, in which the two colors are blended. That configuration prints poorly, if at all. You can use a spot color blended with either white or black, however.

When you want to specify a print job to an outside printer, make sure that the Print to File check box in the Print dialog box is selected. The program then prints to a disk file that you can take to your outside printing service. Otherwise, Publisher uses this printer driver to try to print to your current printer (which may or may not work, depending on its type).

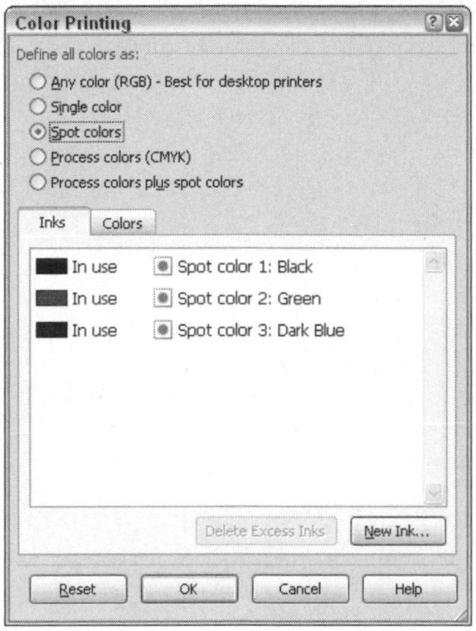

Color Printing

Define all colors as:

○ Any color (RGB) - Best for desktop printers
○ Single color
◉ Spot colors
○ Process colors (CMYK)
○ Process colors plus spot colors

| Inks | Colors |

☐ In use ◉ Spot color 1: Black
☐ In use ◉ Spot color 2: Green
☐ In use ◉ Spot color 3: Dark Blue

Delete Excess Inks   New Ink...

Reset   OK   Cancel   Help

Figure 13-7:
The Color
Printing
dialog box.

Selecting paper

Selecting paper for your publication's printing is a sensual experience that's rare in computer land. Paper has texture, heft, thickness, color, shine, brightness (because of fluorescent chemicals), and even smell. I get excited just thinking about it. (Some would say that it's because I've been locked up in an office writing this book, but I would disagree. I just love paper — especially the green kind with presidents' portraits on it.)

Paper makes up 30 to 50 percent of the total cost of a print job, depending on the number of copies printed and the type of paper stock chosen. Therefore, you can greatly affect the cost of printing your publication by carefully selecting print stock. Your outside printer service can be a big help in selecting the right paper for your publication. Most printers keep sample stock around for you to look at and, in some cases, to test print. Commercial printers have a great deal of experience with using various types of paper and can tell you how well a paper takes ink, folds, or reproduces graphics. Nearly all the larger paper companies distribute sample paper stock kits or paper stock selectors that are strips of sample paper.

Starting your own sampler collection isn't a bad idea. PaperDirect (www. paperdirect.com) will sell you a paper sampler for a $5 shipping-and-handling fee and refund the money in the form of a coupon on your first order. Other paper manufacturers might sell, or even give away, their samplers on request.

Using paper as a design element

When you choose paper for your publication, you must match the paper's characteristics to your publication. Paper size, weight, and thickness — and the methods of measuring these elements — vary with various types of paper. A paper's features related to color, texture, and finish are important to consider when you're deciding on your publication's best presentation. Please note that paper quality is a design element that makes a substantial impression on readers. Here are some guidelines for making a good impression:

- **Buy heavier, better paper when your publication will be handled several times.** A company's annual report is a good example. If your publication will be looked at briefly and then thrown away, however, you can get by with a lightweight, cheaper paper.

- **Choose paper color to enhance your publication.** The most readable text is printed on a soft, yellowish-white paper. For the best accuracy with process colors, use neutral white paper. Brighteners added to paper stock as fluorescent dyes also alter color fidelities. Be aware that the color of the paper affects how your ink color appears on the finished product. To avoid unpleasant surprises, you might want to test the way the ink color you choose will look when matched with your paper color.

- **Print on the side of the paper recommended by the paper manufacturer.** Paper has a grain that makes one side better for printing; reams of paper have a grain indicator on their wrapping with an arrow to indicate which side you should print on. When printing pages, try to keep the grain parallel to the binding edge, to help readers turn pages and to keep the pages lying flat.

- **Choose paper stock weight and thickness that are appropriate for your printing device.** Laser printers typically have a limit of 60-pound stock. If you put heavier paper through a laser printer, you can damage it. Check your printer's documentation for its requirements. If you're printing on two sides of the paper, make sure that your paper is heavy enough that the type from one side doesn't show through to the other side. This *bleedthrough* can make your publication unattractive and difficult to read.

- **Select a coated paper if you need a bit more opacity and better resolution for your printing.** Coated paper costs a little more, but this suggestion is particularly important if you're printing in color or using photographs. You can buy paper stock that's coated on one side (C1S) or on two sides (C2S). C1S is used for labels, packaging, and covers; C2S is used in books and commercial publications. Coated paper withstands higher ink coverage and results in blacker blacks, better color fidelity, and higher resolution. Note that coated paper smudges more easily and might require varnish to keep the color from coming off on readers' hands. Also, note that coated paper exhibits less of the printed image showing through to the opposite side of a page.

More Printing Resources

Printing is a big topic, and I only touch on the subject in this chapter. Fortunately, some great resources are out there to help you. The best book on working with the printing industry, how printers (both mechanical and human) work, and the process of working with printers and graphic arts suppliers is *Getting It Printed: How to Work With Printers and Graphic Imaging Services to Assure Quality, Stay on Schedule and Control Costs,* 4th Edition, by Eric Kenly and Mark Beach (How Design Books). This book should be a standard reference for any desktop publisher.

Another place to read about printing is the more condensed (and dense) book *Pocket Pal: The Handy Little Book of Graphic Arts Production,* 19th Edition, by Michael Bruno (International Paper). You can buy this book at any graphics supply house. This book gives you many pages of technical details on printing, paper selection, printing inks, type, copy preparation, and dozens more subjects. It's particularly valuable for acquiring a detailed, high-level view of the printing industry; I just couldn't do without it.

Part VI
Publishing on the Internet

The 5th Wave   By Rich Tennant

"Someone want to look at this manuscript
I received on e-mail called 'The Embedded
Virus That Destroyed the Publisher's Servers
When the Manuscript was Rejected'?"

In this part . . .

These days, everyone seems to be talking about the Internet. You rarely see a television commercial, magazine ad, or billboard that doesn't have a Web site address plastered on it somewhere (you know, `www.sendmeyourmoney.com`). The two chapters in this part can help you create a Web site of your very own and publish it on the World Wide Web. After all, if I didn't help you publish your work, I might as well title the book *Microsoft Create Great-Looking Publications on Your Computer and Not Let Anyone See It For Dummies*.

Chapter 14

Weaving a Web Site

*Y*ou don't know how to write HTML code but you want to create professional-looking Web pages — Microsoft Publisher 2007 can help. In fact, if you can click a few buttons, you can create some great-looking Web pages in minutes! Read on.

Understanding What a Web Site Is

A *Web site* is a page or group of pages created and published to be viewed on the Internet — specifically, the World Wide Web. A *Web page* is simply a document encoded using HyperText Markup Language (HTML) to describe its appearance. An HTML document can have *hyperlinks* — graphics or text that you can click to move to other documents or other parts of the current document. The Web *server* on which a Web site is published is a computer connected to the Internet running Web server software. For an informational, step-by-step tutorial on creating Web pages, pick up a copy of *Creating Web Pages For Dummies,* 8th Edition, by Bud Smith and Arthur Bebak (Wiley Publishing).

Creating a Web site is only half the battle. If you want to see your Web site on the Internet, you have to publish it to the Web. Chapter 15 discusses how to publish your Web site.

Using the Easy Web Wizard

As I mention in Chapter 1, the easiest way to create a publication in Publisher is to use a wizard. Creating a Web site is no exception. To use the Easy Web Wizard, just click Web Sites in the Publication Types list of the Publisher Catalog on the Getting Started screen. If the Catalog isn't visible, you can restore it by choosing File⇨New. Figure 14-1 shows the Microsoft Publisher 2007 Catalog displaying Web Site templates, with the Use Easy Web Wizard option selected in the Options task pane.

After you click Web Sites in the Publication Types list, Publisher offers you 72 styles of Web sites to choose from in the Web Sites pane. Scroll through the Newer Designs and Classic Designs groups and select the style of the Web site you want to build, and then click the Create button, in the lower-right corner of the Microsoft Publisher Catalog dialog box. Be sure that the Use Easy Web Wizard check box in the Options task pane is selected.

After your computer clicks and grinds for a few seconds (the duration depends on the speed of your PC), Publisher creates the first page of your Web site template and shows you the first panel of the Easy Web Wizard, as shown in Figure 14-2.

Figure 14-1:
The Publisher 2007 catalog with the Use Easy Web Wizard option selected.

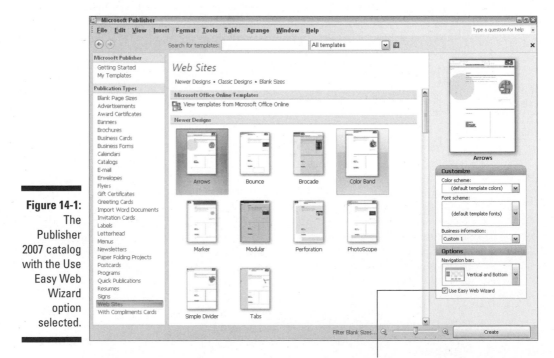

Use Easy Web Wizard option

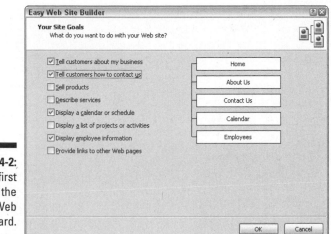

Figure 14-2:
The first
panel of the
Easy Web
Wizard.

The wizard uses this panel to politely ask which kinds of information you want your Web site to provide. How nice! Notice that as you select the check boxes, the wizard adds navigation buttons that represent the corresponding Web pages. Your choices are

✔ Tell Customers about My Business

✔ Tell Customers How to Contact Us

✔ Sell Products

✔ Describe Services

✔ Display a Calendar or Schedule

✔ Display a List of Projects or Activities

✔ Display Employee Information

✔ Provide Links to Other Web Pages

After you select the types of pages to include (by selecting the check boxes), click OK to have the Easy Web Wizard build your Web pages.

When the Easy Web Wizard finishes building your Web pages, it displays the first page along with the Format Publication task pane. Click the Preview Your Web Site link in the Web Site Options to open your Web site in your Web browser. If you like the way the Web site looks, you're done!

Okay, unless you really want visitors to your Web site to see the Publisher 2007 Easy Web Wizard placeholder text and graphics, you aren't done. You still have to edit the publication to include your information. But you don't have to change the color scheme or add pages or make any other changes. When you're ready to edit the Web Wizard's placeholder text and graphics with your own text and graphics, see the section "Adding Text or Picture Objects," later in this chapter.

If you decide that you don't like the template you selected when you started the Easy Web Wizard, you can easily change it. (You think Staples has the only Easy button? Publisher has plenty of them!) Follow these steps:

1. **On the Web Site Options tab of the Format Publication task pane, click the Change Template button.**

   The Change Template dialog box, shown in Figure 14-3, appears.

2. **Pick a different template and then click OK.**

   Publisher displays another dialog box. This one, shown in Figure 14-4, is (oddly enough) also named Change Template. In this one, you get to choose between applying the template to the existing Web site or creating a new one.

3. **After you choose, click OK.**

   If you select the Apply Template to the Current Publication option, Publisher applies the template to your publication. If you choose the Create a New Publication Using My Text and Graphics option, Publisher creates and opens a new publication. The other publication is still open and unchanged. You can switch between the publications by using the Window menu.

Figure 14-3:
The Change Template dialog box.

If you're satisfied with your template choice but realize that you need to add a page (or multiple pages) to your publication, click the Insert a Page link on the Web Site Options tab of the Format Publication task pane. In the Insert Web Page dialog box that appears (see Figure 14-5), select the Web page type that you want to add. Make sure that the Add Hyperlink to Navigation Bars check box is selected if you want Publisher to create a navigation button for your new page, and then click OK.

You can quickly change the fonts used in your Web pages by clicking the Font Schemes tab in the Format Publication task pane and selecting any of the fonts in the Apply a Font Scheme list. Publisher instantly applies your choice to each page in your Web.

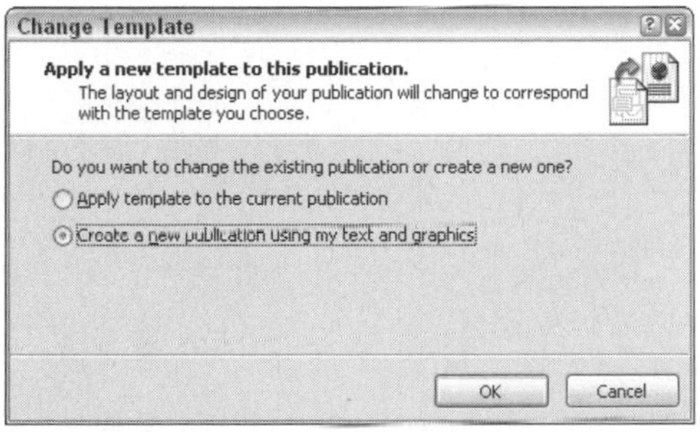

Figure 14-4:
The Change
Template
dialog box
redux.

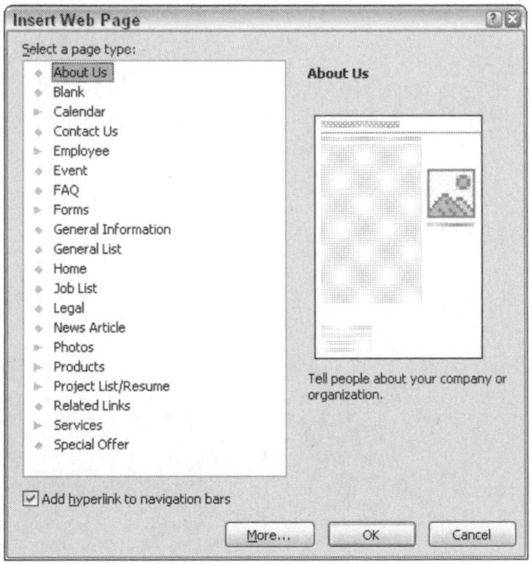

Figure 14-5:
The Insert
Web Page
dialog box.

Changing the color scheme of your Web site is as easy as changing the font scheme. Click the Color Schemes tab of the Format Publication task pane. Publisher lets you choose from more than 90 professionally designed color schemes. Microsoft paid big money to have these color schemes designed, so it's hard to go wrong when selecting one. Still, if you can't decide which color scheme looks best, stick with the default choice.

Figure 14-6 shows the Color Schemes tab of the Format Publication task pane with the Verve color scheme selected.

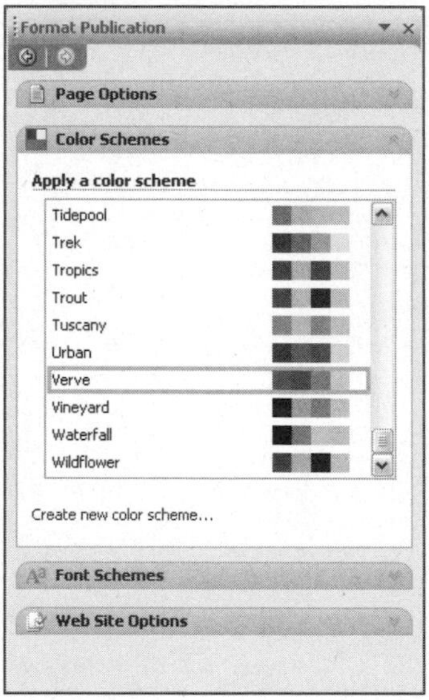

Figure 14-6: Choose from more than 90 color schemes listed in the Format Publication task pane.

Click the color scheme of your choice. Publisher automatically applies the selected colors to every page in your Web site.

Navigation bars contain buttons that allow visitors to your Web site to access the pages of your site. By default, the Easy Web Wizard creates both a vertical navigation bar, usually located to the left of the page, and a horizontal navigation bar, located at the bottom of the page. To change the type of navigation bar that's displayed on your Web site (or to remove them altogether), you have to return to the Change Template dialog box. To do that, select the Web Site Options tab of the Format Publication task pane and click the Change Template button. On the Options pane of the Change Template dialog box (refer to Figure 14-3), click the down arrow next to the Navigation Bar option and choose the way you want the navigation bar to appear. Your choices are

✔ Vertical and Bottom

✔ Horizontal and Bottom

✔ Vertical Only

✔ Horizontal Only

✔ Bottom Only

✔ None

Click OK to display the second Change Template dialog box, and decide whether you want to change your current Web site or create a new one. Click OK again to close the Change Template dialog box.

Unless you're creating a single-page Web site, adding a navigation bar is a good idea.

Adding Color and Texture to the Background

Template? Check. Color scheme? Check. Navigation bars? Check. Background fill and sound? Background fill and sound? And you thought you were done! You've seen Web sites with fancy textures or pictures as the page background behind text. I like plain backgrounds because they make the text easier to read. However, sometimes a more dramatic background is called for. If you're in one of those situations, I'm pleased to inform you that Publisher makes changing Web page backgrounds a snap! (Well, maybe a click.)

To change the Web page background, click the Page Options tab of the Format Publication task pane. Figure 14-7 shows what this tab looks like. Click the Background Fill and Sound link to display the Background task pane, depicted in Figure 14-8.

Click any of the background samples to immediately apply that pattern to the Web page that's displayed. To apply the background to all pages in your Web site, hover the mouse over the background until you see the down arrow to the right of the background. Click the down arrow and choose Apply to All Pages. Click the no-fill background (the white box with the X in the middle) to remove a background. You can modify the color of all gradient and pattern backgrounds by selecting one of the Color Scheme colors at the top of the Background task pane. The More Backgrounds link, at the bottom of the Backgrounds task pane, gives you access to many more backgrounds.

I like fancy backgrounds with bright colors for Web pages that have just a little bit of text, but a plain white background works best for Web pages with lots of text.

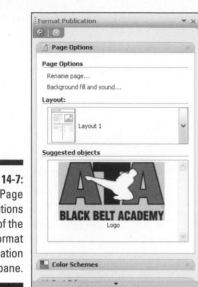

Figure 14-7:
The Page
Options
tab of the
Format
Publication
task pane.

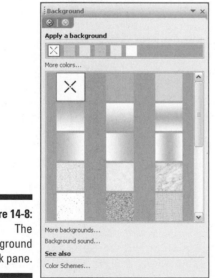

Figure 14-8:
The
Background
task pane.

While you're looking at the Background task pane, I might as well tell you about adding sounds. That way, I can check it off my list. Unless you have a compelling reason to play a sound when your Web page is opened, I recommend that you skip the sound. Sounds can take a long time to download over slow dial-up connections, and looping sounds that play over and over can be annoying. Nothing makes visitors want to move on to another Web site faster than having to wait for an alma mater fight song to download.

If you're determined to add a background sound, here's how it's done:

1. **Click the Background Sound link, at the bottom of the Background task pane.**

   This step opens the Web Page Options dialog box, shown in Figure 14-9.

2. **In the Background Sound section, in the File Name text box, type the full path and name of the sound file that you want to play each time the Web page is opened.**

   If you don't know the name and path, click the Browse button to open the Background Sound dialog box, which you can then use to navigate to (and select) the sound file you want. Click Open to return to the Web Page Options dialog box.

3. **Still in the Background Sound section, select the Loop Forever radio button if you want your sound to play continuously. Or, select Loop and specify how many times the sound should repeat.**

   Remember that just because you can have the sound repeat as many as 999 times doesn't mean that you should.

4. **Click OK to apply your choices and close the Web Page Options dialog box.**

You should keep a couple of concepts in mind about Web page background sounds (other than my recommendation against them). If you want the background sound to play on more than one Web page, you have to repeat the preceding set of steps for each of those pages. Also, you can't hear the sounds in Publisher. View the Web page in a browser (make sure that your sound is turned on) to hear the sound. Each time the page is loaded or refreshed, the sound plays.

Figure 14-9:
Add sound to your Web pages by using the Web Page Options dialog box.

If you have an existing publication (a brochure or newsletter, for example) that you want to place on the Web, you don't have to re-create it as a Web site. Open the publication and choose File⇨Convert to Web Publication. The first panel of the Convert to Web Publication Wizard, shown in Figure 14-10, appears. Decide whether you want Publisher to save your publication before converting it, and then click Next. In the second panel of the Convert to Web Publication Wizard, shown in Figure 14-11, tell the wizard to add a navigation bar. (Unless you're converting a single-page publication, having the wizard create a navigation bar is an excellent idea.) Click Finish. Publisher creates your Web site.

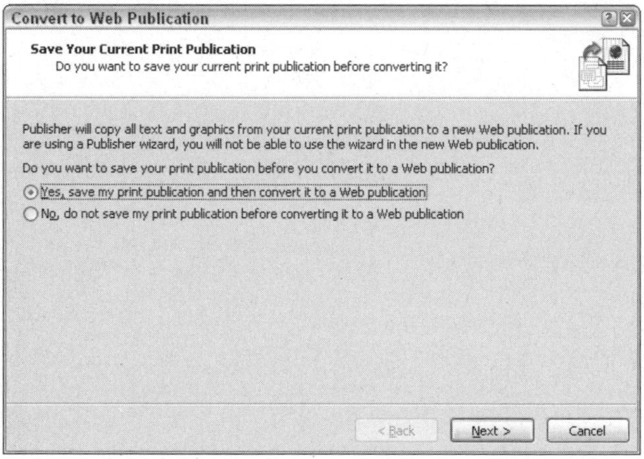

Figure 14-10:
The Convert
to Web
Publication
Wizard.

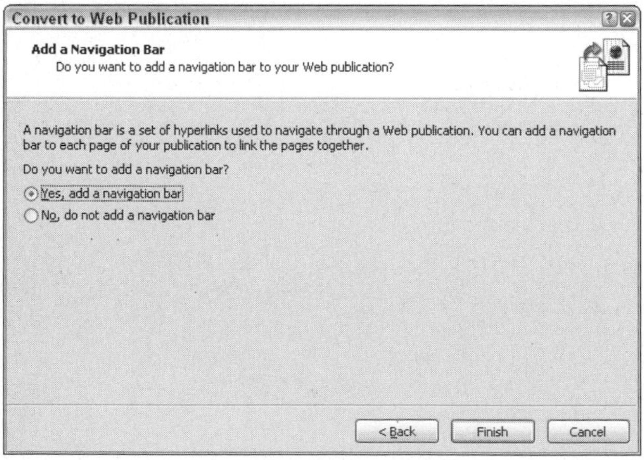

Figure 14-11:
Let the
wizard
create a
navigation
bar for you.

Adding Text or Picture Objects

Adding text or pictures to your Web site is pretty simple. In fact, if you have added text or pictures to a Publisher publication, you already know how to add them to your Web site. If you used the Easy Web Wizard to create your Web site, you probably have several text and picture frames in your publication. (Did I call your Web site a publication? I guess so.)

I strongly recommend that you use the Easy Web Wizard to create your Web site. It's much easier, in my opinion, to create the site by using the wizard and change what you don't like than it is to create the Web site from scratch.

Adding text

To change the placeholder text that the wizard put in your publication, just highlight the text and start typing.

If you don't have any text boxes or don't want to change the text in an existing text box, just create a new one:

1. **Click the Text Box tool.**
2. **Draw the text box.**
3. **Start typing.**

The Easy Web Wizard does a reasonably good job of designing the Web page, but feel free to add, delete, or move objects as you see fit.

Adding pictures

To change a picture on your Web page, follow these steps:

1. **Double-click the picture.**

   The Clip Art task pane appears, and you can select a new picture for your Web page.

2. **In the Search For box, type a word or phrase that describes the clip art you're looking for.**

3. **Choose a collection, and then click a specific category in the list box located to the left of the pictures, if you want.**

   If you aren't sure which collection to choose, pick All Collections to create the largest number of results.

4. **Scroll as necessary and then click the picture you want.**

5. **Click the down arrow next to the clip art image you want and choose Insert from the menu that appears.**

   You return to your Web site.

The procedure for adding a new picture to a Web site is the same as the procedure for adding a new picture to any publication. Adding new pictures is covered in detail in Chapter 9.

Adding and Removing Hyperlinks

Hyperlinks allow the person viewing your Web site to click an object (text or a graphic) and jump to another document on your Web site or elsewhere on the Internet, or to send an e-mail.

Adding hyperlinks

You can add a hyperlink to an object on your Web page in several ways: Add hyperlinks to text, pictures, WordArt, and even the contents of table frames. To add a hyperlink to text box or a table frame, you must first select the individual text that you want to hyperlink. Selecting just the text box or table frame doesn't work.

Follow these steps to create a hyperlink:

1. **Select the object to which you want to add a hyperlink.**

2. **Pick one of these methods: Choose Insert⇨Hyperlink, choose Hyperlink from the context menu, click the Insert Hyperlink button on the Standard toolbar, or press Ctrl+K.**

   No matter which method you choose, the Insert Hyperlink dialog box, shown in Figure 14-12, appears.

3. **Select the type of hyperlink you want from the Link To section.**

   You can choose one of four types of hyperlinks:

   • *Existing File or Web Page:* You need to supply the URL (Uniform Resource Locator, or address) of the document the hyperlink connects to.

   • *Place in This Document:* Select the appropriate page in your Web site.

   • *Create New Document:* Choose to edit the new document now or later.

   • *E-Mail Address:* Supply an e-mail address.

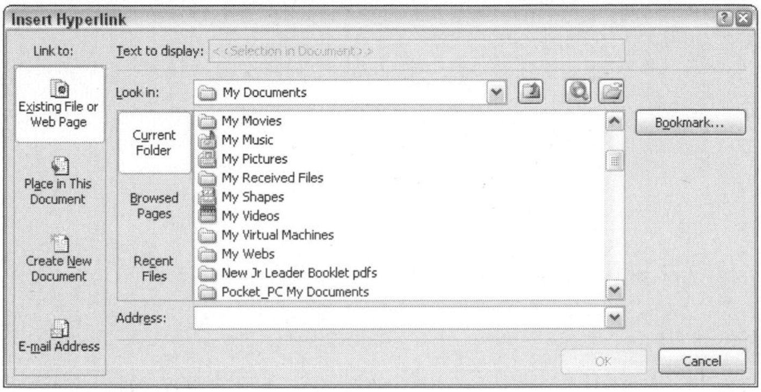

Figure 14-12:
The Insert
Hyperlink
dialog box.

4. **Depending on which type of hyperlink you choose, you may need to browse to the file you want to link to or type an address in the Address box.**

   The Insert Hyperlink dialog box changes, depending on the type of hyperlink you select in the Link To section.

5. **After selecting the type of hyperlink you want and the location it points to, click OK.**

Removing hyperlinks

Removing a hyperlink from an object is a snap:

1. **Select the object from which you want to remove a hyperlink.**

2. **Pick a method: Choose Insert➪Hyperlink, click the Insert Hyperlink button on the Standard toolbar, or press Ctrl+K.**

   This step opens the Edit Hyperlink dialog box, which looks much like the Insert Hyperlink dialog box.

3. **Click the Remove Link button in the Edit Hyperlink dialog box.**

   The Hyperlink dialog box closes, and your hyperlink is removed.

If you're a fan of right-clicking, you can right-click the hyperlink and choose Remove Hyperlink from the context menu that appears.

Chapter 15

Getting Published (On the Internet)

. . . .

. . . .

S o you created a stunning Web site and you're wondering what you should do with it. You have come to the right place! In this chapter, I describe how to preview your Web site in your Web browser and then publish your site.

Previewing Your Web Site

After you create your Web site, you have to preview it to make sure that it meets your expectations before you go to the trouble of publishing it for the entire world to see. You also need to make sure that it looks the way you intended and that all the hyperlinks function correctly.

You must have Web browser software installed and configured in order to preview a Web site.

To preview your Web site, choose File➪Web Page Preview or press Ctrl+ Shift+B. You can also click the Preview Your Web Site link on the Web Site Options tab of the Format Publication task pane. Microsoft Publisher 2007 opens your default Web browser and displays the first page of your Web site. Click the hyperlinks to make sure that they function properly, and view the other pages (if any) of your site. When you finish viewing your site, close your Web browser. You return to Publisher.

Figure 15-1 shows a sample Web site being previewed in Internet Explorer. Notice that the address in the Address box points to a file on a local drive.

Figure 15-1:
Preview of
a Web site
created
with the
Publisher
2007 Easy
Web
Wizard.

Publishing Your Web Site

What's the difference between previewing your Web site and publishing it? When you preview your Web site, Publisher opens the site on your computer and shows you how it will look when it's published on the Internet. Publishing a Web site entails copying it to a computer running Web server software that's connected to the Internet — it's there for all the world to see.

Publisher gives you two options for publishing your Web site to the Internet:

✔ Publish to a location on the Internet.

✔ Publish with File Transfer Protocol (FTP).

Before publishing your Web pages for the entire world to see, run Publisher's Design Checker to find and fix any problems. Here's how to open the Design Checker:

1. **Choose Tools⇨Design Checker.**

2. **In the Design Checker task pane, select both the Run General Design Checks and Run Web Site Checks check boxes. Deselect the Run Commercial Printing Checks check box.**

As soon as you select the type of check to run, the Design Checker starts looking for problems and displays anything that it thinks is a problem in the Select an Item to Fix box of the Design Checker.

3. **Click an item's down arrow in the Select an Item to Fix box to see options for resolving the issue.**

If you aren't sure what the problem is with an item in the Select an Item to Fix box, choose Explain from the drop-down menu. The Publisher Help screen opens with detailed information about the problem item.

4. **Click Close Design Checker when you're finished.**

See Chapter 12 for the complete run down on the Design Checker.

Publishing to a Web location

Publishing your Web site to a folder on your computer and copying it using FTP software is the easiest way to publish to the Web. To publish your Web site on the Internet, you must have Internet access. Most people access the Internet from home by connecting to an Internet service provider, or ISP. If you don't have access to the Internet, you can still publish your Web site to a local drive, which creates all the HyperText Markup Language, or HTML, documents and image files and allows you to copy the files to the Internet later.

Before using the following procedure, make sure that you have all the information you need from your ISP. You need the URL, or address, where you can save files. You also need a username and password.

To publish your Web site to a local drive, follow these steps:

1. **Choose File➪Publish to the Web.**

The message box shown in Figure 15-2 reminds you that you need to have a Web site host in order to publish your Web site. Publisher provides a handy link to a Web site that tells you how to find a Web host. If you already have a Web host, feel free to select the Don't Show This Message Again check box.

Figure 15-2:
Reminder:
You need a
Web host in
order to
publish your
Web site.

Publish to the Web

To publish your Web site, you need to subscribe to a Web hosting provider. If you do not have a Web hosting provider click the link below to find one on Microsoft Office Online. Otherwise, click OK.

Find a Web hosting provider on Microsoft Office Online

☐ Don't show this message again

OK

2. **Click OK.**

   The Publish to the Web dialog box, shown in Figure 15-3, appears.

3. **Type the URL, provided to you by your Internet service provider, of the Web site where you want Publisher to save your Web site files, and then click Save.**

4. **If prompted, enter the username and password you received from your Web host or network administrator.**

   This step connects you to your Web host server.

5. **Select the folder that will contain your Web site and double-click the file to open it.**

6. **Click Save.**

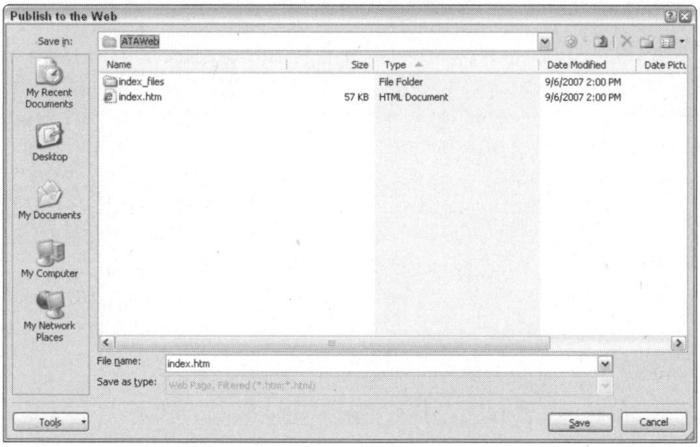

Figure 15-3:
The Publish to the Web dialog box.

Publishing your Web site by using an FTP location

FTP, in the Internet world, is short for File Transfer Protocol, a protocol for exchanging files over the Internet. As I mention earlier in this chapter, publishing your Web site to a folder on your computer and copying it by using FTP software is the easiest way to publish to the Web.

To save your Web site to the Internet using FTP, you must tell Publisher about your FTP site:

1. **Choose File⇨Publish to the Web.**

   If a reminder about needing a Web host appears, click the OK button. Otherwise, you see the Publish to the Web dialog box.

2. **Click the down arrow on the Save In drop-down list and choose Add/Modify FTP Locations.**

   The Add/Modify FTP Locations dialog box, shown in Figure 15-4, appears.

3. **Type the URL of your FTP site in the Name of FTP Site box.**

   Your Internet service provider or Web server administrator should be able to furnish you with this info.

4. **If necessary, click the User radio button, and type your username and password.**

5. **Click Add to add the FTP site to your list of FTP locations.**

   The FTP site you added appears in the FTP Sites list.

6. **Click OK to close the Add/Modify FTP Locations dialog box.**

7. **Click Cancel to close the Open dialog box.**

After you add an FTP site, you can publish your Web site by using an FTP location:

1. **Choose File➪Publish to the Web.**

   If the reminder about needing a Web host appears, click the OK button. Otherwise, you see the Publish to the Web dialog box.

2. **Click the down arrow next to the Save In list box and choose FTP Locations.**

3. **Double-click the FTP location and then double-click the folder in which you want to store your Web site.**

4. **Click OK to have Publisher copy your Web site to the selected FTP location.**

Figure 15-4:
The Add/
Modify FTP
Locations
dialog box.

The amount of time it takes to copy your Web site to your Web server depends on factors such as the speed of your connection to the Internet, the number of pages in your Web site, the number of pictures on those pages, and the speed of the Web server. Try to be patient.

Now that you have published your Web site, you should take a look at it live, over the Internet, to make sure that it looks the way you intended and that all links and buttons function as expected. The URL of your Web site is the same URL to which you published the Web site.

Publishing to a folder on your computer

You may want to publish your Web site to a folder on your computer in addition to publishing it to the Web, for these reasons:

✔ You can test your Web site by using the locally published files before publishing to the Web.

✔ You keep a local copy of your HTML files as well as your Web publication.

To save your Web site to your local machine, follow these steps:

1. **Choose File⇨Publish to the Web.**

   If the reminder about needing a Web host appears, click the OK button. Otherwise, you see the Publish to the Web dialog box.

2. **In the Publish to the Web dialog box, navigate to a folder and click Save.**

When Publisher publishes your Web pages to the Internet, it creates a special version of the files — smaller versions that load faster than typical Web page files, which works well for everyone who visits your Web site. But because the files are "special," you cannot edit the copy directly. If you need to make changes to the Web pages, you should open the original publication and make your changes and then publish it to the Internet again.

Part VII
The Part of Tens

The 5th Wave   By Rich Tennant

Gee, Richard, you'll have to tell me where on the toolbar you found an icon labeled "Overkill."

In this part . . .

Everybody needs lists to get them through the day. I always get my lists from my wife. This part contains lists of ten items on various topics to help you create better printed and online publications.

Chapter 16

Ten Great Design Ideas

Consider these ten general design tips for all your publications.

Borrow the Best Ideas of Others

Ideas cannot be copyrighted, but designs can. The more people you borrow from, the more original it makes you!

Design the Publication with Your Audience in Mind

Your audience is more likely to read your work if it's relevant and appeals to them.

Use a Design Grid

Create a grid guide and align your page elements to it, to impose consistency on your pages. See Chapter 4 for information on how to work with grids.

Use Pictures Well

Pictures are attention getters. If your picture tells your story, your readers get the point more quickly if they see the picture. Give it an appropriate caption and group the two (picture and caption) together. It's an excellent way to get your story noticed.

Check Out the Design Gallery

The Design Gallery has many attractive page elements and other excellent stuff you can use: headlines, sidebars, pull quotes, ornaments, and tables of contents, for example, in several great styles. Use these elements and the Drop Cap feature to break up pages and make them interesting. If you don't find what you like, create your own Design Gallery category and store your own, favorite design elements. You may want to flip over to Chapter 9 for more help in transforming your design into a masterpiece!

Use Master Pages

Put repeating design elements on your master pages. If you put items on the master pages, you don't have to repeat them on every page, and you can't mistakenly delete them or move them. Master pages help ensure consistency throughout your publication and — more important — cut down on your design time. Chapter 4 tells you how to make the most of master pages.

Keep It Simple, Silly!

KISS is a guiding design principle. Simplicity can be elegant, and it lets the reader focus on your message. Make your design consistent and simple to follow by using repetitive elements well.

Create Templates and Use Them

Any design that stands up to time deserves repeating. Save work you like as a template, and then use templates as starting points. Microsoft spent lots of time and money on professional designers to create the sample designs included in Publisher. Make yourself look good — use them.

Use Multicolumn Text Boxes

If you use multicolumn text boxes rather than lots of single-column text boxes, you have fewer objects on your layout to worry about. Text autoflows easily, columns align without strife, and your life flows as smoothly as water flows downhill to the sea.

Live with Your Designs Awhile

Revisiting the scene of the crime is an excellent way of improving your publication: Go back and take another critical look at your work. If you can, show your publication's page proofs to others and get their comments.

Chapter 17

Ten Design Blunders

*B*e on the lookout for these ten design blunders in all your publications.

Not Designing Your Publication for the Right Audience

Not designing your publication for the right audience is the design-blunder equivalent of sending an invitation to file your publication in the circular file (the wastebasket). For example, if you're creating a corporation's annual report, using the Zapf Dingbats font might be deemed an RGE (résumé-generating event).

Not Communicating with Your Print Service Early in the Project

You can prevent a whole range of design blunders by consulting with your print broker or print service from the beginning of your project. For example, some print colors may not be available from your print service.

Using the Wrong Printer Driver

Congratulations! Using the wrong printer driver during the design process gives you the opportunity to reformat your entire document.

Using Too Little White Space

Well-designed publications leave 50 percent of the page for white space. Using less makes your publication seem "busy" and hard to read. That amount might seem like a lot of unused real estate, but it's not, when you consider elements such as margins and the gutter space between columns.

Making Your Publication Too Complicated

A "busy" page with many different design elements can distract readers from the important points of your message. Highlight the important parts of your publication so that readers look at what you want them to see. A common problem is using too many fonts, which creates a "ransom note" effect on your page.

Making Your Pages Too Boring!

Mama always told me that variety is the spice of life. Spice up your pages — add contrast. Add graphics, drop or raised caps, color, rules, and other design elements meant to break up a repetitive page design. This advice is particularly important for long publications that use similar page styles. However, Mama also told me that too much of a good thing is, well, too much of a good thing! Publisher provides you with lots of cool design tools to use — just don't try to use all of them on any single page!

Printing Too Many or Too Few Copies

Printing too many or too few copies of your publication is easy to do, but either case can cause you grief. Try diligently to print the appropriate number of copies. Think hard about just how many copies of a publication are required for your work. For example, try to calculate how many people walking past your trade show booth are likely to pick up your flyer or how many copies of the brochure you will mail out.

Designing a Publication That's Too Expensive

It's easy to overrun your publication's budget. When you're designing your piece, try to substitute less expensive elements or processes. For example, don't use process color if you can't afford it or don't need it. Use spot colors instead. If you're not sure exactly what your final product will cost, you probably should discuss the various pricing options with your print service before you get started rather than wait for your final bill to arrive!

Violating Copyright Laws

Know the source of your graphics, designs, and text, and know your rights to use them. Feel free to use the Publisher templates and clip art in your publications; however, do not "borrow" graphics that appear on someone's Web site unless you have the owner's permission to use them.

Scanning Your Files at the Wrong Resolution

Be resolution-appropriate. Don't waste hard drive space and processing time by scanning a graphic at a high resolution when you're printing at a low resolution. But don't scan the graphic at a low resolution when you're printing in high resolution; the image will look coarse and inappropriate.

Chapter 18

Not Quite Ten Things to Check before Printing

*T*o make your printing process roll smoothly, check out the following advice before you try to print.

Give Color Separations to Your Print Service

Print a set of color separations for your publication and give it to your print service. To do this, set up your publication to print to a print service and choose File➪Print to open the Print dialog box. Click the Advanced Printer Setup button on the Printer Details tab of the Print dialog box. On the Separations tab, select Separations from the Print Colors As drop-down menu and then click OK. Publisher prints one page for each color in your publication.

Show Your Publication Around

Show your publication to several people. The more eyes that see it, the greater the chance that mistakes will get noticed.

Use the Pack and Go Wizard

You can use the Pack and Go Wizard to prepare your publication to take to a commercial printer. You can choose to have the wizard embed TrueType fonts and include your graphics so that you don't forget to take them with you. (Chapter 13 has more on the Pack and Go Wizard.)

Give Your Print Service All Original Materials

Make sure that you collect in your submission all the original materials your publication needs. If your print service requires a photograph or drawing for reference, don't forget to include it.

Run the Design Checker

I don't like hidden objects, empty frames, and other page elements that don't print properly. And, I have a devil of a time finding them without this useful tool. Choose Tools⇨Design Checker to run the Design Checker. It does an excellent job of identifying problems in your publication and helping you fix them.

Specify the Correct Printer Driver

Ensure that you have specified the correct printer driver for your publication and your printer. In other words, make sure that you're submitting the print job formatted for the printer that will print it. The current printer driver shows up in the Name list box of the Print Setup dialog box.

Use Printing Marks on Master Copies

Make sure that your master copies have *crop marks* on them. Crop marks let the print service know exactly where the paper will be cut. These marks help immensely in preparing the final printed matter quickly and correctly.

Check for the End of the Story

As you reformat text boxes, you can easily — and accidentally — move text at the end of your story so that it's out of view. To keep this situation from affecting your final publication, ensure that all story endings are properly included on their last connected text boxes. One way to do this is to check the continuation mark on the last frame of a story. (And no, this is not the end of this story.)

Chapter 19

Ten Questions for Your Print Service

Ask the following questions as you screen and select a print service.

Do You Work with Microsoft Publisher 2007?

Publisher has been around for quite a few years now. Although it isn't as popular as some of the more complex desktop publishing packages, it's still worth asking about. If your commercial print service uses Publisher 2007, producing the output you expect will probably be a simple task. Just use the Pack and Go Wizard and give the print service a copy of your publication.

How Do You Want to Receive My Files?

If your print service can't work with Publisher files, does it need or want EPS or PDF files? A service can work with Publisher files only if it has a copy of the program on hand. Many print services don't keep Publisher around. Therefore, you can give shops without Publisher an EPS of PDF file that they can print as is, without having the program on hand. The disadvantage of using these files is that the print service cannot always make changes to the file if a problem arises.

What's Your Usual Turnaround Time?

When do you need your publication, and what will you be charged if you need it quicker? This question helps you plan your production and submission schedule.

What Kind of Imagesetter Do You Use?

This question tells you the particular printer driver to use. Publisher has a generic imagesetter driver named MS Imagesetter. If you know the particular imagesetter that your print service has, however, using the real printer driver (for that imagesetter) produces superior results and fewer errors.

Which Kind of Equipment Do You Have in Your Shop?

Does the print service have a high-quality scanner, a Xerox DocuTech Publisher high-volume printer, or a color laser copier? The type of equipment that the service has available factors into the price and the kind of work that the print service can do.

Do You Have the Fonts in My Publication?

If not, you need to supply the fonts or avoid using ones that the print service doesn't have. Without all your required fonts available, the print service may give you printed output that has substitute fonts in place of the ones you specified in Publisher.

Do You Have the Creator Applications for the EPS Graphics 1 Create?

Without the creator application (one that can create new EPS or PDF files), your print service cannot correct any problems in your files. The printed results are your responsibility.

How Much Do You Charge?

Get a quote in writing — it's your insurance that you pay for what you get and get what you pay for. Most print services print an *overage,* a specific number of copies above your print order, to be on the safe side. Some services charge for the overage — make sure that you know when they do. An overage charge of more than 15 percent of the print price is excessive.

Can You Outsource the Work You Can't Do?

If your print service works with commercial printers and other businesses, you can use that single source to manage your entire print job and save you hassles and headaches.

Can You Give Me Some References?

Who are the print service's clients? Is the shop happy with the work? Ask to see samples of the printed work.

Chapter 20

Ten Ways to Save on Printing Costs

*L*ook over these money-saving tips for ideas to help you save on printing expenses.

Talk to Your Print Service

Printers know how to save you money. Specify your budget, and then ask how to meet it. Also ask what else you can do to lower your costs.

Choose an Appropriate Print Service

Get recommendations for a print service from other people, and choose a service that's appropriate to the kind of printing you do. Each printing establishment specializes in a particular kind of printing. Some are good at low- or high-volume printing; others specialize in careful color work. Select a print service accordingly.

Solicit Three Written Bids for a Print Job

Get competitive bids for your print job. Make the process meaningful by providing a complete disclosure of your printing requirements. Select the print service whose bid seems the most reasonable, and get everything in writing: deadlines, delivery, and storage costs, for example. Don't necessarily select the cheapest bid, but don't overpay, either.

Make a Careful Paper Selection

You can find paper bargains out there if you try. Let your print service help you make a paper selection.

Provide Your Print Service with Everything It Needs

The further you can go in the printing process, the less you pay and the fewer variables can make things go wrong. If you can, supply your commercial printer with camera-ready art and copies of your fonts. If you're using a custom color, supply the Pantone color, too.

Ask for a Cash Discount

If you pay immediately with cash, you should pay less. Hey, it's worth a try.

Don't Print Close to Your Deadline

Don't cut your deadline too close; leave some time for back-and-forth discussions between you and the print service. For example, if you have enough time, you can request a press proof and examine it. That way, you see a sample printed with the inks and press that your service will be using for your print job, and you can check it carefully for errors.

Use Special Paper to Print in Color without Having to Print in Color

Although the paper from PaperDirect (www.paperdirect.com) is more expensive than common stock, you can run its colored designs through an inkjet or laser printer and do short-run printing. You can get outstanding results, and only other desktop publishers will know that you did it. I won't tell — honest.

Use a Print Broker for Large or Expensive Print Jobs

Is your print job especially large, expensive, or complicated? Using a print broker can save you money if your job falls into one of these two categories. A *print broker* is a middleman who works between a customer and a print manufacturer. Brokers work as free agents and have the flexibility to represent several companies for you. You would expect your rep to add value to your print project through effective planning and management. You rely on that person's judgment on timing and knowledge of manufacturing materials and processes and workflow issues.

Minimize the Amount of Setup Work Your Printer Must Do

If your printer has a three-color printing press, don't use four colors. That requires an extra print run and will cost you more money.

Index

• *N* •

WITHDRAWAL